SIKHS

SIKHS

THE STORY OF A PEOPLE, THEIR FAITH AND CULTURE

Editorial Team Avanika, Nayan Keshan, Vatsal Verma
US Editor Sharon Lucas
US Executive Editor Lori Hand
Senior Art Editor Bhavika Mathur
Project Art Editor Devika Awasthi
Senior Jackets Coordinator Priyanka Sharma
Jacket Designer Suhita Dharamjit
Picture Researcher Mamta Panwar
Senior Picture Researcher Sumedha Chopra
DTP Designers Rajdeep Singh, Satish Gaur,
Mohd Rizwan, Rakesh Kumar
DTP Coordinator Tarun Sharma
Pre-Production Manager Balwant Singh
Production Manager Pankaj Sharma
Picture Research Manager Taiyaba Khatoon
Managing Editor Chitra Subramanyam
Managing Art Editor Neha Ahuja Chowdhry
Managing Director, India Aparna Sharma

Consultants Roopinder Singh,
Davinder S. Toor

Writers and Researchers Saanika Patnaik,
Nehal Agarwalla

First American Edition, 2023
Published in the United States by DK Publishing
1745 Broadway, 20th Floor, New York, NY 10019

Copyright © 2022 Dorling Kindersley Limited
DK, a Division of Penguin Random House LLC
23 24 25 26 27 10 9 8 7 6 5 4 3 2 1
001–334508–Apr/2023

A catalog record for this book is available
from the Library of Congress.

ISBN 978-0-7440-7752-0

Printed and bound in India

For the curious
www.dk.com

Publisher's Note

Sikhs is a celebration of Sikh culture and people, and
an exploration of the different experiences and
interpretations of identities and legacies that make up
the faith. While no one book can encapsulate an entire
people and every experience, the team behind the
book has tried to present the faith in a responsible,
respectful, and representative way. In order to do so,
they have consulted several experts so that the book
can present a detailed, reflective, and inclusive
meditation of this inspiring culture. We hope that you,
the reader, consider it so as well.

Contents

CONSULTANTS

Roopinder Singh
Author and Senior Journalist

Roopinder Singh is a reputed author and Indian journalist. He served with *The Tribune*, Chandigarh, for three decades, where he retired as Senior Associate Editor. He launched the Internet Edition, wrote extensively, and also headed magazines and book reviews. Prior to this, he was an Assistant Editor at *India Observer* in New York, USA. He earned his undergraduate and postgraduate degrees in Philosophy from St. Stephen's College, University of Delhi. He has published many books, including *Sikh Heritage: Ethos and Relics* (co-author), *Delhi '84*, *Guru Nanak: His Life and Teachings*, and *Arjan Singh DFC: Marshal of the Indian Air Force*. He regularly speaks at literary and cultural events.

Davinder S. Toor
Author and Art Collector

Davinder Toor is a leading figure among Indian and Islamic art collectors. He has acted as a consultant to major private collectors, auction houses and institutions such as the British Museum, Victoria and Albert Museum, and Wallace Collection. Objects from the Toor Collection of Sikh Art have been exhibited at major global institutions including at the Kunst halle der Hypo-Kulturstiftung (Munich), Art Gallery of Ontario (Toronto), Asian Art Museum (San Francisco), Virginia Museum of Fine Arts and the Brunei Gallery (London). He was also featured on the BBC's *Lost Treasures of the Sikh Kingdom* (2014) and *The Stolen Maharajah: Britain's Indian Royal* (2018) documentaries.

CHAPTER 6

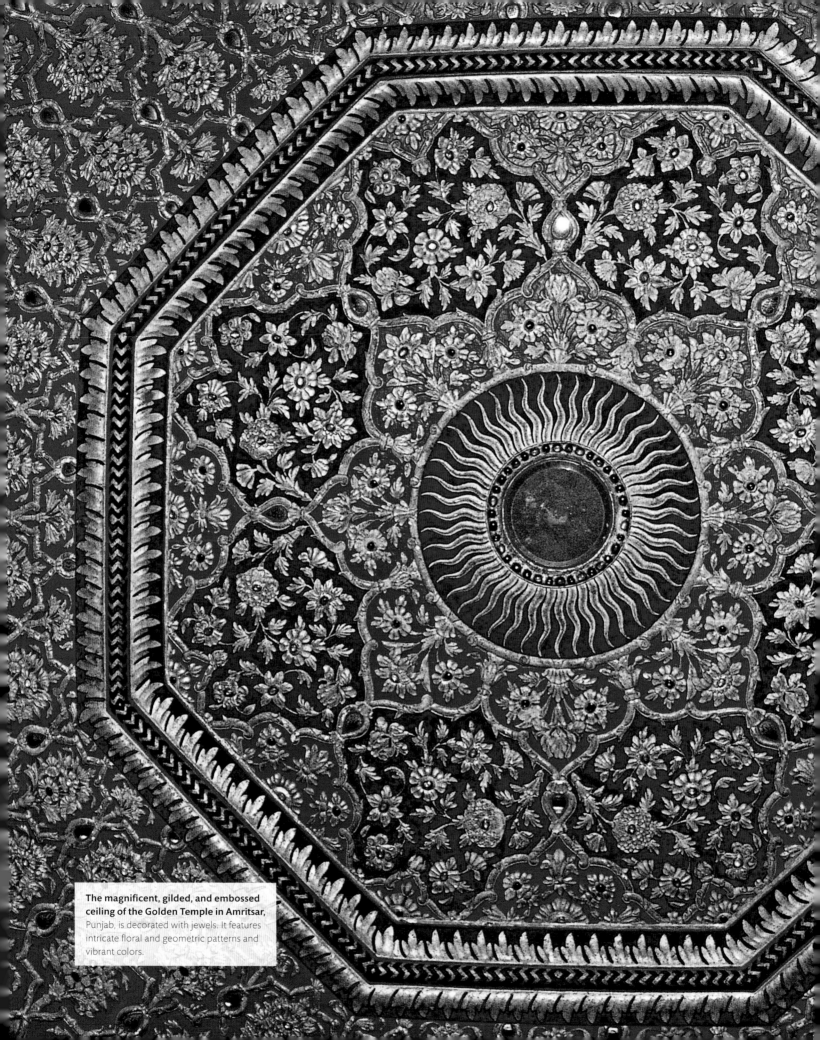

The magnificent, gilded, and embossed
ceiling of the Golden Temple in Amritsar,
Punjab, is decorated with jewels. It features
intricate floral and geometric patterns and
vibrant colors.

Introduction

Sikhs are present in every part of the world and have made their mark in fields as diverse as the colors of their turbans that mark them as truly unique. A religion that traces its origins five-and-a-half centuries back, Sikhism has left an imprint on humanity. The lucidity of precepts as given by the 10 Gurus, the centrality of equality and service in the ethos, and the accomplishments of adherents of the religion—all combined to provide the world with a distinct, definitive denomination.

Sikhism started in Punjab and spread to the world. The history of the Sikhs is intertwined with the region of its founder Guru Nanak Dev's origin. He traveled widely to spread his message; so did the successive Gurus, although they did not travel as far as he did.

The Sikhs today are well dispersed all over the world, and wherever they go, they take the fundamentals of their faith and their observances with them.

As the reader flips through the pages of *Sikhs: The Story of a People, Their Faith and Culture*, a rich picture of the diversity of thought within the unity of mission unfolds. Guru Nanak set forth his ideas with rare clarity and candor. He visited established centers of faith and held discussions with the learned people and the clergy, even as he expounded his thoughts, often by singing his hymns to Bhai Mardana's rabab.

Guru Nanak's successors built on the solid foundation that he set up. They consolidated the faith and provided the framework that allowed the message to permeate a broader number of people. As society and people evolved to a stage where Guru Gobind Singh formalized the Khalsa, the religion held sway over the Punjab region. In the two centuries between Guru Nanak and Guru Gobind Singh, the transformation of the Sikh followers was significant. Even as they imbibed the core spiritual values of *gurbani*, they became more organized and learned military skills, which, in time, enabled them to establish their own rule.

The Sikhs spread out to the world in the 19th century, often as soldiers. They found opportunities in faraway lands, such as Kenya, Canada, the UK, and the USA. Now, in many countries, they are political leaders, jurists, administrators, scholars, and sportspeople—around the globe, they are represented in all walks of life.

Sikhs: The Story of a People, Their Faith and Culture explores the world of the Sikhs, their religion, and history. It takes the reader on a journey that starts in Punjab before Guru Nanak, into the origins of the faith, the challenges faced by Gurus, the rise and fall of the Sikh Empire, how Sikhs fared in the British Empire, and then to India after its independence in 1947. The diaspora, literature, and arts are explored, and enhanced by relevant illustrations in this compendium of vignettes. Together, they give us this volume, which readers will find both illustrative and educative as they discover a fresh perspective on the Sikhs and their faith.

ROOPINDER SINGH
Author and Journalist

1

Before Guru Nanak

Until 1469

Lush fields, settlers from across the lands, the plurality of cultures, and a melting pot of ideas and faith systems exemplified *Punj-ab*, which translates to mean the land of five rivers. It was this that helped the region, once a part of the Indus Valley Civilization in 3000 BCE, become the site of a new religion's genesis.

The story of Punjab

From the ancient Indus Valley Civilization that thrived on the fertile plains of the region, to the early Aryan invaders, the Greeks, and the Ghurids of Afghanistan, Punjab has always been at the center of the rise and fall of many polities.

Located on the northwestern side of the Indian subcontinent, the land of five rivers, Punjab is defined by its geography. There is some debate as to whether this spatial definition of Punjab holds true over history. The Rig Veda refers to the Sapta Sindhu, the seven rivers, while the Zoroastrian text, the Avesta, talks about the Hapta Hendu (seven rivers). The emphasis in both is on rivers rather than the land. However, the spatial definition of Punjab by seven rivers comprising the Indus, or Sindhu, its tributaries, and the legendary Saraswati river, cannot be denied. Mughal Emperor Akbar extended the province of Lahore to cover the valleys of the five Indus tributaries and called it Punjab. For the British, this was a neat definition of the territory.

▲ **A gold coin** from the reign of Chandragupta II c. 400.

A matter of geography

There is general consensus, however, that the Yamuna River forms the region's eastern boundary. The Aravalli Hills lie to the south and the dry stretch of the Thar desert in the southwest. To the north and northwest rise the high walls of the Himalayas, the ice caps and glaciers of which feed the Indus and its tributaries.

It is here, to these rich alluvial plains, that migrants from Central Asia arrived after crossing the Hindu Kush ranges. The plains are categorized into three distinct areas, which are Malwa to the south of the Sutlej River; Majha in the interstices of the Ravi, Beas, and Sutlej Rivers to the west of the region; and Doaba, the region between the Beas and Sutlej Rivers in the east.

In brief

c. 3300 BCE
The Indus Valley Civilization develops

c. 1500 BCE
The Aryans immigrate to the subcontinent

c. 518 BCE
Darius makes Punjab part of Persian Empire.

c. 321 BCE
Formation of the Mauryan Empire

1001
Mahmud of Ghazni enters the Indian subcontinent

1451
The Lodi Dynasty comes to power

The history of Punjab

The earliest human settlement here, in the Soan River Valley between the Indus and Jhelum Rivers, dates back to the Palaeolithic Age. From 3300 BCE, the Indus Valley Civilization emerged on the northwestern fringe of the subcontinent and several of its settlements such as Harappa, Rupar, and Ganweriwala developed in the region of Punjab.

By the middle of the second millennium BCE these cities began declining and were replaced by settlements of the Indo-Aryan populations that arrived from Central Asia. This was the Vedic period that saw the composition of the Rig Veda, a key Hindu sacred text. In the sixth century, the Persian army under Darius the Great ruled the region between the Indus and Jhelum rivers. Two centuries later, the Greek Alexander the Great succeeded the Persians and asserted control up to the Beas River. As Greek authority waned, parts of the region came under the Mauryan Empire that followed. With the decline of the Mauryas came the Greco-Bactrians and then the Kushanas. In the first eight centuries CE, different parts of the region were ruled by the Gupta Dynasty, the Huns, the Harsha Empire, and the Taank Kingdom. Mahmud of Ghazni arrived from Central Asia in the 11th century and annexed Punjab. A century later, the Ghurids came from Afghanistan and established the Delhi Sultanate over the north of the Indian subcontinent.

At the time of Guru Nanak's birth in 1469, Punjab was under the control of the Delhi Sultans of the Lodi Dynasty, with the exception of Multan which was under the Langah Sultanate.

"… towns of the **Indus Culture** began to **decline** in the second millennium … a slow but sure **movement up** the river valleys, and into the **lower Himalayas**, was made possible."

J.S. GREWAL, *THE SIKHS OF THE PUNJAB*, 1990

A lithograph depicting the drift sands in the interiors of the Sindh Sager Doab in Punjab. The print shows the sandy desertlike area, dotted with mostly shrubs and a few trees.

The people of Punjab

The fertile plains created by the abundant river system in the region have seen human settlement since prehistoric times. While the mountains of the Hindu Kush range formed a barrier into the subcontinent, the passes through them brought both migrants and invaders from Central Asia and as far away as Greece.

"The **Jat** is ... most important of the Panjab peoples ... **Rajput** who comes next ... while the two **together** constitute **27 percent** of the whole population of the **Province**."

UMAIR MIRZA, *PUNJAB CASTES*, 1916

By the 15th century, the population of the Punjab region was significantly heterogeneous and while the communities were varied and settled in different parts of the plains, intermingling was not uncommon. The Pathans and Balochs, hailing from parts of present-day Pakistan and Afghanistan, settled around the banks of the Chenab River in Multan. The Kharal and Sial tribes, nomadic subcastes of the Jat or Rajput communities, could be found in the lower reaches of the doabs between the Chenab and Beas Rivers. Other Rajput clans were settled along the border with Rajasthan and along the Shiwalik foothills.

Along the upper reaches of the Indus River, almost along the foothills in the Sindh Sagar Doab, resided a large number of warring tribes, including the Gakkhars, Awans, Janjuas, and Bhattis, who were embroiled in an incessant conflict over control of the land that continued for centuries thereafter. It is often difficult to arrive at the actual origins of these tribes, who claimed to be subcastes of larger groups such as the Jats or Rajputs, and variably ascribed to different faiths such as Hinduism, Islam, and later Sikhism.

The Jats and the Rajputs

The Jats were a diverse community of largely agricultural nomads from the Sindh region in the lower reaches of the Indus Valley. Used to a nomadic lifestyle, they migrated northward over time, passing through Rajasthan to arrive at Punjab where they found fertile land. This started a process of settlement through various shifts toward settled agriculture. The Jats gradually came to own large tracts of land, making them a powerful force in the region.

The Jat migration into Punjab saw the displacement of a large number of Rajput and Gujjar clans. While it was largely the Jats on the eastern side of Punjab who gained wealth through sedentary agriculture, those on the western front continued their nomadic lifestyles. For both, the migration prompted exposure to the mainstream religions of Hinduism and Islam, and paved the way for subsequent conversions to Sikhism after the 15th century (see pp.269–270).

The Rajputs comprised a wide array of warring tribes who held territories across the northern part of the subcontinent, including Punjab, although it was the Rajput kingdoms in what later came to be known as Rajasthan that gained historical fame. Over the years, the banner of the Rajputs came to assimilate various tribes settled in different parts of Punjab, who claimed to hold allegiance to both their tribe as well as their Rajput status. Although greatly outnumbered by the Jats, the Rajputs were another significant agricultural group in the region.

A painting attributed to 19th-century artist Bishan Singh, depicts a scene from the daily life of women in Punjab. Here, they can be seen on a horse-drawn carriage.

The religious landscape

Punjab witnessed not just the amalgamation of ancient beliefs into the multistranded philosophy of Hinduism, but also the arrival of Islam.

Fifteenth century Punjab was no stranger to a variety of religious beliefs and practices, having been populated for centuries by communities that ascribed to a diversity of faiths. It was also the frontier that faced Islam when it entered an "invader" as opposed to its peaceful arrival on the western coast earlier.

Hinduism

The prevailing faith in the subcontinent at the time was Hinduism. However, its tenets are difficult to define. There is no single personality around which it evolved, nor a clear, authoritative creed on which it is based. It is more a philosophical construct that grew organically, assimilating along the way the varied beliefs and values of the people it came into contact with. It is, in the words of philosopher and the first president of India, S. Radhakrishnan, "a medley of rites, a mere map… It meant one thing in the Vedic period, another in the Brahmanical, and a third in the Buddhist."

In the centuries after the arrival of the Indo-Aryans in the subcontinent in the second millennium BCE, their propitiation of natural phenomenon—the rising sun, the full moon, thunder and lightning—gradually came to be integrated with the diverse pantheon

This gum tempera painting c. 1800s, depicts the Hindu deity Shiva, identifiable with the all-seeing third eye on his forehead, along with his consort Sati, both seated on a lotus blossom.

> "[Hinduism] may be **described** rather as an **encyclopedia** of religion than as a **religion**."

NICOL MACNICOL, *INDIAN THEISM: FROM THE VEDIC TO THE MUHAMMADAN PERIOD*, 1915

of deities worshipped by people of the Indus Valley. The Hindu pantheon includes innumerable gods and goddesses, all accepted as aspects of the one Supreme, who is, in varied manifestations of energy, the creator, preserver, and destroyer. It is for this reason that Hinduism is often perceived as a fusion of various customs that likely predated the Vedas, its earliest scriptural texts, stretching back to prehistoric times.

The earliest institutionalization of the Vedic tradition was marked by the composition of the Rig Veda in the doabs around the Indus Valley. Other texts, such as the Dharmashastras and Upanishads, were added to the Vedic corpus over time, defining religious duties, rites and rituals, codes of conduct, moral precepts: every aspect of knowledge essential to live a dharmic, or dutiful, life.

With the institutionalization of beliefs and codes of conduct came the emergence of a hierarchy, the caste system, an almost inviolate division of society into brahmins (priests), kshatriyas (warriors), vaishyas (merchants), and shudras (artisans and laborers). Over the years, strands of Hinduism were patronized by different kingdoms; deities rose to prominence at different periods in different parts of the subcontinent. The one constant, however, was the acceptance of essential philosophy laid down by the sacred texts that defined a way of life—a person's *dharma*.

Islam

Islam was born in 7th-century Arabia, when the Prophet Mohammed founded a community of followers in Mecca after a divine vision. A Muslim (believer) accepts absolute surrender to the will of Allah, who is the one and only God. Worship in Islam centers on the basic tenets of reverence to the messenger of God, the Prophet Mohammed, and the sacred text known as the Quran. Strict monotheism, collective reading at the mosque, fasting in the month of Ramadan, and the pilgrimage to Mecca are essential practices, which together create a sense of universal equality, brotherhood, and solidarity among Muslims.

As Arab traders regularly crossed the Arabian Sea to the Indian subcontinent, the new religion did not take long to reach its western shore. Moreover, there had always been some Arabs who preferred to stay instead of returning with their ships. The first Arab-Muslim settlements were established along the Malabar coast as early as 636 CE. Mosques were built and the community grew peacefully, converting the local populace as it expanded further inland toward the south and north.

With Mahmud of Ghazni's campaign in India in the 11th century, traces of Islam began seeping into Punjab and Muslim forces came to be seen as the enemy. The number of Muslims in the region increased in the 12th century when Islamic rule was perpetuated after Muhammad Ghori's first conquest in Punjab, which established the Delhi Sultanate.

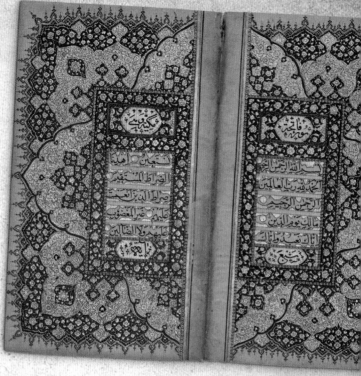

▲ **This Quran manuscript is from the late 18th or** early 19th century. The beautiful blue and gold illumination is found at the opening to the nine *suras*, or chapters.

BUDDHISM

Gautama Buddha or the "Enlightened One" founded a new school of nontheistic religious thought in North India in the late 6th century and the early 4th century BCE. He taught the "Middle Way": that the course to a life without suffering is a path between slavish attachment to material desires and asceticism. Patronized by the Mauryan king Ashoka, Buddhism spread rapidly through the north of the subcontinent. According to author D.C. Ahir, Buddhism came to Punjab with Buddha himself and enriched the region's culture. However, its popularity waned in the face of Hindu sects and the advent of Islam by the end of the 7th century CE.

A 15th-century statue of a seated Buddha from Thailand.

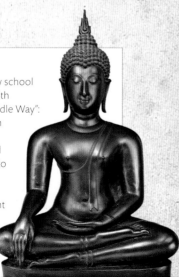

Catalysts of a new faith

A religion is never born in a vacuum. It is ensconced within the emergent trends of its time. This maxim holds true for all new religions, especially within the subcontinent, which developed by breaking away from the mould of mainstream belief systems.

The 6th and 7th centuries BCE witnessed great intellectual and spiritual upheaval in the subcontinent. In addition to numerous states ruled by monarchs, there were also independent republics whose rulers were chosen by the people. Vedic traditions were challenged by freedom of thought and diversity that developed in response to the rapid urbanization that this period experienced. New social groups were assimilated into the Hindu fold, and it is possible that they were unconvinced about their caste positions. Philosophers and spiritual masters emerged who questioned the rigidity of the caste system and the oppressive and discriminatory practices to which it gave rise.

Renunciation and the practice of austerities

Many new religions took root in this fertile soil. Buddhism, Jainism, and Ajivikism are all situated within this context of philosophical and social upheaval. Each one was deeply embedded within the renunciatory tradition of the Sramana movement that based itself on the concepts of *samsara* or the eternal cycle of birth and death, and *moksha* or the breaking of this cycle to achieve liberation. The Sramanas believed that it was possible for an individual to attain *moksha* through renunciation, penance, and the practise of austerities directed at cleansing their essential energies. Most of the religions that emerged under this umbrella died out or were reabsorbed into Hindu traditions; Buddhism and Jainism are two that have survived.

A personal relationship with God

By the 15th century, the Bhakti movement had spread across the north of the subcontinent, having gradually migrated from the south where it had been born in the 7th century. Bhakti emerged from within the traditions of Vaishnavism (where Vishnu is the supreme deity) and Shaivism (where

▲ **Prayer wheels, like the ones seen here at** the Buddhist Lamayuru Monastery at Leh in India, are an important part of Buddhism. The religion originated in the Indian subcontinent nearly a millennium before Sikhism.

"The **weaver** is forever
Fetching his clay-pot,
Forever **plastering** his kitchen.
He **cares** not for his loom or shuttle;
He is **raptured** by the bliss of saying
Hari, Hari."

KABIR (TRANSLATION BY NIRMAL DASS,
SONGS OF KABIR FROM THE ADI GRANTH, 1992)

the supreme deity is Shiva), but it was in essence a reform movement. Once again, the orthodox practices of mainstream Hinduism ignited a backlash, which seethed around a personalized devotion that largely transgressed caste and class boundaries.

The appeal of the Bhakti movement was its focus on one God, the only reality in a world full of illusion. Bhakti laid emphasis on the deep emotional bond between God and devotee. The passionate devotion and complete surrender to His will was the way to serve Him and navigate one's way to salvation. It was through meditation, chanting, and the singing of hymns in the praise of God that the devotee could truly express their intense devotion.

Bhakti found itself echoed in the teachings of the Sufi mystics who believed in the all-embracing presence of God, devotion to whom implied a complete surrender or merging of one's own identity with God. Such a mystic experience could be realized through meditation; *zikr*, or the chanting of God's name; as well as singing and dancing. While the Sufi mystics' advent into the region followed the invading Muslim armies, their attitude was very different. They did not believe in killing nonbelievers or destroying places of worship but extended warmth, friendship, and love to all. Not surprisingly, both Bhakti and Sufi saints found most of their followers among the lower castes and classes, who found a familiar yet liberating release within these forms of worship.

It was in this milieu of an age of questioning and lowering of barriers that Guru Nanak was born and lived in Punjab before founding his own religion in the latter half of the 15th century.

Guru and guruship

The concept of a teacher or guide who imparts and exemplifies knowledge is as ancient as religion itself. Its essence is manifold because the guru's role is manifold: as a guide, a parental figure, a mentor, and sometimes, even an exemplar.

The variance in the meanings and origins of the word "guru" epitomizes the rich diversity of roles the individual sustained in real life. This is why it is challenging to capture the plurality in the concept of the guru within any western framework of belief.

In most Indic systems, the concept of a teacher falls under the nomenclature of a Guru. Such an individual's role and purpose could be interpreted in accordance with one's faith. In English, the word "guru" translates to "teacher," but its Sanskrit roots have several other connotations. The syllable "gu" means ignorance and "ru" means one who dispels. So, a guru enhances their disciple's knowledge, not just of religious teachings, but also of myriad skills, including music, dance, and martial arts.

Guru in the Sikh philosophy

The Sikh faith moulded the understanding of the guru in a different way. The task of the Sikh Guru was to guide followers on a spiritual path, without discriminating on the basis of caste, gender, age, or class. The Guru instructed the Sikhs on the nature of Truth, and instilled in people the value of labor while stressing the equality and oneness of humanity; adherence to these beliefs lifted the follower's spiritual merit.

> "Guru is **God, ineffable, unsearchable**. He who follows the Guru **comprehends the nature of the universe**."

J.S. GREWAL, *SIKH IDEOLOGY POLITY, AND SOCIAL ORDER: FROM GURU NANAK TO MAHARAJA RANJIT SINGH*, 2007

The most distinguishable characteristic was the separation of the guruship and the guru. While the former was an eternal state, the latter was metamorphic, implying that the guru could transform. This allowed followers to conceptualize a unity between Guru Nanak, the first Sikh Guru (see pp.32–33), and his successors, all of whom carried his knowledge. Moreover, the Sikh Gurus were central figures of the religion, which became a marker of its self-identity and distinction.

The word "guru" itself also denotes "heavy" or "ponderous," implying the moral and spiritual weight that a Guru carries in that capacity. It is an allusion to the extent of knowledge that the figure possesses and the influence they exert on their followers. "Guru" might have also been derived from "giri," referencing "one who calls." This implies that the Guru bears an association with the "divine call," or the idea that spiritual service and nurturing are tasks bestowed upon someone by divine powers.

Guru in Hinduism

"Guru" had a different connotation within the various strands of Hinduism, with the exact meaning and purpose of the individual varying. Generally, a *shishya* (student and disciple) would rely on the guru to guide them toward the attainment of *moksha* (liberation from rebirth). This was because only the guru had the means to simplify the complex understanding of Truth for common people. The two main aspects of guruship were the system of initiation of *shishyas*, and the tradition of succession to perpetuate this order. According to Hindu texts, the guru orally taught Vedic knowledge, which was beyond the *shishya's* access. The process involved dialogue, contemplation, and physical service, often in the gurukul, a school run by the guru. There was an intimate connection between the guru and the *shishya*, marked by reciprocal dependence, mentorship, affection, and devotion, which at times conflated the former with a parent and with the Divine.

This is exemplified within the Bhakti tradition of Hinduism, which placed less emphasis on learning based on the Vedas, the ancient religious texts, and instead venerated its saints who would impart knowledge through the music and the poetry they composed. Within the more heterodox Tantric tradition, which presented itself as an antithesis to the Vedas, the guru was essential as knowledge was more esoteric than in mainstream Hinduism.

◀ **A watercolor painting, c. 1780,** from Hyderabad in Andhra Pradesh, imagines a gathering of Sikh Gurus. The first Sikh Guru, Guru Nanak, sits under a tree, surrounded by the other Gurus and his companion Bhai Mardana, seen holding a stringed instrument, in the far left.

Splintering of the sultanates

By 1469, the year of Guru Nanak's birth, the political landscape had transformed. Punjab was now surrounded by regional polities that had asserted their rule since the 14th century, and was itself being governed by the Delhi Sultanate.

At the turn of the 15th century, Punjab lay under the reign of the Indo-Turkic Tughlaq Dynasty. However, the Delhi Sultanate, as the Empire was called, had started floundering.

The fragmentation

An attack from Timur's Turko-Mongol army in 1398 had destabilized the sultanate, already reeling from internal threats. As the might of the sultanate waned, regional polities sprung up. The last Tughlaq ruled until around 1412 and was succeeded by the next dynasty, the Sayyids.

Under the Sayyids, the sultanate continued to assert dominance over the regions of Punjab and some parts of Sindh. However, their weakness became evident when they failed to suppress the rebellions of the hill tribe of Khokars in Punjab and others in the doab region between Punjab and Delhi.

In 1451, Bahlul Lodi overthrew Alauddin Alam Shah of the Sayyids, establishing the Lodi Dynasty, which became the final dynasty of the Delhi Sultanate. The Mughals replaced them in 1526.

▲ **A watercolor painting c. 1600** depicting the Timur army fighting Nasir al-Din Mahmud Tughlaq.

Regional states

Many regional states emerged in the 14th century, often as a result of local rebellion by former administrators, and became independent successors of the sultanate. One of the earliest formations was the Bahmani Sultanate, in the Deccan in 1347. In Bengal, power was wrested from the sultanate midcentury by the Ilyas Shahi Dynasty, which was in turn overthrown by the Husain Shahi Dynasty in the last decade of the 15th century. Similarly, just outside Delhi, Jaunpur asserted its sovereignty in 1396. A few decades later, the region of Malwa, situated next to Gujarat, broke away from Tughlaq hold. A local sultanate was established in Gujarat under Ahmad Shah around the same time.

The landscape around Punjab continued to swarm with rebellion through the 15th century, even as the centralized authority of the Delhi Sultanate tried its best to retain its hold over its kingdom.

On the north and south

To the north of Punjab lay the hill terrain of Kashmir, which had become home to several Muslims arriving from Central Asia since the 11th century. It was in 1338 that the first

In brief

1396
Jaunpaur state
is formed

1411
Ahmad Shah becomes
ruler of Gujarat

1412
Sayyid Dynasty
comes to power

1451
Lodi Dynasty
comes to power

THE SULTAN OF MULTAN

The Delhi Sultanate ruled Multan, a city on the banks of the Chenab River in eastern Punjab, from the time it was established in the 12th century. As the sultanate weakened, the residents of Multan supported Sheikh Yousaf Qureshi as their next ruler and he came to power in 1438. Seven years later, the Langah clan wrested power from him and established the Langah Sultanate, inviting conflict with the Lodis. The Langah Sultanate continued until the 16th century.

Muslim kingdom was established in the valley under Shah Mir. Through the 14th and 15th centuries, the Shah Mir Dynasty ruled in the region, only coming to an end after Kashmir came under the Mughal Empire in the 16th century.

This period was also marked by the rise of a new group of polities just south of Punjab in the region of Rajasthan—the Rajput states. The first of these to be formed was Mewar under the Sisodiya Rajputs. The Rajputs in Rajasthan identified themselves as kshatriyas (warriors or the ruling class), and they need to be differentiated from the Rajputs settled in Punjab, who were mostly agriculturally oriented.

The 7th-century Chittorgarh Fort in Rajasthan, India, was initially built by the Rajputs. Over the years, it was attacked by many invading dynasties.

2
Origins
1469–1606

In 1469, a child was born who, it was prophesied, would rise to eminence, with his name resounding across the skies. His name was Nanak, and he would go on to become the founder of the Sikh faith. Over the next century, the Sikh Gurus that came after him spread his message far and wide, welcoming thousands into the folds of the new religion.

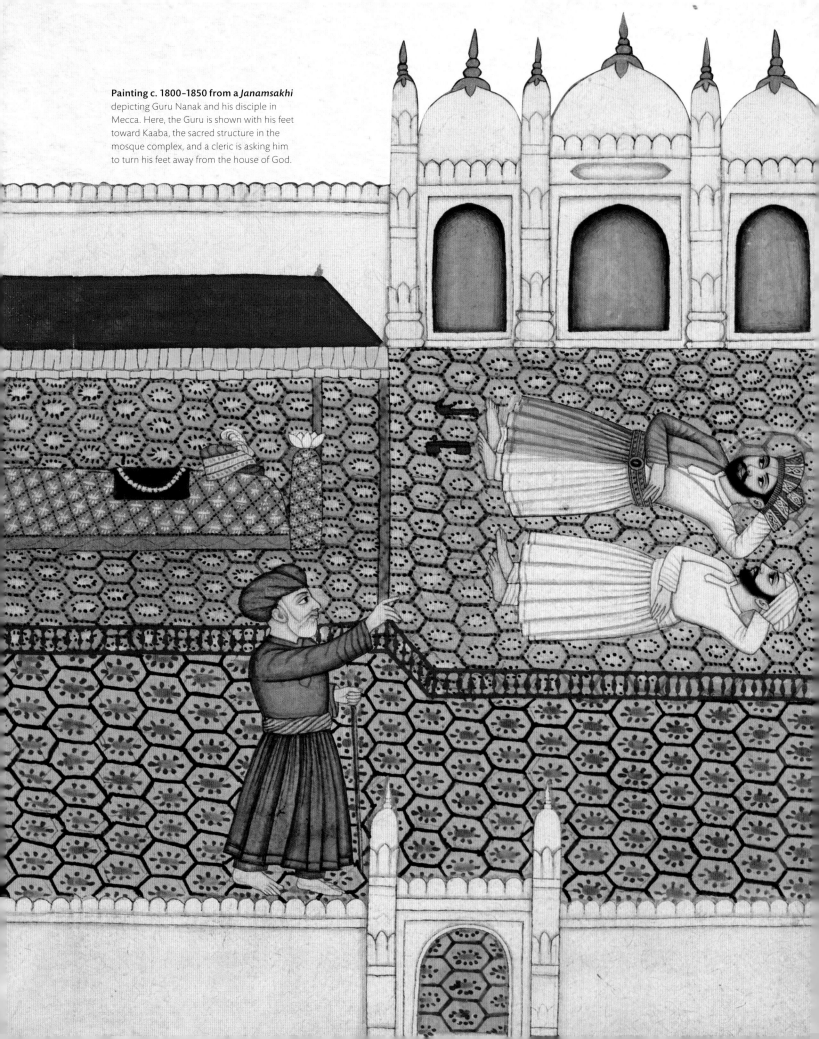

Painting c. 1800–1850 from a *Janamsakhi* depicting Guru Nanak and his disciple in Mecca. Here, the Guru is shown with his feet toward Kaaba, the sacred structure in the mosque complex, and a cleric is asking him to turn his feet away from the house of God.

The first Guru

Legends narrate that a holy figure declared at Guru Nanak's birth that he would attain greatness and acknowledge only the true Divine Being. The first Guru in the Sikh faith dedicated his life to preaching the message of God.

In a milieu of religious strands that focused on attaining oneness with their God, Guru Nanak's understanding of the Divine stood out. Instead of focusing on how to "meet" God, he spoke of the presence of one formless, eternal Divine Being. "There is no Hindu, no Mussalman," he declared at a young age.

Nanak was born in the month of Baisakh according to the Hindu and Sikh calendars; this date is generally considered to be around April 15, 1469. He spent his childhood in the hamlet of Rai Bhoi di Talvandi (now known as Nankana Sahib), about 40 miles (64 kms) southwest of Lahore. His father was a *patwari*, or a revenue records keeper. Most of his childhood was spent much like other children, but Nanak developed an interest in meeting holy figures, Hindu or Muslim, passing through his village.

Early influences

Perhaps the strongest influence in young Nanak's life was his older sister, Nanaki. When she moved away from their childhood home after her marriage, it left him without a close confidante. Author Roopinder Singh in *Guru Nanak: His Life & Teachings* writes that Nanak became withdrawn and distracted. His father wished for his son to learn the skill of accounting. Instead, the young boy turned to poetic compositions, some of which are now a part of the Guru Granth Sahib.

Nanak was proficient in multiple languages through his exposure to teachers of other faiths. His friendship with neighbors and travelers led to a mindset of egalitarianism and equality, an ideology still rare at the time.

Spreading the word

As Guru Nanak's ideas around God and religion cemented, he believed he needed to spread the word. Accompanied by *rabab* player Bhai Mardana (see p.28), he undertook *udasis*, or journeys. Though the exact itinerary of his travels is uncertain, Sikh sources indicate that he visited places of pilgrimage in all four directions.

> "The **sky** is the **salver**
> And the **sun** and the **moon**, the lamps. The luminous **stars** on the **lamps** are the **pearls**."
>
> GURU NANAK'S "AARTI," GURU GRANTH SAHIB (TRANSLATION BY ROOPINDER SINGH IN *GURU NANAK: HIS LIFE AND TEACHINGS*, 2004)

He went as far as Kamrup, now Assam, in the east, to Mecca in the west; and from Ceylon, now Sri Lanka, in the south, to Ladakh in the north. They had to cut through Central India forests, where there would be no habitation for days.

During these travels, the pair took part in local rituals and witnessed holy events. There are stories of Guru Nanak questioning socio-cultural practices where they went, such as refusing to recognize the "low" caste of Lalo, a carpenter with whom he stayed, when prompted by other villagers. He also questioned an Islamic cleric who asked him not to point his feet toward Mecca, and thus God, while lying down. What direction should he point his feet to, Guru Nanak asked the holy man, so that they were not pointing toward God, when the Divine was everywhere?

Journeys of miracles

There are many tales of his mystic abilities from his travels, including the story of a frozen lake in Sikkim, where he struck his staff to get water to the locals. It is said that a part of the lake still does not freeze. Roopinder Singh notes that the journey to Mecca, Medina in Saudi Arabia, Afghanistan, and Iran was his longest. On the way back, they came upon the army of Emperor Babur who had invaded India. Guru Nanak and Bhai Mardana were captured by soldiers during the raid on the town of Saidpur. Like other captives, he was put to manual work, but word of his miracles and his reputation as a spiritual authority had reached the captors. Upon being offered a release, Guru Nanak insisted that the others be freed as well. This marked the end of his *udasis*. Thereafter, he lived in Kartarpur, where he founded a community.

The first community

After nearly two decades of preaching the word of the Divine across the subcontinent, Guru Nanak founded the town of Kartarpur and made it his home. It is here that his followers would gather and live. They would distance themselves from the existing ideas of caste and class, and follow the precepts of Sikhism.

The town of Kartarpur, along the western banks of the Ravi river in Punjab, became a haven for those seeking spiritual guidance. The community's lack of religious orthodoxy was essential to its popularity. Guru Nanak's faith was inclusive to all and so, Hindus as well as Muslims found solace here.

Genesis of a religion
The formation of the commune in Kartarpur marked the beginning of the religion and the end of the journeys he had undertaken across the subcontinent. In fact the town's name translates to "abode of God." After moving here, Guru Nanak established the first *dharmsal*, a sacred space for the Sikhs. It is here that they worshipped and distributed *langar*. It is in this space that Guru Nanak's followers brought into practice key elements of his philosophy. They believed in *kirt karo*, or doing work; *naam japna*, or meditating on the Divine Word; and *wand chako*, or being charitable.

Guru Nanak's idea of equality found resonance in congregational worship, or *sangat*, including the performance of *kirtans*, devotional singing as a group, and in the emphasis on *langar*, or the practice of eating together in a community kitchen. The act of *langar* shattered Hindu caste barriers that forbade upper-caste members from eating with those considered to be of a lower caste. Instead, *langar* inculcated the values of humility and equality among the Panth, the Sikh community (see p.307). In this sense, Kartarpur played an important role in furthering Guru Nanak's vision.

The community also moved away from Hindu idol worship and rituals, such as fasting. Instead, it embraced Guru Nanak's doctrines and prioritized work and family.

Guru Nanak as the Divine
Symbolically, Guru Nanak embraced the garments of a common man. He preached that the life of a person engaged in the household was more rewarding than that of an ascetic. He advocated and participated in working in the fields. He also wrote several of his compositions during his years at Kartarpur.

Indian historian and expert in Sikh studies, J. S. Grewal in his book *Sikh, Ideology, Polity and Social Order: From Guru Nanak to Maharaja Ranjit Singh* noted that "...Nanak the Guru stands in a special relationship with [God], sharing the traits of an avatar and a prophet, but distinct from each." The epithets that Guru Nanak used for the Divine power were later reinvented and used for the Guru by those that followed him.

For them, the Guru was the guiding light that would lead them to the "Truth" (see p.41). His compositions of *shabad*, or the holy word, sung to followers at the new center, were integral in binding the community together.

In brief

1469
Guru Nanak is born

1525
Guru Nanak establishes community at Kartarpu

1526
Babur becomes the Emperor of India

1539
Guru Nanak names Bha Lehna, later called Guru Angad, as successor

1539
Guru Nanak passes away in Kartarpur

BHAI MARDANA
Guru Nanak's companion was often depicted in paintings with a rabab, a string instrument. Born into a Muslim family of minstrels, Bhai Mardana grew up in the same village as Guru Nanak, and was his friend from childhood. He accompanied the Guru on his long journeys and played the rabab for Guru Nanak's singing of poetic compositions. One of Bhai Mardana's verses even appears in the Guru Granth Sahib in *Bihagare ki Var*. The *Janamsakhis*, Sikh hagiographies, are replete with stories of Bhai Mardana's unreserved devotion for Guru Nanak.

"The **Primal Lord** revealed the **Divine Word**, and **It** eradicated all **fears** and **anxieties**."

GURU ARJAN, *SHABAD*, GURU GRANTH SAHIB

Legends of Nanak

The evocative and metaphorical import of various mythical stories narrated in the *Janamsakhis* played a fundamental role in spreading Guru Nanak's philosophy and elevating his position in the Sikh faith to that of a divine figure.

There is a famous story about Guru Nanak often told to children. It tells of the time the Guru was traveling with his companions, Bhai Bala and Bhai Mardana, and they came upon a body of water so vast it seemed uncrossable. A large, monstrous fish helped them navigate the waters much to the horror of the Guru's companions. It was only later that they realized the creature was a lost soul seeking redemption, freed after it received blessings from the Guru.

The story, often told orally, is part of the *Janamsakhis*, hagiographic accounts of the life of Guru Nanak. Sometimes they demonstrate his otherworldly qualities and supernatural ability, or exemplify his status as an enlightened being.

There are various forms or renditions of the *Janamsakhi*, with the earliest dating back to the late 16th or early 17th century. Some of the key versions include the *Bala*, *Meharban*, *Adi*, and *Puratan*. They all have one thing in common—they depict the Guru's life in the form of mythical stories. Sikh-studies scholar Nikky-Guninder Kaur Singh notes that there is no denying the functional utility of these myths as they reveal essential elements of Sikh culture.

"To **whichever direction** I turn my eyes there **It is**, Whosoever I see, there **It pervades**, Wherever I see there is a **singular reality**, Whoever I see **there are You**, Ignorant is the one who does not realize **Reality visually**."

GURU NANAK, GURU GRANTH SAHIB
(TRANSLATION BY NIKKY-GUNINDER KAUR SINGH)

ਮਾਲਨੇ
ਚਰ ਲਿ

ਸ੍ਰੀ ਗੁਰੂ
ਨਾਨਕ
ਸਾਹਿਬ ਜੀ
ਉਮਰ ੧੦
ਸਾਲ

▶ **A mural from a gurdwara in Amritsar, Punjab** portrays the 10-year-old Nanak as a farmer. This depiction is one of many based on the *Janamsakhis*.

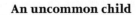

An uncommon child

There are several stories and legends associated with Nanak's early life. One of them is of an encounter with a *pandit* or Hindu spiritual teacher after seven-year-old Nanak refuses to be taught by him. He instead argues the futility of worldly learning and emphasizes his belief in the value of the Divine Word as being the ultimate "Truth." The *Meharban Janamsakhi* elaborates on the same legend. In it, the *pandit* believes that Nanak is too wise for his age and should thus decide what is best for himself. In another tale, 11-year-old Nanak, born into a Hindu Khatri family, refuses to wear the *janeu* or sacred thread customary for upper-caste Hindus. He argues that a person's inherent qualities and deeds define them and not such caste insignia. Nanak's early years of growing up in the town of Talwandi, in present-day Pakistan, become a center for miraculous legends. Each seeks to reinstate his divinity, spiritual force, and the power to transcend the material world. One such tale is of a paddy field, destroyed by Nanak's buffaloes while he was meditating, but miraculously restored. There is also an episode in the *Puratan Janamsakhi*, where Nanak's shadow, while he is asleep under a tree, remains constant with the setting sun.

Communion with the Divine

The *Bein Pravesh* (entry into the Bein rivulet) story from the *Puratan Janamsakhi* represents Sikhism's core concept of "ultimate truth" being transcendental and formless. It describes a young Nanak's religious experience in the Bein rivulet, where he would go to bathe. One morning, he does not return, and everyone fears the worst. He emerges two days later and tells people that he spent the time in communion with God. His first words upon return were: "There is no Hindu, no Mussalman (Muslim)."

Sikh scholar Harbans Singh, editor-in-chief of the *Encyclopaedia of Sikhism*, notes that this is significant as it showcases a vision for shared humanity in a society ripped apart by conflicts and hierarchies. Guru Nanak's journeys, or *udasis*, as an adult, to spread the "Word" of God are also documented, as are his interactions with different gurus, saints, and ascetics. His prophesied death also acquires a dramatic narration: Guru Nanak sits on a withered acacia, which blossoms at once when he perishes.

▶ **A 1960 oil painting** of Guru Nanak by Indian artist Sobha Singh.

Guru Nanak

The founder of Sikhism, Guru Nanak was the first spiritual leader of the faith. His indelible ideas of social organization, theology, and literature have endured through the ages and form the bedrock of the Sikh religion.

Guru Nanak created a socially involved religion that was based on the tenets of equality, service, and humanity. He also established a community quite distinct from others in the subcontinent. Sikh accounts narrate that before founding the religion, Guru Nanak was a man deeply devoted to serving God. Born within the milieu of heterodox religiosity, illustrated by the Bhakti, Sufi, Sant, and Nath movements that moved away from mainstream interpretations of Hinduism, Guru Nanak's early forays into theological ideas led him to craft an original faith that was opposed to the stringency as well as ritualistic aspects of Puranic Hinduism and orthodox Islam.

Historians note that he undertook journeys across India at the turn of the 15th century, interacting with people of other faiths. This helped him shape his own interpretation of divinity. It is evident from his subsequent writing that he had an acute understanding of the human condition, which in turn equipped him with the metaphors he used to preach his message to the masses.

With Sikhism, Guru Nanak forged a new social order based on his cherished values of equality and humanitarianism, an overt demonstration against the evils embedded in the religious systems that he saw around him. Sikhism, however, hinged on a framework of equilibrium in caste, gender, economics, and age, forging a radical community with a distinct sense of identity that Guru Nanak's successors built upon. This self-identity was reinforced by the stress on collective action and liberation, which was unusual at that time.

A noteworthy leader

By instituting practices such as *langar*, Guru Nanak distinguished himself from other medieval poet-saints who did not really challenge the system beyond their verses. He stood out for his unique philosophy that blended monotheistic worship with sociocultural service. From his compositions on the nature of a good leader and proper governance,

> "Guru Nanak was clearly and lucidly the **spirit behind Sikh ideology**, a fact that is recognized in multiple ways in the unfolding **evolution of the panth**."

LOUIS E. FENECH, "THE EVOLUTION OF THE SIKH COMMUNITY," IN *THE OXFORD HANDBOOK OF SIKH STUDIES*, 2014

it is evident that his concern for social equality went beyond the religious to oppose the tyranny of political authority as well: the subcontinent had undergone changes in power and foreign rulers, such as the Mughals, had institutionalized new, unequal policies.

The community at Kartarpur, now set in Pakistan, was a representation of his political ideals, of a fraternity based on social liberation, which would aid in his religious mission. As the Guru, Nanak initiated a schedule for followers to pray, meditate, cook, share food, and work to earn; this was replicated at other centers through subordinate leaders. The system gained the support of the community and became a way of distinguishing Sikhism from other religions.

The architect of a faith

Guru Nanak passed away in 1539 at Kartarpur, leaving behind ideas, such as the *panj khand* (five realms) philosophy of spiritual progress that leads one to the Divine Truth." His poetry, enriched with imagery, captured the beauty of the universe created by the Divine. His successors built upon his poetry, philosophy, and structure to further strengthen the religion.

Guru Nanak set the fundamental beliefs that are followed to date in Sikhism, and his *gurbani*, or words, inspired the compositions of later Sikh Gurus as well, demonstrating his central position in Sikh history. His tenets have been read, scrutinized, and reinterpreted in many contexts across centuries, which has enabled the first Guru to survive in memory long after his passing. However, most importantly, it is the values of humanity and equality enshrined by Guru Nanak into the Sikh ethos that memorialize him as an extraordinary individual.

▼ This 1858 engraving after a painting by British artist W. Carpenter depicts devotees reading the Guru Granth Sahib at a Sikh temple in Amritsar.

Poetry of faith

Guru Nanak's compositions encapsulate his teachings on equality, peace, honesty, and kinship, capturing the imagination of people. They form the backbone of the faith and are still recited today as a marker of the Sikh community and their belief.

While no manuscript written in Guru Nanak's own hand has survived the vagaries of time, his poetry is immortalized through compilations of the gurus that came after him. One collection is the Adi Granth, where the verses are arranged according to 18 ragas or melodies. Guru Arjan, the fifth Guru, took on the task of selecting the hymns of his predecessors. He chose 985 poems of Guru Nanak for inclusion in the Adi Granth. One such composition is the opening of the *Japji Sahib*, which is the first composition of the founder of Sikhism and appears at the beginning of the collection. It also formed the core of the faith:

> *There is One God*
> *His Name is Truth.*
> *He is the Creator*

The power of simplicity

Guru Nanak chose to compose his poems in colloquial Punjabi, with a sprinkling of Persian and Sanskrit, the languages that the Hindu and Islamic faiths were taught in. These were spoken and understood by members of the different communities in Punjab, lending to their accessibility. The poems were also put to music, making them easy to remember. The repeated melody played the role of coaxing the listener to engage with the words and their interpretation, while slowly arriving at the meaning. In many ways, the realization of divinity became intrinsically connected with mellifluous enjoyment.

Guru Nanak's poems are also direct in style, despite the complexity of ideas and profundity of his writings. They follow the logic of common sense, allowing them to be appreciated by everyone. This demonstrates his keen understanding of human existence, augmented as a result of the various *udasis*. These equipped him to write about the Divine Truth in a manner that would appeal to all classes and communities, as illustrated in the following verse from the *Japji Sahib*. Here, the emphasis is on prayer and action as a way to cleanse one's soul of past deeds.

As hands or feet besmirched with slime,
Water washes white;
As garments dark with grime
Rinsed with soap are made light;
So when sin soils the soul
Prayer alone shall make it whole.

Rich imagery

Guru Nanak's poems echo the style of the *Nirguna bhagats*, holy figures from the Bhakti movement (see p.41). They also used short and simple verses, while weaving in aspects of the local *Khari Boli* dialect to make their ideas accessible. Guru Nanak distinguished his works with the use of folk idioms and imagery. For instance, Guru Nanak's "Bara Mah" captures the yearning for God through the year. Here, he writes in the voice of a woman awaiting the Divine.

When the bough adorns
itself anew
The wife awaits the coming of her lord
Her eyes fixed on the door.

The use of imagery as epitomized in "Bara Mah" is especially pertinent since it evokes scenes familiar to his followers. The poem succinctly relates the weather to the search for the *Akal Purakh*, and later became the basis for the Nanakshahi calendar, the tropical solar calendar that Sikhs use. In the poem, Guru Nanak locates God all around, but ultimately encourages his followers to look within to find the answer to liberation.

Guru Nanak asks: "Whither seekest thou the Lord?
Whom awaitest thou?
Thou hast not far to go, for the Lord
Is within thee, thou art His mansion."

There is no doubt, as academic Susnigdha Dey notes in the essay "Guru Nanak as a Poet" that Guru Nanak's compositions are the most significant demonstration of the Sikh belief that "The Word of the Guru is the Inner Music."

> "…The **beloved** seeks the **cool of the evening**. If the comfort she seeks be in **falsehood**, There will be **sorrow** in store for her. If it be in **truth**, Hers will be a life of **joy everlasting**."

ASADH VERSE, "BARA MAH," *HYMNS OF GURU NANAK*
(TRANSLATION BY KHUSHWANT SINGH)

Gagan Mein Thaal, a painting by contemporary Indian artist Seema Kohli depicts Guru Nanak and his companion Bhai Mardana (shown strumming the rabab). It is based on "Aarti," a *bani* (hymn) by the former where the sun and moon are likened to lamps, and the sky to a platter. The stars are considered the adornments, the sandalwood trees the incense, and the flowers, the garland offered up to the Divine.

"Bhai Gurdas confirms that 'with the accompaniment of ... **rabab** (stringed instrument) the **praises** (of Baba Nanak) are **sung** in every home.'"

GURNAM SINGH, "SIKH MUSIC," *THE OXFORD HANDBOOK OF SIKH STUDIES*, 2014

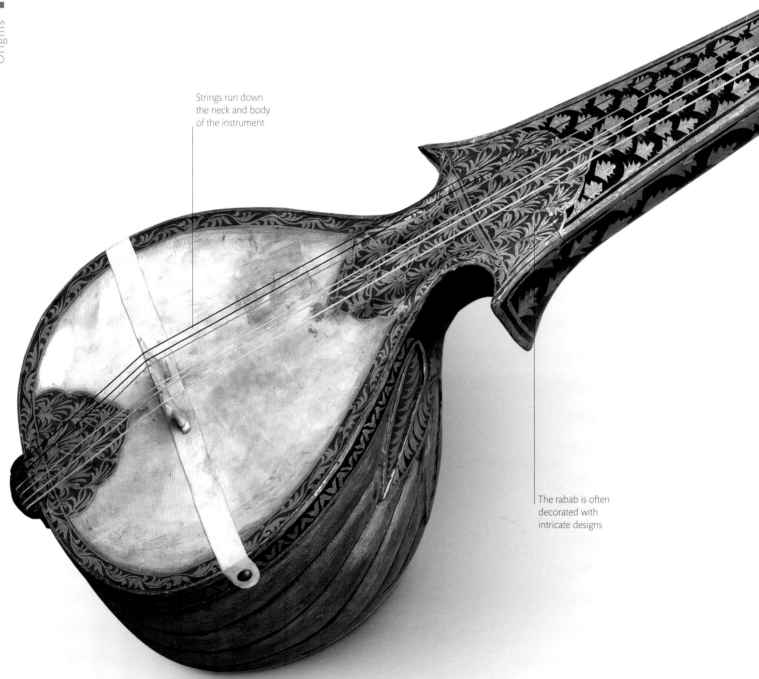

Strings run down the neck and body of the instrument

The rabab is often decorated with intricate designs

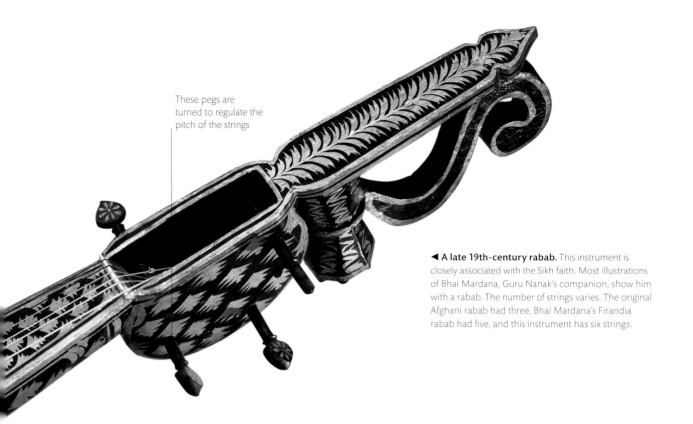

These pegs are turned to regulate the pitch of the strings

◄ **A late 19th-century rabab.** This instrument is closely associated with the Sikh faith. Most illustrations of Bhai Mardana, Guru Nanak's companion, show him with a rabab. The number of strings varies. The original Afghani rabab had three, Bhai Mardana's Firandia rabab had five, and this instrument has six strings.

Rabab

The first Sikh musical instrument

The Sikh Gurus used singing as well as instruments to evoke spiritualism among the listeners. The first musical instrument that was used for this purpose was the rabab: a pear-shaped, lutelike device.

The Firandia rabab

Guru Nanak adopted the rabab as a spiritual tool to instil divine mysticism in his devotees. Popular Sikh accounts indicate that his sister, Bebe Nanaki, had the instrument custom-made by Bhai Firanda, a skilled carpenter, before gifting it to Guru Nanak. The Guru then presented the instrument to Bhai Mardana (see p.28), a Muslim minstrel who provided musical expression to Guru Nanak's verses for almost three decades during their travels. Whenever Guru Nanak sang, Bhai Mardana played the rabab with grace. This resulted in the tradition of *shabad kirtan* (singing of scriptural hymns) that was continued and refined by the successive gurus.

Bhai Mardana's Firandia rabab (named after Bhai Firanda) was a longer variation of the original instrument from Afghanistan.

A plucked instrument with gut strings running down its neck, the Firandia rabab was about 3 ft (0.9 m) long and fashioned of 'Tunn' wood, with a hollow base encased in goat hide. It made a pleasant yet striking sound.

Its structure and design made it suitable for Guru Nanak's travels for spiritual propagation. Bhai Mardana could effortlessly play three octaves without having to retune his strings. His rabab had a fretless composition, larger fingerboard, and five strings (in comparison to the traditional three strings that Afghani rababs had). A two-in-one instrument, the rabab carried the tune as well as the rhythm. This provided Bhai Mardana with the versatility to perform a variety of musical styles, as Guru Nanak traveled through places with distinct cultures and musical traditions.

An instrument designed to accompany the divine hymns that came through the Guru, the Firandia rabab of the Sikhs started a long tradition of Sikh music and the same model of rababs remained in use up to the period of the tenth Sikh Guru, Guru Gobind Singh.

Guru Nanak's idea of the Divine

Diverging from the mainstream understanding of divinity at the time, Guru Nanak preached that the Divine, or *Akal Purakh*, which translates to the Timeless Being, is *Ik Onkar*, or the Absolute One—singular, eternal, and formless.

The repeated use of the numeral one in Guru Nanak's compositions shows his conviction hat there is no second "supreme being." The Divine was the creator of everything and the end goal of everything, and it is the Sikh purpose to accept and achieve this result.

This is perhaps best personified in the expression *Ik Onkar*, which translates to "there is only one God." Here, the word *onkar* transcends the English meaning of God to signify the essence of the Divine and the ultimate Truth.

Also, Guru Nanak did not ascribe any form to the *Akal Purakh*, or the eternal God, choosing instead to perceive it as *nirankar* or without shape. This epitomized the ineffable nature of the Divine as it was unfathomable by human consciousness, although still accessible to humans because of its merciful grace and the word of the Guru. In Sikh writings, *Akal Purakh* has many names and is of different genders, ages, and faiths, adding to the discourse that the Divine is omnipresent, yet not physical.

Finding parallels

There were two distinct religions, Hinduism and Islam, in the Indian subcontinent around the time Guru Nanak began preaching his faith. These had divergent strands as well. One such strand that emerged from Hinduism, *Nirguna* Bhakti, shared some interesting similarities with Sikhism.

Though it evolved from within Hinduism, the *Nirguna* school of Bhakti did not ascribe to orthodox Puranic practices that revolved around the worship of deities, such as Vishnu, Shiva, and their incarnations. Much like the *Akal Purakh*, *nirguna* too meant "without material attributes" and referred to the worship of a formless deity.

Guru Nanak, too, was keen to establish a religion opposed to the ritualistic practices of Brahmanical Hinduism, such as the system of caste under the *varnashramdharma* and the notions of purity upon which it operated. The notions that fire, water, cow dung, salt,

◀ *Kirtan* **is the recitation of devotional songs** of the Sikh faith, set to Indian ragas and performed by singers and instrumentalists. Depicted here is one such *kirtan* underway at the Gurdwara Sis Ganj Sahib in New Delhi, India.

THE BHAGATS AND GURU NANAK

The Adi Granth includes the hymns of 15 Bhakti saints, or Bhagats, who lived during Guru Nanak's time. Of these, 13 were Hindu, including Namdev, Ravidas, and Surdas. The remaining two were the Sufi saint Farid and the poet Kabir, who stood on the interstices of Hinduism and Islam.

A Mir Kalan Khan painting of prominent Bhakti saints, with Namdev in the center, c. 1770–1775.

and ghee were free from pollution were an illusion. For him, God created everything as equal and no one belonged to a low or a high caste. It is why his followers were expected to forego social status, engage in egalitarian practices, such as *langar* (see p.56), and search for the Divine Truth within themselves.

Poetry from the *Nirguna* school of the Bhakti tradition bore similar expressions as well, whether it was in the yearning for the Divine or reimagining oneself as a woman pining for God, visualized as a lover.

The idea of liberation

Many religions subscribe to the common understanding that all living beings possess a soul. Belief systems are equally concerned with that soul's path to emancipation—from the body onto a higher plane to avoid the cycle of rebirth or purgatory. Sikhism is no different.

Guru Nanak contemplated the journey that the soul takes at length. He concluded that the only way for the soul to obtain liberation from the body was through its unity with the Divine Being, the *Akal Purakh*.

The foundational word

Guru Nanak believed that following the will of the Divine was the only way to realize the soul's emancipation. Purity of mind and perseverance were paramount in order for the soul to connect to God. The most important way to achieve this was by repeating the *shabad*, or foundational word, using a technique known as *naam japna*. This allowed one to understand God better, but never in totality since the Divine is beyond human comprehension. The root formula *ik onkar* (see pp.44–45), thus became the *shabad*.

◀ A gouache painting depicts devotees paying their respects to Guru Nanak (top right) while a *langar* is underway. Lettering in English on the painting identifies some of those portrayed; these include Maharaja Ranjit Singh of the Sikh Empire, and Sir Donald Mcleod, Governor General of Punjab in the late 1800s.

Following the Guru's words as recorded in the *gurbani* could also enable a deeper understanding of God.

The meditative quality of recitation was necessary to open up the mind. Practices such as fasting and penance, Guru Nanak asserted, were not suitable for this. This was instrumental in creating a clear distinction between Sikhism and the other religious practices of the time.

Guru Nanak saw asceticism as only an escape from the universe, ineffectual as it only served to distance the devotee from the Divine. Recitation made the *shabad* comprehensible to the devotee. It also guided them away from the influences of *haumai* (the ego) and onto the state of *sahaj* (spiritual liberation).

In his book *Hymns of Guru Nanak*, author Khushwant Singh translated one of the most apt verses from the *Japji Sahib*, which appears in the Guru Granth Sahib. It states that for those who hear the *shabad*, "sorrows end and sins disappear."

Life of a devotee

Guru Nanak advocated a sociable life for the devotees of the faith, including participation in daily activities. It was important to fulfil material obligations as work enabled one to appreciate the true essence of the universe. It also promoted the mind to the next realm of expanded knowledge, where one became more intuitive about the Truth and themselves. Everyone had to uphold a certain lifestyle and demonstrate certain qualities, such as the values of morality, service, humility, honor, charity, and collective action.

As the devotee advanced further in the journey to emancipation, the grace and presence of the *Akal Purakh* became more conspicuous, a blessing that elevated the virtues of the devotee, preparing the soul for liberation. Ultimately, Guru Nanak held that the soul drifted to the abode of the Divine to unite with the *Akal Purakh*.

"He cannot be proved, for He is **uncreated**;
He is **without matter**, self-existent.
They that **serve** shall **honored** be,
O Nanak, the Lord is **most excellent**."

VERSE 5, *JAPJI SAHIB*, *HYMNS OF GURU NANAK*
(TRANSLATION BY KHUSHWANT SINGH), 1990

ਅੰਗ ੧੩੪੬

Devotees approach Harmandir Sahib, or the Golden Temple, in Amritsar. The main sanctum of this important pilgrimage site is encased in gold leaf.

▶ **The first phrase in the Guru Granth Sahib,** *Ik Onkar* is one of the most sacred aspects of the Sikh faith.

Written in Gurmukhi, it means, "There is but one God."

Ik Oankar | Sat Nam | Karta Purkh | Nir Bhau | Nir Vair | Akaal Moorat | Ajooni | Saibhang | Gur Parsaad

"There is one God, truth by name, the creator, without fear, without hate, timeless in form, beyond birth, self existent, (known by) the grace of the Guru."

MOOL MANTRA, GURU GRANTH SAHIB
(TRANSLATION BY ELEANOR NESBITT, *SIKHISM: A VERY SHORT INTRODUCTION*)

Ik Onkar
The nucleus of Sikh philosophy

Ik Onkar is a Sikh religious symbol and a phrase that popularly adorns the walls of gurdwaras and Sikh households and appears on clothing, badges, and books. Transcribed as a single symbol—ੴ—with an open upward-reaching arc in Gurmukhi, it is represented by the numeral one (1) and the boundless infinity (k). *Ik Onkar* literally means "one ultimate entity." It is the first epithet of the Mool Mantra (root formula), the opening verse of the Sikh holy scripture, Guru Granth Sahib. The Mool Mantra, a collection of different epithets, encapsulates the essential theological concept of the Sikh faith through multiple characterizations of the formless, omnipresent Divine, the *Akal Purakh*. Believed to be the first composition uttered by Guru Nanak, it contains the message that he taught his followers. He emphasized the all-pervading nature of one supreme deity (*Ik*), with no second being. As a staunch monotheist, he denied the notion of avatars (incarnations) by preaching that by being the sole creator, all creation is subsumed within Him and all creation emanates from Him. This belief in the unity and oneness of God shapes the Sikh theological worldview and *Ik Onkar*, in seed form, represents all scriptural revelation.

Beloved of the people

Guru Nanak's emphasis on social emancipation attracted Hindus and Muslims, people from all communities, across various caste classifications. Also among his followers were the Jats, who played a crucial role in the faith's history.

Guru Nanak believed in equality and liberation, preaching against the injustices of social hierarchies. He laid emphasis on this philosophy even within his religious doctrine. It is why his early followers found in him a teacher and a value system that diverged from the mainstream religions of the time.

The appeal of Sikhism

Guru Nanak's birthplace, Talwandi, had become a center of Islamic and Hindu communal activities. He chose to establish his community elsewhere. Kartarpur, a town in present-day Pakistan, became the preferred option and Guru Nanak preached to his followers from here. They came from diverse social and religious backgrounds, a marker for his faith's distinctiveness. The community advanced his aims of consolidating a religious doctrine and presented him with a way and the space to preach to a wider audience.

Guru Nanak's humanitarian approach presented an easy contrast to the social and political tyranny of the caste system, class segregation, and Mughal oppression. This was likely the prime appeal of Sikhism. Another reason could have been Guru Nanak's emphasis on honest labor over social standing as the path to spiritual liberation.

Along with the universality of Guru Nanak's message, there were other reasons for associating with him as well. He composed poems in vernaculars that the people of the region were familiar with. Peppered with metaphors from many religious strands, this universal language gave the population a sense of representation and eased their access to his teachings. Guru Nanak also held a deep admiration for Punjab and its landscape. This becomes apparent from his poetic compositions where he describes the geographical charm of the region, which would have certainly appealed to the agriculturalists and others rooted to the land.

Diversity of followers

Guru Nanak's early followers were largely Hindus, specifically from his own high-caste community. Beyond this hegemonic group, the majority of those that chose to follow him belonged to the Hindu lower castes and nomadic groups of the region, and a large number of Muslims. Among them was Bhai Mardana (see p.28), often identified by the rabab (see pp.38–39), a string instrument, in his hands. Best known as one of the first few Sikhs, he was also Guru Nanak's childhood friend. Many followers also came from within the high concentration of agriculturalists in Punjab.

> "As a beggar goes a-begging,
> **Bowl** in one hand,
> staff in the other,
> Rings in his ears,
> in ashes smothered,
> So **go thou forth** in **life**."

VERSE 28, *JAPJI SAHIB*, *HYMNS OF GURU NANAK*
(TRANSLATION BY KHUSHWANT SINGH), 1990

Nanak believed that the reformative tenets of his faith would appeal to this community of peasants and farmers. After all, it gave an alternative to those religions where their place in the social heirarchy was rigid.

The Jats

Hindu Khatris sustained ties with the Jats (see pp.114–115), which engendered their entry into the Sikh fold. This justified the motivation for social emancipation. Though economically dominant as landowners, the Jats were placed within the lower-caste echelons of society owing to their nomadic roots. Around this time, they also began to have conflicts with the Mughal state over the collection of land revenue. Sikh solidarity for them might have been advanced by Guru Nanak, who came from a similar agrarian background.

By the time of Guru Nanak's death, a large number of Jats had entered the Sikh community, cementing a relationship that would continue for years. For instance, Nanak's son established the Dehra Baba Nanak village on land gifted by a Randhawa Jat, and Guru Angad, the second Guru, established a Sikh center at Khadur, a Jat stronghold. Such historical solidarity explains why, in the later centuries, the Jats sided with the Sikhs in the wars against the Mughals, the Persians, and then the Afghans.

▶ **Guru Nanak meets a devotee** along with his companions Bhai Mardana and Bhai Bala in this late 19th-century painting from Guler, Punjab Hills.

A worthy successor

Moved by his disciple Bhai Lehna's devotion and piety, Guru Nanak chose to appoint him as his successor. Guru Angad, as he was later named, took over and successfully fortified the religion through his emphasis on the founder's message and the formalization of Gurmukhi.

Guru Nanak picked Bhai Lehna, a trader from Khadur, over his own sons, to succeed him as the Guru of the Sikhs. Guru Nanak renamed him Angad (meaning one's own body part), symbolic of the successor as a physical extension of the first Guru.

Guru Angad's appointment was significant to the Sikh faith as it implied that there was no difference between the founder and the successor. This act was unique, breaking away from the contemporary religious hierarchical norm of either nominating a new leader posthumously, or passing the seat to an eligible heir or family member.

The Udasi challenge

Not everyone believed that Guru Angad was capable of being the next spiritual leader. It is why his succession as the religious head after Guru Nanak was contested. One of the reasons was that he was an outsider, a devout Hindu before joining the Panth. The most

▶ **This painting c. 1850–70 shows** Guru Nanak's son Sri Chand reading scriptures to his community of abstinent followers in a hermitage.

severe opposition came from Sri Chand, who considered himself the legitimate heir as Guru Nanak's elder son and direct descendant.

As a reaction to Guru Angad's selection, Sri Chand formed his own order of breakaway followers. They called themselves the Udasis, derived from the Sanskrit word for detachment or journey, and reflective of the group's more ascetic views. Sri Chand, along with his father's teachings, emphasized his own tenets of renunciation and celibacy. After Guru Nanak's death in 1539, he also exercised claim over Kartarpur, the center of faith established by the Guru.

True to the philosophy

Meanwhile, prompted by Guru Nanak, Guru Angad returned to Khadur where his wife and children lived. By staying true to Guru Nanak's message, he persuaded his followers to remain with him and earned the support of the Sikhs. He advanced the founder's philosophy about leading pure lives and performing material duties, instead of adopting asceticism.

Perhaps one of Guru Angad's primary contributions lay in strengthening the existing institutions within Sikhism. Not only did he preach the same message as set by Guru Nanak, he also followed it as an example to his followers. Several bards, such as Bhai Santokh Singh, Bhai Satta, and Balwand, have hailed Guru Angad's devoted lifestyle in their compositions.

LANGARS UNDER MATA KHIVI

Guru Angad was keen to support Guru Nanak's tenets of *sangat* (congregation) and *pangat* (communal eating) within his Panth. He appointed his wife, Mata Khivi, to manage the *langars*, communal kitchens, that exemplified these philosophies. Her successful implementation of the *langar* advanced equality among the Guru's followers and also reinforced the solidarity of the Sikh community. Writers Bhai Satta and Balwand describe Mata Khivi as a noble woman who gave "soothing, leafy shade to all" through her service.

"Your name is **Angad** son, you are **wholly mine** and you will not be separated from my body (**ang**). You were **born from my body**."

TRANSLATION BY W. H. MCLEOD, *THE B40 JANAM-SAKHI*, 1980

A lasting legacy

There was no doubt that Guru Angad possessed an understanding of his Guru's compositions. So, to preserve the verses for posterity, he adopted a new script called Gurmukhi (see pp.54–55). Translated to mean "from the Guru's mouth," it was a collection of letters from other scripts of northern India. In so doing, he gave the Panth a written language distinct from other religions. The script continues to serve its purpose and is still used today. In fact, Guru Nanak's *gurbani*, meaning "Guru's utterances," was also recorded in Gurmukhi. Guru Angad made several efforts to popularize the script in the community. Soon enough, Khadur transformed into a center of learning for the Gurmukhi alphabet. He also designed special primers to help teach children. In addition to preserving Guru Nanak's *bani*, Guru Angad also composed 63 *shlokas* (verses), where he expressed Guru Nanak's ideas in a simplified form. These eventually formed part of the holy text Guru Granth Sahib.

Keen on physical fitness, Guru Angad also contributed to the Panth by establishing an *akhara* (wrestling arena) in Khadur. Followers took part in exercise, such as wrestling, which strengthened their spirit and laid the foundation of the Sikh martial tenor, characteristic of later centuries.

He created a rich legacy that he passed on to his successor, Guru Amar Das, just before his death. In doing so, he followed Guru Nanak's footsteps and appointed a devoted follower instead of his own kin.

▶ **In this painting from the 1830s, Guru Nanak,** dressed in white, blesses Guru Angad and his followers as they take their leave.

► **A miniature painting** of Guru Angad depicts him reading the scriptures, with an attendant waving the fly-whisk behind him.

Guru Angad

A staunch devotee of Goddess Jwalamukhi until an audience with Guru Nanak transformed his religious beliefs, Bhai Lehna became the first Guru's most fervent follower. Guru Angad, as he came to be known, undertook the task of guiding and fortifying the Sikh Panth, which was still in the early stages of development.

A trader from Punjab, Bhai Lehna was on a pilgrimage to the temple of the Hindu goddess Jwalamukhi, when he heard about Guru Nanak from some ascetics. Intrigued by the Guru's divine nature and message, he decided to meet him.

It was at Kartarpur, Guru Nanak's center for Sikh congregation, that Bhai Lehna absorbed Guru Nanak's beliefs and tenets. They made enough of an impression on Lehna to prompt him to join Guru Nanak's Panth as his disciple. He showed his allegiance to Guru Nanak in ways that exceeded the actions of most other followers.

No task was too menial for him, nor too difficult. He prevailed in all the tests of commitment, surpassing even the Guru's sons. This earned him Guru Nanak's appreciation and he soon became one of his most trusted aides. Eventually, the Guru chose him as his successor. He gave Bhai Lehna the name "Angad," which means limb, as Guru Angad was seen as a part of Guru Nanak's person, and the chosen one to continue his work.

This move on the Guru's part was crucial as it established an enduring tradition wherein the nomination for the office of the Sikh Guru would be on the basis of eligibility rather than kinship. Guru Nanak's appointment of Guru Angad, a relative outsider, as

> "Guru Angad was **proclaimed**, and the **True Creator confirmed** it. Nanak merely changed his body; he still **sits on the throne**, with **hundreds of branches reaching out**."

GURU GRANTH SAHIB

his successor also accorded critical insight into the nature of the Sikh community that chose to uphold duty and devotion above all else. It reveals the possibility of transgressing caste and filial relations to assume leadership within the Panth. After all, Guru Nanak prioritized piety and service as the ultimate qualities by choosing Guru Angad over his own sons. Guru Angad finally received the *gurgaddi*, or guru's seat, upon Guru Nanak's passing in 1539.

Consolidating the Panth

Guru Angad asserted his guruship by proving his piousness as a Sikh and by crafting a symbolic unity between his predecessor and himself. He exemplified his life to his followers by strictly adhering to the tenets prescribed by Guru Nanak. This asserted his legitimacy and created the basis for all his work. Remarkably conversant with Guru Nanak's teachings, Guru Angad wrote

his own compositions as an extension of his predecessor's philosophies, while creating distinctively short verses in the name of Guru Nanak. He reiterated the Guru's ideas, and in doing so reassured Guru Nanak's followers while amassing a following of his own, considerably enlarging the Panth in the process.

His dedication to Guru Nanak became apparent through his development of the Gurmukhi script (see pp.54–55), which was used to faithfully preserve the founder's compositions, and would later act as the foundation for the Sikh canon.

A seamless transition

Guru Angad continued the tradition of *langar*, a community kitchen, which engendered equality in the community by serving meals to all without any discrimination. He also kept alive a strict regimen of meditation, recitation, and worship for his followers. This pontificate was more than a simple replication of Guru Nanak. It was a statement of Guru Angad's sharp understanding and response to the circumstances of his succession. It required him to return to the original basics of the religion to assert his authority over the Panth. *Gurbani*, or his writings for the spiritual, and the *akhara*, or the wrestling arena that he set up for the physical development of Sikhs, stand as epitomes of his capable presence.

◄ **Devotees light oil lamps** in the Golden Temple to pay homage to Guru Angad Dev on his birth anniversary.

This miniature painting from the famous *B-40 Janamsakhi* depicts a young Guru Nanak (in yellow), with his father Mehta Kalu in a school. Children can be seen in the foreground with wooden writing tablets in their hands, engaged in play.

Janamsakhis

The tales about Guru Nanak's life written by his followers emerged in the 16th century to address the need of the Sikh community to make the faith more personalized. These texts facilitate a deeper understanding of Sikhism.

Janamsakhis, meaning birth stories, are short hagiographical accounts of the life of Guru Nanak. These tales feature mystical experiences, miraculous acts, and travel anecdotes from Guru Nanak's life. They are generally divided into three parts, documenting the Guru's early life, his travels after enlightenment, and his work in Kartarpur. However, they vary across artist, time, and region. They are accompanied by hymns from the sacred Adi Granth (see pp.74–75) to contextualize their creation. The stories were derived from legends about Guru Nanak that spread across Punjab subsequent to his travels.

Role in Sikhism
These texts form an intrinsic part of the Sikh literary tradition. Given the centrality of Guru Nanak in Sikhism, *Janamsakhis* have been historically popular within the community. They are widely read, often recited at religious gatherings, or passed down as sacred tales to the next generation. They were written across centuries, long after the demise of the Guru, and came to be revered by Sikhs as part of their understanding of his divinity and the tenets of Sikhism.

These stories, rich in metaphor and symbolism, help devotees understand and connect with who the Guru was, how he led his life, and how they also must lead their lives in keeping with the traditions he established to achieve the religious goals he revealed. These also allow them to visualize the Guru and get a glimpse *(darsan)* of his person. By highlighting the life and instructions of Guru Nanak, the *Janamsakhis* reaffirm Nanak as the moral exemplar for Sikhs.

> "Then sing I the **praises** of the **most exalted** Guru Nanak. I sing the praise of the **most sublime** Guru, the **ocean of bliss**, the **destroyer of sin** and the fountain of the Lord's Name."

GURU GRANTH SAHIB
(TRANSLATION BY MANMOHAN SINGH)

The creation of Janamsakhis
While the primary Sikh corpus documented the compositions of the Sikh Gurus, the absence of Guru Nanak's life stories and contexts prompted his followers to record and preserve it in the form of *Janamsakhis* for posterity. They emerged with borrowings from oral traditions surrounding the Guru in varied editions, from the late 16th century onward.

The primary Janamsakhis
There are several *Janamsakhis* in circulation. *Bala Janamsakhi* was widely read in the 18th century, and is believed to have been penned in the end of the 16th century by Bhai Bala, a companion of Guru Nanak who wrote the hagiography to describe the founder's life to Guru Angad, the second Sikh Guru (see pp.50–51). The *Meharban Janamsakhi* is attributed to Meharban, the leader of the schismatic Mina sect, who was a nephew of Guru Arjan, the fifth Guru. Additionally, the *Janamsakhi* of Bhai Mani Singh is an 18th-century text credited to a close companion of Guru Gobind Singh, the tenth Guru. Also part of this historic tradition are two composite manuscripts known today as the *Puratan Janamsakhi* and the *Adi Janamsakhi*. The *Puratan,* meaning ancient, is considered to be a more realistic account of the Guru's life, drawn from sources dating to the late 16th century. The *Adi,* meaning first, is considered to be one of the earliest compilations in the tradition.

Another type is the *B-40 Janamsakhi*, which is thought to be the third oldest extant manuscript. It is referred to by its assigned catalog number after the India Office Library acquired it in 1907. Although it shares some common sources with the *Puratan* and *Adi Janamsakhis*, *B-40* offers distinct stories that warrant its separate inclusion.

Material differences
The Sikh community generally considers the *Janamsakhis* as credible sources of history because they deal with matters concerning the life and philosophy of Guru Nanak. However, there are several disparities that arise from the fact that each *Janamsakhi* is written from the independent perspective of its author, with variable focus on different elements of the Guru's life. This has resulted in multiple interpretations around Nanak's life. However, these texts are crucial to the Sikh discourse as they lay down the model of life that the Sikhs are expected to follow, and shed light on the identity of the community.

> "Angad's compilation ... gave the Sikhs a written language **distinct** from the ... language of the Hindus or the Mussalmans and ... fostered a sense of their being a **separate people**."

KHUSHWANT SINGH, *A HISTORY OF THE SIKHS (VOLUME 1)*, 2004

Gurmukhi
The sacred script

The primary script in all Sikh writings after the 16th century, Gurmukhi is still in use today. It is the official script of the state of Punjab. Its name is closely tied to the concept of *gurmukh*, or the ideal Sikh personality, embodied by the Gurus. The script developed under Guru Angad and is associated with the Adi Granth, a corpus of writings from the Sikh Gurus. Later Sikh scriptures as well as the *gurbanis*, the poetic compositions of the Gurus, were recorded in Gurmukhi and added to the Adi Granth.

The significance of Gurmukhi transcends its literary use. While it bears religious importance as the script of the divine teachings of Gurus, it is also seen as an assertion of Sikh identity and individualism. The theological base of the script is manifested in the character for 'one,' representing Ik Onkar, being the first letter.

A place in history

The script also gave Sikh literature and scriptures lexical unity, especially from the 17th century onward. Initially developed to compile the teachings of the Gurus, Gurmukhi became the script of preference to record several compositions and hymns that were orally transmitted in the Punjab region. It also enabled communal solidarity, which burgeoned in the face of persecution, and later found a critical space in the Sikh nationalist discourse. The advancement of Punjabi in Gurmukhi also became a crucial marker of Sikh identity.

Expanding its scope further, Gurmukhi has been employed in various literary modes from scriptures and poems to reports and newspapers, thereby establishing its identity beyond religion to embrace secular aspects as well. Punjabi was among the languages used in Maharaja Ranjit Singh's kingdom, both in Shahmukhi (modified Perso-Arabic script) and Gurmukhi scripts. Moreover, the Patiala state encouraged the use of the Gurmukhi. The Singh Sabha movement (see pp.232–233) led to the establishment of newspapers in Gurmukhi such as the *Khalsa Akhbar* and the *Khalsa Samachar*. Sikh scholars Gyani Gyan Singh's *Panth Prakash*, *Twarikh Guru Khalsa*, and Kahan Singh's *Guru Sabdaratnakar Mahankosh* are significant literary milestones in Gurmukhi, as is novelist and poet Amrita Pritam's "Ajj Aakhaan Waris Shah Nu." Writer Giani Gurdit Singh's *Tith Tihar* and *Mera Pind da Jiwan* won UNESCO awards.

▶ **A rare *hukamnama* (official document)** c. 1845–48, written in Gurmukhi. It was issued to appeal to the Sikh community for donations.

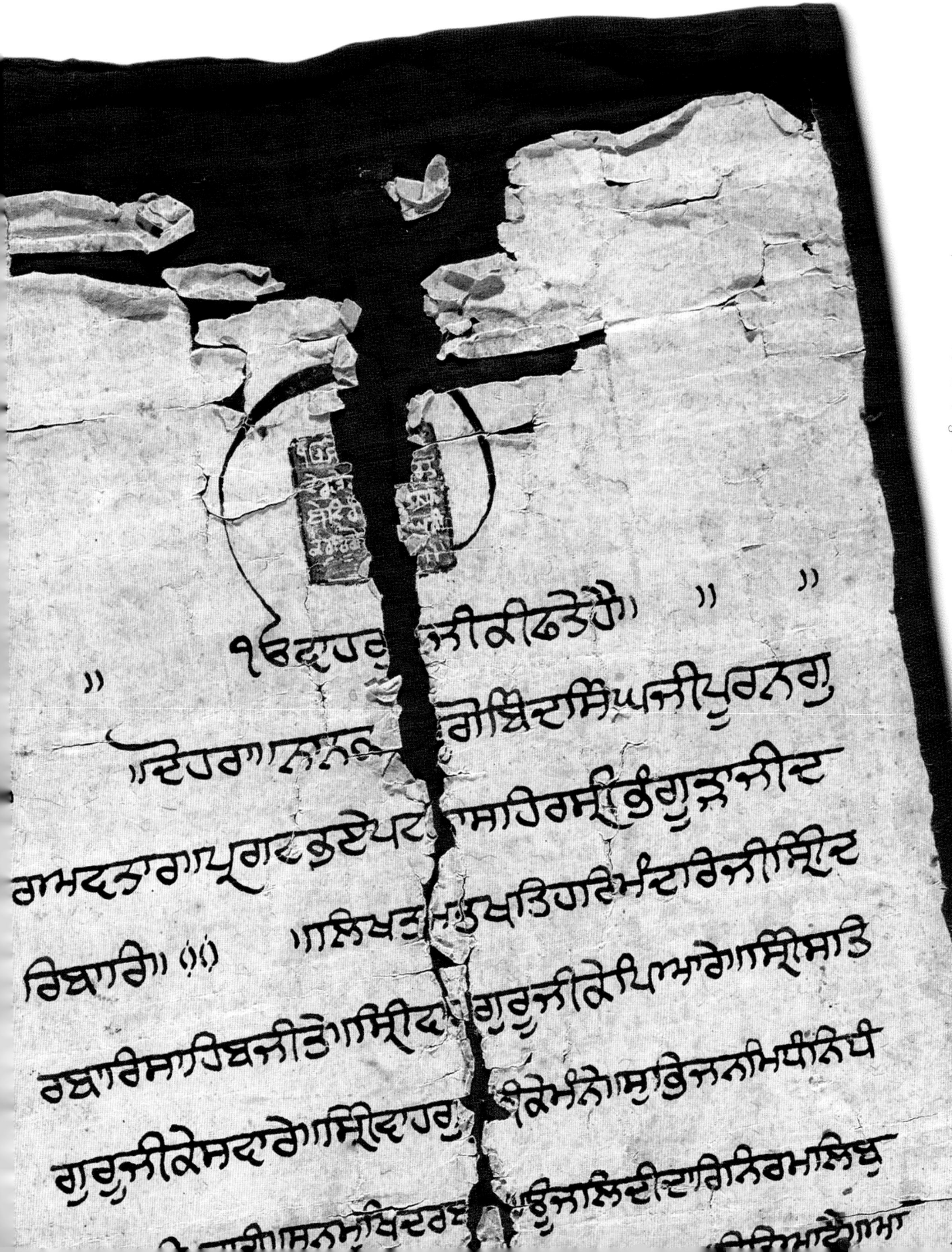

The pious one

Guru Amar Das took over the leadership of the faith at the age of 73. The third Guru was crucial for the development of several institutions, which strengthened and consolidated the Sikh religion in profound ways and created the framework for future developments.

◀ **Portrait of Guru Amar Das at Goindwal,** depicting him with flowing robes and a halo to signify his simplicity, piety, and divine position.

Guru Amar Das was first exposed to Sikhism when he was around 60 years old. His nephew's wife was the daughter of Guru Angad, the second Sikh Guru (see pp.50–51). He had heard her reciting Guru Nanak's hymns and it sparked his interest, even though he was a follower of the Hindu god Vishnu at the time. Stories say that a priest advised him to find a spiritual guide, and so he requested for a meeting with Guru Angad. Moved by his philosophy, Guru Amar Das quickly became his disciple, and spent the next few years in the devoted service of the second Guru, who was younger to him in age. He only assumed the *gurgaddi*, or seat of the Guru, at the age of 73.

Guru Angad's choice of Guru Amar Das was in continuation of Guru Nanak's tradition of appointing a follower rather than his kin as the next spiritual guide of the Panth.

Institutionalizing Sikh traditions

Guru Amar Das emphasized tangible elements in the faith so that Guru Nanak's philosophical message would become more accessible. These pragmatic interventions helped him consolidate the scattered congregations across Punjab, strengthen the connection between guru and follower, and distinguish Sikhism from other prominent faiths.

However, just as Guru Nanak's sons opposed Guru Angad's guruship, Guru Angad's sons opposed Guru Amar Das's appointment and forcefully established themselves at Khadur. As a result, the new Guru moved his religious center to Goindwal, a village on the banks of the Beas river.

Here, he introduced the tradition of pilgrimages to *tiraths* (sacred sites) on auspicious occasions, such as Baisakhi and Diwali to encourage Sikhs to celebrate together. The *tirath* at Goindwal was centered around an 84-step *baoli* (stepwell), constructed under his instructions, to foster a connection among his followers. He also initiated rituals to commemorate the births and deaths of previous Sikh Gurus. He institutionalized the tradition of *langar*, insisting that those who wished to see him had to eat there first, to stress upon the tenets of equality of life and service.

Popular accounts speak of a time when Mughal Emperor Akbar arrived at Goindwal and sought an audience with the Guru.

In brief

1479
Birth of
Amar Das

1539
Amar Das meets
Guru Angad

1552
Guru Amar Das
becomes the
third Guru

1574
Guru Amar Das
passes away, Guru
Ram Das becomes
the fourth Guru.

MASANDS

The tradition of the *masands* was an innovative contribution of Guru Amar Das, carried forward by his successors. *Masands* were the representatives appointed to govern the 22 *manjis* or seats of administration, each coinciding with the jurisdiction of a Sikh congregation. Their role involved fostering the faith of the devotees by scheduling daily worship and maintaining the religious community, or *sangat*, by collecting offerings. The system not only promoted the unity of the scattered Sikhs, but also offered a direct connection with the Guru to the followers through his appointed representative.

A print of Gurdwara Baoli Sahib, the 84-step stepwell at Goindwal, dating from 1931–33. The stepwell stands beside the main hall or Darbar Sahib, which houses the holy book, the Guru Granth Sahib.

Guru Amar Das refused to meet with him until Emperor Akbar had taken *langar* along with the rest of the community.

A key development was the formation of the *manjis*, seats of religious administration overseen by the Guru's representatives, the *masands*. They collected *dasvandh* (a tenth of a person's income) as revenue, which provided the Guru with the resources to pay for religious centers, armies, and cultural events.

Literary spiritualism

Guru Amar Das laid the foundation for Guru Arjan's compilation of the Adi Granth, which eventually became the Guru Granth Sahib (see pp.74–75). He wrote several hymns, collected those composed by his predecessors, and included selected verses of some of the prominent saints of the Sufi and Bhakti traditions, such as Kabir and Namdev. This collection is known as the *Goindwal Pothis* or the *Mohan Pothis*. It made him instrumental in developing some key Sikh literary traditions.

Guru Amar Das was focused on expanding the reach of Sikhism beyond Goindwal, and aiding his followers' ability to interact with the faith. His compositions were essential in spreading his philosophy. He highlighted his belief in the *sat-sangat* (true communion) that

facilitated the emancipation of the soul in his writings. He spoke of the virtues of reciting the *shabad* (holy word) and listening to the *banis* (hymns) sung by minstrels.

Anand Sahib

Among Guru Amar Das's compositions, perhaps the most distinctive is the *Anand Sahib*, which demonstrates the essence of his philosophy. Translated to mean "the revered song of joy," this hymn is set to Raga Ramkali, a classical melody in Indian music, and has 40 stanzas. The honorific "Sahib" was added later as a marker of the hymn's importance within the Sikh tradition.

Today, it is a part of the morning prayers and is considered to have inspired the *Anand Karaj*, the Sikh marriage ceremony. Parts of it are still

> "... Sing a **hymn to the Lord** who is housed in your hearts. What **bliss** I can feel, Nanak says, I have found my **true guru**."

ANAND SAHIB, *TEACHINGS OF THE SIKH GURUS*
(EDITED BY ARVIND MANDAIR, CHRISTOPHER SHACKLE), 2013

▼ **Guru Amar Das instituted the celebration of major festivals** such as Diwali and Baisakhi. This tradition has continued over the centuries. Seen here is the Harmandir Sahib, or Golden Temple complex, lit up for Diwali.

recited during Sikh funeral and wedding rituals and the hymn has been incorporated within the Adi Granth.

Written in a mix of local dialects, the *Anand Sahib* highlights the idea of bliss that devotees experience upon the realization of the Divine and the liberation of the soul. This process is said to quell all suffering and worries and help devotees achieve a state of *anand* or delight. The hymn stresses the need for performing collective rituals and strictly following the mandates of the Guru to successfully unify the soul with the Divine. In its verses, the hymn underlines the nature of the Divine and the path that all Sikhs should follow.

Breaking established traditions

Guru Amar Das was keen to usher in reforms in the society. His focus on communal liberation points to his belief in a caste-less, gender-neutral, and classless society for the Sikhs. He opposed social practices such as *sati* (self-immolation of a widow), which was part of some Hindu traditions until modern times, female infanticide, and the consumption of liquor. He espoused widow remarriage, the abolition of the purdah system, and monogamy. A Sikh hagiographical account even suggests that Mughal Emperor Akbar revoked the tax imposed

on the Hindu pilgrimage to Haridwar at the Guru's request. Guru Amar Das chose his son-in-law, Bhai Jetha (see pp.66–67), who was later known as Guru Ram Das, as the next spiritual guide of the community.

▲ **A Sikh attendant waves the Chaur Sahib**, or the ceremonial whisk, over the Guru Granth Sahib on the occasion of Baisakhi at a gurdwara in Los Angeles, USA.

► This modern-day portrait of Guru Amar Das depicts him in contemplation. A faint halo wreaths his head.

Guru Amar Das

The third Guru, Guru Amar Das, established Goindwal as a major religious center and an enduring pilgrimage spot for the Sikh community. He also compiled the writings of this predecessors, which formed the basis for the Adi Granth.

For most of his life, Amar Das was a devoted worshipper of the Hindu god Vishnu and went on several pilgrimages to the holy city of Haridwar. According to legends, it was while returning from one such trip that a saint encouraged Amar Das to find a guru. Around this time, he overheard his nephew's wife Bibi Amaro, who was Guru Angad's daughter, chanting a hymn by Guru Nanak. He persuaded Bibi Amaro to introduce him to her father. The meeting prompted the 60-year-old Amar Das to become a Sikh disciple.

A devoted Sikh

Born in the village of Basarke in 1479, to Tej Bhan and Bakht Kaur, Amar Das grew up in a devout Hindu family. He later married Mansa Devi, who was also from the same community, and the couple had four children—two sons and two daughters.

In spite of his previous religious background, Amar Das was known for his devotion to the Sikh Guru after becoming his disciple. Sikh accounts narrate that every day, despite hardships, he collected water for Guru Angad's bath. He spent hours in the community kitchen and every other moment in worship. It was this dedication that earned him Guru Angad's affection and paved the path for his succession.

The pragmatic Guru

Guru Amar Das became the third Sikh Guru a few days before Guru Angad's death in 1552. All his actions were guided by a keen sense of pragmatism, encouraged by his motivation to simultaneously strengthen the Panth and its piety. Every decision was ensconced within a sharp sensibility toward making Sikhism more accessible, while strengthening the foundation of the community, avoiding disruptions and fractures.

His first aim was to facilitate devotion among the followers, which he accomplished through a compilation of the writings of the earlier Gurus as well as eminent

> "Heavenly **music** resounds in that fortunate house, It resounds in that **fortunate house** which is filled with **His power.**"

ANAND SAHIB, *TEACHINGS OF THE SIKH GURUS*
(TRANSLATION BY CHRISTOPHER SHACKLE AND ARVIND-PAL SINGH MANDAIR)

poet-saints from other religious traditions. This became the basis for the Adi Granth (see pp.74–75).

He kept his teachings simple and logical, while fostering the values of equality and justice. The new Guru encouraged the practice of *langar*, and the elevation of women through appointments. He did not support following Hindu practices, such as the purdah system and widow self-immolation, or *sati*.

He achieved his second objective of further consolidating the Panth by instituting the *manji* system (see p.56), and establishing his center in the strategically situated town of Goindwal (see p.56). He was able to fortify his central position as the third Sikh Guru by encouraging followers to congregate at Goindwal on specific occasions and make pilgrimage to the new stepwell, which was considered as a sacred site for ablutions. Guru Amar Das also traveled to familiarize himself with the consciousness of his followers.

It was because of these measures that he was able to revitalize the Panth by the end of his term, when it was passed to his son-in-law Bhai Jetha.

▼ The golden-domed Goindwal Baoli (stepwell) is paved with 84 steps. A dip in the well is believed to lead devotees to salvation.

Legacy of Guru Ram Das

From composing 638 hymns, which form part of the Guru Granth Sahib, along with four stanzas of the *Anand Karaj*, to establishing the cornerstone of the present-day, famous town of Amritsar, Guru Ram Das's contributions to the Sikh tradition are indelible.

One of the most significant contributions that the fourth Guru, Guru Ram Das, made to the Sikh faith lay in his literary works. Sikh Gurus and scribes had already established a strong foundation with their compositions by the time Guru Ram Das became the Guru. However, the considerable amount of hymns he composed, elucidating his philosophy, only added to the extensive corpus of Sikh literature.

Guru Ram Das's verses

The Guru demonstrated his literary ability by composing verses in nearly 30 different ragas (traditional scale or pattern of notes). These hymns laid down the steps to be followed by all Sikhs and addressed a range of topics, whether it was meditating on the Lord's name to wash away one's sins or ridding oneself of pride and ego.

Among all his works, two compositions dealing with the theme of Sikh marriage have transcended religion, and have since been incorporated into the social fabric of the Sikh community: the *ghorian*, a wedding song, was meant to be recited on the day before the wedding, while his *lavans*, four hymns of four lines each, pertained to the solemnization of a marriage in Sikhism. Even today, the *lavans* are recited during the four circumambulations made by the couple around the Guru Granth Sahib during the *Anand Karaj*, or the Sikh wedding ceremony (see pp.64–65).

Religious strands in literature

Guru Ram Das's compositions emphasize the centrality of the Guru, styling him as a parent figure from whom the devotee imbibes honor and respect by association. The importance of the Guru is reiterated through the stress on the true *bani* (spoken word), which was in contrast to all other sayings termed as the *kachi bani* (false or "unripe" words), thus enforcing a strict set of guidelines for the devotees. Guru Ram Das encouraged them to become *Gursikhs* (pious, devoted, and observant Sikhs) and show allegiance to the congregation as this vested them with divine grace.

His compositions provided a distinct identity to the Sikhs by drawing on the meditative and non-meddling nature of the devotee. The emphasis on staying true to the path alluded to a historical presence of dissension and threats to the guruship.

Perpetuation of authority

Guru Ram Das tried to consolidate the Panth by building a strong Sikh center at Ramdaspur (see pp.68–69), which later evolved to become Amritsar. Here, he commissioned a *sarovar*, or tank, in the Harmandir complex for devotees' bathing purposes. Through his sermons at the center, preserved today as his writings, he preached an inclusive message that would appeal to all and prompt them to adopt the more egalitarian Sikh religion.

Before his death in 1581, Guru Ram Das nominated a successor, naming his youngest son Arjan Dev as the next spiritual leader.

In brief

1574
Guru Amar Das appoints Guru Ram Das as the fourth Sikh Guru

1577
The Guru founds Ramdaspur, later known as Amritsar

1581
Guru Ram Das passes the guruship to his youngest son Arjan Dev

"They are not said to be **husband** and **wife**, who merely sit **together**. They alone are called husband and wife, who have **one light** in **two bodies**."

GURU RAM DAS, GURU GRANTH SAHIB

◄ **A 19th century gouache painting** depicting Guru Ram Das, the fourth Sikh Guru, with followers, including some seen playing musical instruments.

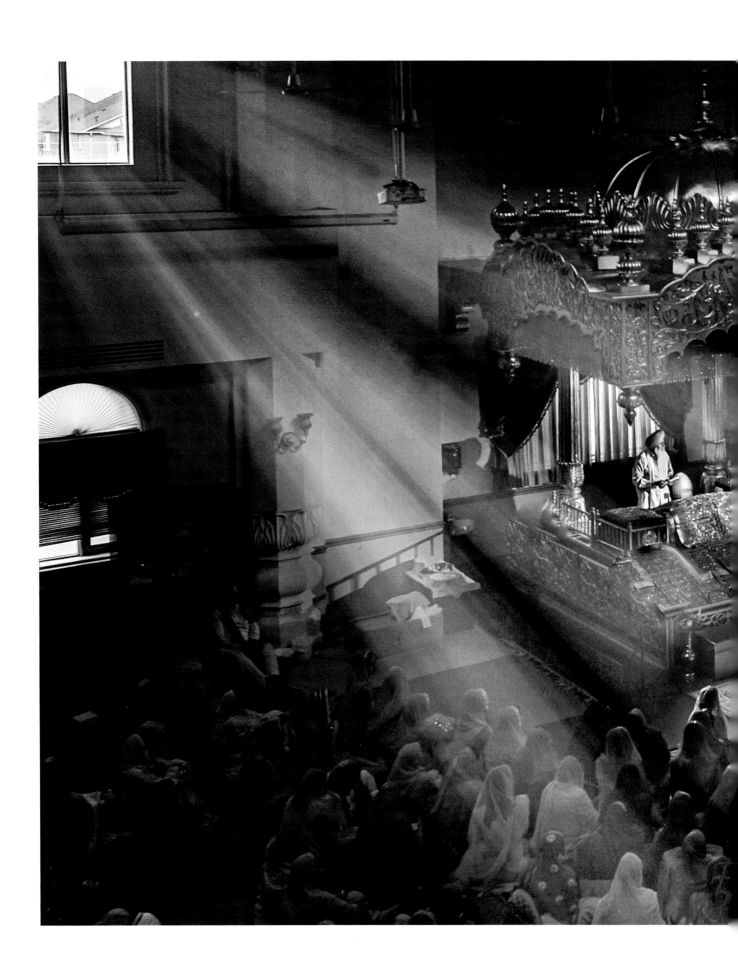

A Sikh wedding ceremony takes place at Gurdwara Dasmesh Darbar
in Brampton, Canada. Called the *Anand Karaj*, "blissful action", it features
the four hymns that Guru Ram Das composed. The ceremony is usually
held in a gurdwara's main hall, before the Guru Granth Sahib. It is
officiated by an *Amritdhari* Sikh, an individual initiated into the Khalsa.

▶ **Portrait of Guru Ram Das,** the fourth Sikh Guru and the founder of the holy city of Amritsar.

Guru Ram Das

Remembered as the founder of Amritsar, the holiest city of Sikhism, Guru Ram Das was the fourth in the line of ten Sikh Gurus. His musical innovations set him apart and his compositions added to the Sikh corpus.

Guru Ram Das may have served as a Guru only briefly, yet his legacy transcends the annals of time. While he is mostly associated with what later became the holy city of Amritsar, his contributions toward further strengthening the community and composing spiritual texts are undeniable.

A life of servitude

As a young Hindu boy, Jetha Mal left Lahore following the death of his parents and moved to the holy town of Goindwal, Guru Amar Das's religious center. He began practising Sikhism after meeting Guru Amar Das. His meritorious disposition impressed Guru Amar Das so much that he was betrothed to the Guru's younger daughter, Bibi Bhani. Following the wedding, Jetha Mal became Guru Amar Das's ardent votary and spent most of the forty years of his life in the service of the Sikh community.

Guru Amar Das, before his death in 1574, renamed Jetha Mal as Guru Ram Das and appointed him as the next Guru.

Establishing Ramdaspur

Guru Ram Das had a large artificial pool constructed on the land gifted by Emperor Akbar and this became the nucleus of a new town, known as Ramdaspur, in northern India. As the number of Sikh followers surged in the town, Guru Ram Das invited many economic groups, such as merchants, artisans, and shopkeepers to make the town their home and provide for the needs of the community. He also commissioned another *sarovar*, the Amritsar tank, which was to be built at the center of the town. This later expanded to also house the Golden Temple (see pp.68–69), or the sacred Harmandir Sahib.

Today, the town is known as Amritsar, one of the biggest cultural, religious, and economic hubs in the state of Punjab in India, with the Golden Temple, the holiest place of pilgrimage for Sikhs, its biggest draw.

"[His] **qualities** I will sing, [his] qualities I will spread, [his] qualities I will tell, O my mother! The **disciple** who tells [his] qualities, is my friend; having joined [this my] friend, I will sing the qualities of **Hari**! A **diamond**, having met with a diamond, is perforated; in deep red color I will **bathe**!"

GURU RAM DAS, SIRI RAG MAH. IV., SABD III. IV. (LXVII) [TRANSLATION BY ERNEST TRUMPP, *THE ADI GRANTH OR THE HOLY SCRIPTURES OF THE SIKHS*, 1877]

Building a community

The expansion of Ramdaspur and the construction of the *sarovar* were based on the donations made by the followers of the Guru. For the purpose of establishing and expanding his community, Guru Ram Das utilized the system of resource-collection through representatives known as *masands*, who would gather offerings from followers who could not visit themselves.

Compositions of Guru Ram Das

Guru Ram Das composed nearly 640 hymns, which later made up about ten percent of the holy text, the Guru Granth Sahib. His hymns were set to new and innovative musical notes. They described the allegiance to the Divine and the Guru as a hallowed act. In his compositions, he empathized with the hardships faced by different communities—specifically the lower castes, peasants, traders, and women. He also sanctified the Sikh identity by emphasizing distinctive social practices among the Sikhs, such as meditating, which set them apart from contemporary ritualistic religions.

▼ **The Amrit Sarovar at the complex** of the Golden Temple in Amritsar, which was commissioned by Guru Ram Das, translates to "pond of immortality."

Birth of the Golden Temple

The holiest place of pilgrimage for the Sikhs, the Golden Temple or Harmandir Sahib, is in the town of Amritsar in northern India. Steeped in history and religious tradition, the temple complex has endured the ravages of time and endures as a lasting testament to Sikh piety.

In the late 16th century, toward the last years of his predecessor Guru Amar Das's leadership, Guru Ram Das, the fourth Sikh Guru, was tasked with establishing a new center of pilgrimage for the growing Sikh community.

Guru Ram Das began by commissioning the construction of a *sarovar* (sacred tank), later named Santokhsar, on land granted by Mughal Emperor Akbar. He moved from Goindwal and settled down near the tank. A town soon started developing around it, and it came to be known as Ramdaspur, known today as Amritsar.

Before its settlement, the site was an uninhabited low-lying area surrounded by forests and small villages. In order to further expand the town, Guru Ram Das invited members of various economic groups, such as traders and artisans, to relocate here.

Initial structure

Eager to make the town a pilgrimage site, Guru Ram Das commissioned another tank, named Amritsar, to be built near the Santokhsar tank. Devotees bathed in these tanks as a means of symbolically cleansing themselves.

Amritsar's name comes from the words *Amrit* or nectar, and *sar* meaning *sarovar*. After Guru Ram Das's death, Guru Arjan, the fifth Sikh leader, continued the development at

"The **Akal Takht** was the
locus of miri (temporal authority);
the **Harmandir** the epicentre
of *piri* (spiritual authority).
The **Guru** was the holder of both."

MICHAEL HAWLEY, "SIKH INSTITUTIONS",
THE OXFORD HANDBOOK OF SIKH STUDIES, 2014

Ramdaspur. Eventually, the Amritsar tank was enlarged and Harmandir Sahib (Temple of the Divine), or the Durbar Sahib (Hall of the Divine), was constructed at its center. It is believed that Harmandir Sahib was built in brick and set at a level lower than the peripheral land. Devotees enter by going down a number of steps—symbolically shedding their ego before meeting the Guru. The square complex is open on all sides with four gates to emphasize the fact that everyone is accepted and welcome. The sanctum within the pool is connected by a bridge.

At the turn of the 17th century, the compiled Adi Granth (see pp.74–75) was ceremoniously placed within its halls, thereby sanctifying it. Together, the tank, the temple, and the text established Harmandir Sahib as a holy site in Sikhism.

The Akal Takht

Under the administrative control of Guru Arjan, Ramdaspur rose in prominence as an autonomous town and Harmandir Sahib flourished as a pilgrimage site. These developments drew the ire of the Mughal Empire, as they considered it a threat to their authority in the region. The new Mughal Emperor, Jehangir, disapproved of Guru Arjan's popularity and had him executed at the beginning of the 17th century. The violence strengthened the significance of Harmandir Sahib as an anchor for the Sikh community.

It was then that Guru Hargobind, Guru Arjan's son and the sixth Guru, took over the leadership and started training an army. He built the Akal Takht (Throne of the Timeless Divine), a raised platform at the time, directly in front of the Harmandir Sahib. Here (see pp.278–279), he discussed ideas for military activity with the congregation. This eternal throne was symbolic of the Guru's temporal power.

The temple's later history

The 16th and 17th centuries witnessed many conflicts over the temple's control, alongside several desecrations by Sikh adversaries, including the Mughals, Persians, and Afghans. By the 18th century, the temple had become the rallying center for Sikhs and this was evidenced by the many efforts made by its followers to protect, control, and rebuild it.

The reconstructions during this period added more structures around the complex for residence, worship, and spiritual education of the Sikhs. In 1808, the Sikh ruler Maharaja Ranjit Singh (see pp.182–183) added gold plates to the exterior of the upper storeys as well as marble in the interior and the walkways of the Harmandir Sahib. This gave it a modern façade and a new name, the Golden Temple. Despite its long history of conflicts and external constructions, the complex has managed to preserve the original structures of the temple and the *sarovar* built by the Gurus.

◄ **Detail from the golden doors of the Harmandir Sahib** shows scenes from the lives of the Sikh Gurus. The doors, rarely shown to the public, were added to the temple by Maharaja Ranjit Singh who established the Sikh Empire.

Emergence of new towns

In the late 16th century, Guru Arjan established a string of new towns in Punjab, northern India, which became centers of spiritual authority. These cities have now become major pilgrimage sites for Sikhs and keep the legacy of the Sikh Gurus alive even today.

The establishment of new cities have played a key role in the diffusion of the Sikh faith. The Sikh Gurus founded new religious centers that became popular as places of pilgrimage. These formed the basis of spiritual activity where seekers would travel for an audience with the Guru, consequently attracting more people into the Sikh fold.

The ten Sikh Gurus led congregations from different places in Punjab. For instance, Guru Nanak, the founder, settled Kartarpur on the right bank of River Ravi, which also became his final resting place. Guru Ram Das, the fourth Sikh Guru, established Ramdaspur, now known as Amritsar and the location of the Golden Temple, the holiest of pilgrimages. The founding of new urban spaces provided Sikh Gurus with additional centers where they could preach, and offered the growing Sikh community more sites of pilgrimage and accommodation. In the late 16th century, several townships came up under Guru Arjan, the fifth Guru. These included

Tarn Taran, Kartarpur (different from Guru Nanak's Kartarpur), and Sri Harigobindpur. These have had a lasting legacy, surviving centuries after their founding, and kept alive through pilgrimages. While traveling in central Punjab for the establishment of these townships, Guru Arjan expanded the number of his followers significantly.

A pool of salvation
Of all the townships Guru Arjan established, Tarn Taran is perhaps the most famous. In 1590, Guru Arjan came upon a natural pond, about 15 miles (24 km) from Amritsar, between the Beas and Ravi rivers, with immense natural beauty, vast grassy lands, and clear water. Here, he started the digging of a *sarovar* (tank). He blessed it as Tarn Taran, meaning "the boat that takes one across (the ocean of existence)." The tank's water soon earned a reputation for having healing properties and it became

> "God is my **sacred shrine** or place of pilgrimage and pool of purification; I wash my mind in **His name**."

GURU AMAR DAS, GURU GRANTH SAHIB (TRANSLATION BY RAJINDER S. JUTLA IN "PILGRIMAGE IN SIKH TRADITION," *TOURISM, RELIGION AND SPIRITUAL JOURNEYS*, 2006)

a site of pilgrimage, especially for those afflicted with leprosy. It took six years to dig the tank, after which Guru Arjan ordered a shrine, a hall for sermons, and a leprosarium to be built next to it. Soon a city of the same name developed around the tank.

Another city of God

After establishing Tarn Taran, Guru Arjan founded another town in 1594. It was set in the Jalandhar Doab, between the Beas and Sutlej rivers, on a piece of land granted to him during the reign of Emperor Akbar. Guru Arjan named it Kartarpur (after the center established by Guru Nanak, near Lahore). Here too, the Guru constructed the Gangsar *sarovar*, which helped with the of shortage of water for agriculture. The sixth Guru, and Guru Arjan's son, Guru Hargobind, took residence here briefly.

In the mid-17th century, the Sikhs fought a three-day battle here, after the local *faujdar*, military commander, attacked the city. Following this incident, Guru Hargobind moved to the hill town of Kiratpur. His grandson, Dhir Mal, stayed back in Kartarpur, forging his own sect as a self-anointed Guru. The original copy of the Guru Granth Sahib (see pp.74–74) prepared by Guru Arjan and other relics are still preserved in the old residence of the Gurus here, in the Shish Mahal.

A thriving township

After Kartarpur, Guru Arjan built another town on the banks of the River Beas, which he named after his son Hargobind, as Sri Hargobindpur. After becoming the sixth Sikh Guru, Guru Hargobind developed a carefully planned walled-township here. A gurdwara was constructed along with a mosque for Muslims and a temple for Hindus. The Guru even built his home and settled here with his family for a while. In 1630, the Mughals fought a battle against the Sikh forces because of Guru Hargobind's growing popularity (see pp.116–117). The Damadama Sahib Gurdwara commemorates the site of the battle in the town. Later, Sri Hargobindpur became the capital of the Ramgarhia *misl*, a Sikh sovereign state.

A vintage, engraved illustration dated 1836 and published in *Le Magasin Pittoresque, Vol 4*, depicts a scene at the Golden Temple. This is believed to be one of the earliest European portrayals of the iconic gurdwara. Devotees can be seen praying in the foreground. The busy city of Amritsar is shown in the background.

▶ **A folio from an illustrated Adi Granth,** late 17th–early 18th century, at Takht Sri Harimandir Sahib, Patna, bearing the *nisan*, or handwriting, of Guru Gobind Singh, the tenth Sikh Guru.

> "Whoever **seeks** to have a sight of the Guru the **holy Granth** must **behold**; Should he seek to have converse with the **Guru** the **Granth** must he study with **devoted heart**."

CHAPTER 5, *GURU BILAS PADISHAHI CHHEVIN* (TRANSLATION BY GURBACHAN SINGH TALIB, *AN INTRODUCTION TO SRI GURU GRANTH SAHIB*, 2011)

Guru Granth Sahib
The holy scripture

The Sikh hymns are collected in a volume known as the Guru Granth Sahib. This sacred book contains 5,894 *shabads* (hymns) across 1,430 pages, arranged into 31 sections set to ragas, which were sung. Written in Gurmukhi (see pp.54–55), the Guru Granth Sahib contains the "*bani*," or utterance, of the Sikh Gurus as well as saints from other faiths (see p.41), such as Kabir, a 15th-century Hindu mystic poet-saint, and Baba Farid, a 13th-century Muslim mystic saint. In each section, the hymns are grouped according to the Guru who wrote them, with those by non-Gurus featured at the end.

Compiling the holy scripture
The Guru Granth Sahib's compilation was a culmination of a long process that had begun with Guru Nanak's compositions in the Sikh liturgy. The threat of the circulation of false words (*kachi bani*) by schismatic groups obliged the Gurus to hire scribes and prepare copies of the Gurus' hymns. With the religion expanding to other parts of Punjab, the fifth Guru,

Guru Arjan Dev, fulfilled the need for an authentic collection of scriptures for Sikhs. To lay to rest concerns over whether or not certain texts were genuine compositions of the early Gurus, Guru Arjan began to gather the true manuscripts in order to validate their authenticity. Possessing an exceptional talent for devotional poetry and music, he himself composed a large volume of hymns and added elucidatory annotations to the large corpus of sacred verses. Then he and his follower Bhai Gurdas compiled them into one volume. In 1604, the text was finished and installed in Harmandir Sahib, or Golden Temple, in Amritsar. Guru Arjan's followers regarded the book, the Adi Granth (the primal book), as the divine work of the early Gurus. Almost a century later, the tenth Guru, Gobind Singh, revised it, adding hymns of the ninth Guru, Tegh Bahadur. In 1708, before his demise, Guru Gobind Singh conferred his authority upon the Adi Granth (see pp.132–133) as the Sikhs' final Guru. This Granth contained the banis of his predecessors and it came to be known as the Guru Granth Sahib.

▶ **Guru Arjan is seated in a courtyard** expounding on the Guru Granth Sahib in this painting from Guler, Punjab Hills, c. 1790.

Guru Arjan

Guru Arjan's impact on the Panth is immense. Not only did he compile the holy scripture, Adi Granth, he also built the Harmandir Sahib as the fifth Guru. His execution by the Mughals became a defining moment in the history of the faith.

Guru Ram Das founded Amritsar, the holiest of cities for the Sikh community. His youngest son, Guru Arjan Dev, cemented the structure of the Panth. Under his father's mentorship, Arjan acquired a strong understanding of the Sikh doctrine. His commitment to the tenets of the faith and devotion to God convinced his father to nominate him as his successor. Guru Arjan Dev assumed the office of the Guru after his father's passing in 1581.

The Harmandir Sahib
One of Guru Arjan's key contributions was the development of the Harmandir Sahib. In the 1580s, he undertook the construction of the Amritsar *sarovar* (tank) at Ramdaspur (see pp.68–69), a town established by his father. Soon, the Harmandir Sahib, which translates as the Temple of God, was built in the center of the *sarovar* in 1588. Persian and Sikh accounts of the time indicate that Guru Arjan invited a Muslim saint from Lahore, popularly known as Mian Mir, to lay the gurdwara's foundation stone—a testament to the diversity and acceptance of all religions within the Sikh faith.

Author Khushwant Singh writes in *A History of the Sikhs* that Guru Arjan raised funds for its construction by asking all Sikhs "… to donate a tenth of their income (*dasvandh*) in the name of the Guru." The *masands* were tasked with collecting donations from far-flung areas. Ramdaspur became known as Amritsar, and the gurdwara

became a sacred place of pilgrimage as well as a rallying center for the growing Sikh community.

Centres of religion
Not long after Harmandir's completion, Guru Arjan toured the Majha and Doaba regions of Punjab. He founded three new towns during this five-year journey, which became strong centers of religion (see pp.70–71): Tarn Taran, Kartarpur, and Sri Hargobindpur. He also brought in many members from the peasant communities into the Sikh fold, groups with diverse socio-economic profiles, solely united by a shared belief in the way of life preached by the Guru. He promoted trade relations and established an asylum for those suffering from leprosy.

▲ **A fresco from Amritsar's Gurdwara Ramsar Sahib,** depicts Guru Arjan Dev being anointed with a *tilak* (colored mark).

The eternal gift
In 1595, Guru Arjan immersed himself in the compilation of the compositions and writings of his predecessors into one text, known as the Adi Granth (see pp.74–75). Upon its completion in 1604, it was placed in the inner sanctum of the Harmandir Sahib. The community came to recognize the repository as an equal and legitimate form of divinity. Over a century later, Guru Gobind Singh proclaimed the Adi Granth as the immortal Guru in 1708, and it came to be known as the Guru Granth Sahib.

Martyrdom
Emperor Jehangir acceded to the Mughal throne in 1605. Within a year of his rule, he instated policies of religious intolerance. Especially hostile toward the growing Sikh community, he had Guru Arjan arrested on flimsy charges and subjected the Guru to severe torture that led to his martyrdom the same year (see pp.80–81). Guru Arjan's passing changed the fabric of the Sikh Panth forever. It led to the militarization of Sikhs in order to defend themselves against oppression.

"Guru Arjan was the **first Guru** to be **born** into a **Sikh household**… tutored to **acknowledge** the **Divine Presence**… His 25 years of reign was marked by **far-reaching institutional developments** within the Panth, and his **death** became a **turning point in Sikh history**."

PASHAURA SINGH, *LIFE AND WORK OF GURU ARJAN*

The secular royal

Mughal Emperor Akbar's tolerant ideology, combined with his stable politico-administrative arrangements and the kingdom's economic prosperity, helped in the development of Sikh religion and its institutions.

In 1552, four years before Jalal-ud-din Muhammad Akbar's ascension to the Mughal throne, Guru Amar Das was anointed the Sikh Guru. He moved the spiritual center from Khadur to Goindwal, located on the route from Lahore to Delhi, which were important towns in the northern part of the subcontinent.

In 1569, when Akbar was passing through Punjab, he decided to meet the revered Guru. Late-18th century Sikh historian Sarup Das Bhalla in *Mahima Prakash* (a versified account of the ten Sikh Gurus) notes that the Emperor walked barefoot to the location, forgoing the silks his attendants had laid out for him as a mark of respect for the Guru. The Mughal royal joined devotees to enjoy a meal at the *langar* or community kitchen at Goindwal. Akbar and some of his officials sat in rows alongside the other devotees. He was pleased to see that the kitchen was open to everyone, irrespective of their caste, class, or faith. Impressed, he is said to have offered a royal land grant, which the Guru refused to accept. Guru Amar Das invoked the Sikh philosophy of "*wand kay shako*," which translates to sharing one's earnings with the community.

Akbar's tolerant beliefs

The third Mughal Emperor came to the throne in 1556, and is widely regarded as the greatest of the Mughals to rule over India. This was not just for the Empire's expansion to nearly all areas of the subcontinent. His importance in the pages of history also stems from the sense of religious tolerance in the Empire under his rule.

Sikhism, still in its early years then, benefited from his policies and governance. His popularity was only augmented by the wealth of the treasury in his reign. All these factors enabled Akbar to maintain a stable government and fostered the expansion of Sikhism, then a new religion. Three of Guru Nanak's successors lived and expanded upon the Sikh ideology at the time of Emperor Akbar's reign. These were Guru Amar Das, Guru Ram Das, and Guru Arjan.

Granting the land of Ramdaspur

The town of Ramdaspur, which is present-day Amritsar, acquired its name after the fourth Sikh Guru, who shifted the spiritual center of Sikhism here. This town was built on land gifted by Emperor Akbar to Guru Amar Das on the occasion of his daughter's marriage. In the Adi Granth, Ramdaspur is likened to "*Ram-Rajya*" in Hinduism, where

> "One who **works** for what he eats, and **gives** some of what he has—O Nanak, he knows the **Path**."
>
> GURU NANAK, GURU GRANTH SAHIB
> (TRANSLATION BY DR. SANT SINGH KHALSA)

due to the grace of the Guru, neither *jizya* (a tax on non-Muslims of the region) nor any other tax was levied by the state. The administration of the town was entirely under Guru Ram Das. Essentially, Ramdaspur existed as an autonomous town within the larger framework of the Mughal Empire.

Final years of Akbar's reign

The notion of freedom was evident in the Guru's ability to preach without the threat of persecution. This was a significant factor in bolstering the development of Sikhism. In *Ain-i-Akbari*, Abul Fazal notes that Akbar's tolerance gave way to increased state support for other religions, which was for the development of spirituality.

The final Sikh leader to have his guruship overlap with Akbar's rule was Guru Arjan. He also received the same unwavering support from the state under Akbar. According to Sikh scholar J. S. Grewal, the Mughal Emperor's approach towards Guru Arjan had a "sheltering impact." In November 1598, while on the way back from Lahore after a long stay, Akbar visited the Guru in Goindwal. The heartfelt reception that he received and the hymns that were chanted impressed him deeply. As a result, he consented to the Sikh request to reduce the provincial revenue rates by one-sixth, bringing them back to where they were before his protracted stay in Lahore.

Grewal notes that by the time Akbar died, the Sikh Panth had been organized as a state inside the Mughal Empire, owing in large part to his religious generosity and tolerant policies. However, while this helped the faith's growth and spread, it couldn't be protected indefinitely. The Gurus and the religion itself would soon face intolerance and persecution at the hands of those in positions of power.

The start of state hostility

The period after Emperor Akbar's reign saw increased state interference in the affairs of the Sikhs, from Guru Arjan's martyrdom and Guru Hargobind's imprisonment at the hands of Emperor Jehangir to armed conflicts with Emperor Shah Jahan. This resulted in a period of immense socio-political transformation that both shaped and reshaped Sikh ideology.

By the time of Emperor Akbar's death, the Sikh Panth had transformed itself into a state within the larger Mughal Empire. A self-reliant government had evolved where the Sikhs did not vie for patronage or look at external sources for financial help. The Gurus collected taxes, held court, and were declared *sacha padshah*, true king. The Mughals soon perceived this organizational unity as a threat to the imperial structure.

Growing antagonism

When Emperor Jehangir came to the Mughal throne, it became clear that Akbar's benign religious policies had aided and sheltered the development of Sikhism (see pp.78–79), notes Sikh historian J. S. Grewal.

The reasons for Jehangir's religious bigotry are often debated among historians, who usually cite political and economic reasons for his hostile treatment of non-Muslims. However, there is no doubt that the growing popularity of the Sikh faith compounded this intolerance, because Jehangir assumed that Guru Arjan Dev had lured the people into converting to Sikhism. Historian G. S. Nayyar asserts that certain Mughal noblemen further incited the Emperor by claiming that their religion was in danger.

TUZUK-I-JAHANGIRI (1605–27)

Also called the *Jahangir-Nama* or the memoir of Jehangir, this Persian text is an autobiographical account of the life of the fourth Mughal emperor. It is the most important source of Mughal historical reconstruction during his reign. He wrote it in stages during most of his life, until he fell ill in 1624. Mutamad Khan, a military commander, was given the responsibility of continuing the memoir during the seventeenth year of Jehangir's reign and wrote it until the reign's nineteenth year.

Jehangir's angst against Guru Arjan Dev grew even further after he believed that the Guru supported his son Prince Khusrau, who had unsuccessfully challenged his rule.

Execution of Guru Arjan

One of Jehangir's primary anti-Sikh actions involved fining Guru Arjan Rs 20,000 for "acts of deviance." The Guru refused to pay, so Jehangir had him captured and imprisoned at the Lahore fort. He confiscated the Guru's property and handed his children to the Mughal nobleman Murtaza Khan. The Guru was then ordered to convert to Islam.

Guru Arjan Dev refused, and Sikh records note that he was starved and made to sit on a large, metal plate placed on top of a fire. The torture continued for five days. There are several accounts of Guru Arjan's torture. One version says he was later sent to cool down in a nearby river but never returned. Another narrative, a letter dated 1606, as recorded in *Sicques, Tigers or Thieves*, is by Jesuit missionary Father Jerome Xavier, who claimed

to be present at the torture. He briefly mentions how some supporters tried to appeal to Jehangir to free the Guru, but could not change his mind. Though other accounts cite different incidents, a common assertion is that the Guru earned the Mughal state's disfavor, which Jehangir's memoir, *Tuzuk-i-Jahangiri*, also attests.

Redefining the Sikh faith

Guru Arjan's martyrdom led to a radical transformation within the Sikh Panth. His execution was a turning point that ushered in a new era of Sikh self-consciousness, militarization, and sectarianism.

Guru Hargobind, who succeeded Guru Arjan, reacted to his father's death by emphasizing military might as the way to assert the faith's position. He equipped himself with two swords, the *miri* and *piri*. One symbolized his spiritual authority and the other his temporal power. He also constructed the Lohgarh fort for defense purposes, and had the Akal Takht built near the Harmandir Sahib to conduct his temporal duties (see p.84).

Emperor Jehangir imprisoned the 14-year-old Guru Hargobind at Gwalior Fort, where political prisoners were usually detained, on the pretext that the fine imposed on his father had not been paid. Sikh accounts state that the Guru was eventually released, it is speculated, in 1619.

Subsequently, his army fought four battles against the Mughal state, defeating them each time and destroying the idea that the imperial rulers were invincible. Guru Hargobind's military success roused the peasantry and brought even more followers into the Sikh fold.

In brief

1605
Emperor Akbar's death

1605
Jehangir's ascension to the Mughal throne

1606
Execution of Guru Arjan Dev

1609
Guru Hargobind is imprisoned at Gwalior Fort

1621
Sikhs and Mughals clash in the Battle of Rohilla for the first time

1635
The fourth Mughal–Sikh battle, last to be led by Guru Hargobind, is fought

◀ **The imposing Gwalior Fort in Madhya Pradesh,** Central India, where Emperor Jehangir held the young Guru Hargobind as prisoner.

ਸੁਰਤਨਾਜੀ

ਪ੍ਰਸਨਨਰਾਮਸਤਰੋਤਰਨੇਤਰਭ

ਜ਼ਤਿਕਤਾਤਿਸਰਬਨਾਮਕ

ਦਨਕਰਮਨਾਮਬ੍ਰਨਤਸੁਅਤਾ॥੧

ਪ੍ਰੁਖਾਰਤੁਰਾ ਧਾਮਸਤੋਅਕਾਲੇ

ਕ੍ਰਿਪਾਲੇਧਾਮਸਤੋਅਰੂਪੋਧਾਮਸਤੋ

ਧਾਮਸਤੋਅਰੂਖੇਧਾਮਸਤੋਅਲੇਖੋ

ਕਾਲੇਧਾਮਸਤੋਅਜਾਲੇ॥੨॥ਧਾਮਸ

ਜੋਨਧਾਮਸਤੋਅਤੇਜੋਧਾਮਸਤੋ

ਧਾਮਸਤੋਅਕਾਮੋ॥੩॥ਧਾਮਸਤੋ

ਕਮੀਰਧਾਮਸਤੋਅਧਰਮੀ

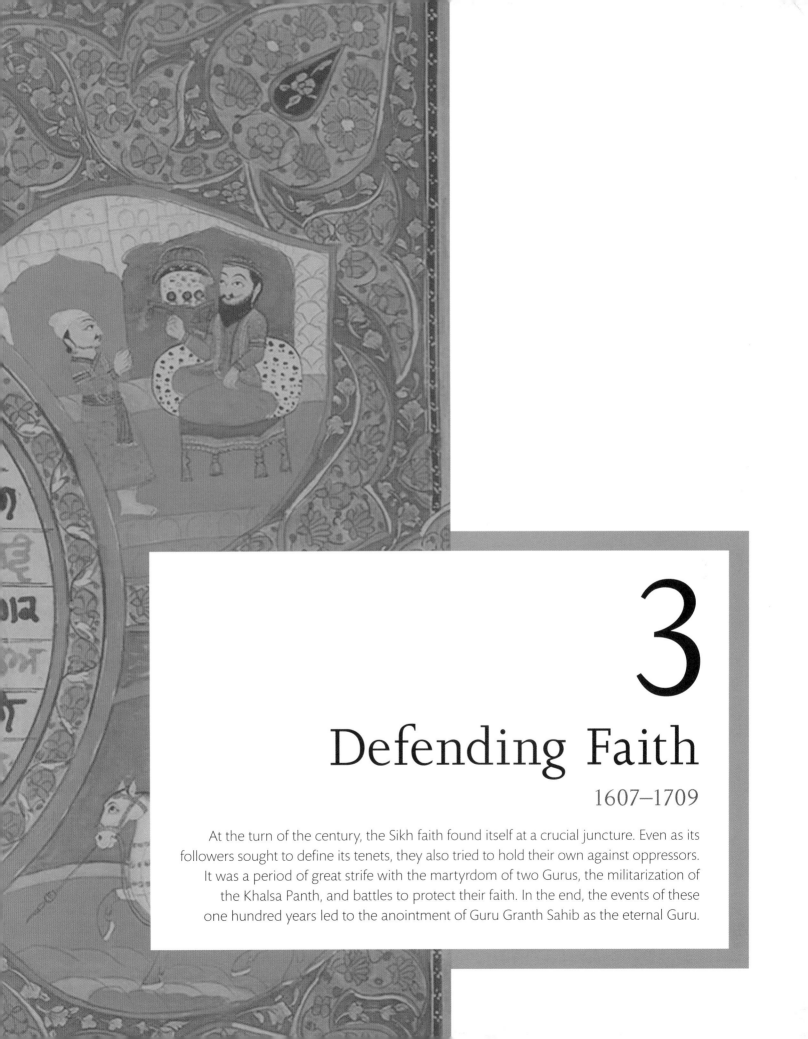

3
Defending Faith
1607–1709

At the turn of the century, the Sikh faith found itself at a crucial juncture. Even as its followers sought to define its tenets, they also tried to hold their own against oppressors. It was a period of great strife with the martyrdom of two Gurus, the militarization of the Khalsa Panth, and battles to protect their faith. In the end, the events of these one hundred years led to the anointment of Guru Granth Sahib as the eternal Guru.

Building military strategies

Guru Arjan's execution made Guru Hargobind realize the need to reform the Panth as a way of changing the dynamics within the Mughal–Sikh relationship. The relationship, fraught during Emperor Jehangir's reign, only turned worse when Shah Jahan came to power in the first half of the 17th century.

In his book *A History of the Sikhs*, Indian author Khushwant Singh explains that the death of Guru Arjan at the hands of the Mughals was meant to subdue the Sikhs for a while. Officials had not arrested his family assuming that they would not cause any trouble. In the years following the Guru's death, the Sikh community rallied behind his family, offering support to the elders of the faith and the Guru's son, who was also his successor.

Changes to the Panth

Guru Hargobind assumed guruship in 1606, when he was 11 years old. Despite his young age, he realized that reforms were necessary in order to strengthen the position of the Panth and build a strong defense against its detractors. He introduced the doctrine of combined temporal and spiritual authority, embodied by two swords, the *miri* and *piri,* to cement his novel position. He also built the Akal Takht outside the Harmandir, which signified the supreme temporal authority possessed by the Guru. Here, he discussed military strategies with the Panth. He invested in training a body of soldiers in martial exercises and urged the community to donate weapons and horses instead of money. These developments marked a time when Sikhs first began to exercise martial organization and warfare.

◄ **A portrait of Emperor Shah Jahan** painted soon after his ascension to the Mughal throne, c. 1630, depicts him with a beard, dressed in royal finery.

BABA GURDITTA

Baba Gurditta was the first son born to Guru Hargobind and Mata Damodari in 1613. His father taught him the religious doctrines of Sikhism and trained him in martial arts, hoping to hand over the spiritual mantle to him in due course. Gurditta was deputed to move to Kartarpur after his marriage to Ananti, and was later commissioned to oversee the development of Kiratpur, where the Guru eventually retired. Beyond his service to his father, Gurditta valiantly fought in the battle at Kartarpur, and also succeeded Sri Chand as the head of the Udasi sect. He passed away in 1638 leaving behind two sons, Dhir Mal and Har Rai.

Initial opposition

Local officials began to warn Emperor Jehangir of Guru Hargobind's activities. The Mughal ruler decided to quell the Guru's influence. He used the unpaid fines imposed upon Guru Arjan as an excuse to imprison Guru Hargobind in the Gwalior Fort, and ordered the dissolution of his army. Historians remain divided as to why Guru Hargobind was released, some believing that Jehangir's policies grew more tolerant in the later years of his rule. Upon his release, Guru Hargobind consolidated his followers and continued to train a cavalry and an artillery. Subsequently, his offensive against the Mughals at Rohilla resulted in a victory for the Sikhs.

The Guru also toured the north of India, where he urged people to follow the message of Guru Nanak and fight beside the Sikhs. He received a plot of land in the foothills from the Raja of Bilaspur, where he deputed his son, Baba Gurditta, to build the settlement of Kiratpur.

Internal rivalry

Guru Hargobind's authority and position as "*miri-piri da malik,*" which translates to "lord of the temporal and the spiritual," was seen by his critics, especially those whose familial claims had been ignored for the Guruship, as a divergence from the norm. A key figure who intermittently undermined his authority was Prithi Chand, the eldest brother of Guru Arjan.

He claimed his right to the seat of spiritual authority, which was later asserted by his son Meharban as well. Others, such as Guru Hargobind's grandson Dhir Mal, also chose to showcase their allegiance to the Mughal throne rather than to the Guru.

Facing Shah Jahan's army

The conflict with the Mughals continued under Shah Jahan, when local administrators in Punjab complained about the Guru's hunting activities. Orders were sent for his arrest at Ramdaspur, resulting in an incursion between the Mughals and Sikhs, and eventually Guru Hargobind left for Kartarpur. The Sikh army had to encounter the Mughal forces on several occasions here.

Shah Jahan's transgressions continued to incite anger among the Panth. Sikh accounts claim that he destroyed an important Sikh *baoli* (stepwell) in Lahore, which did not help relations between the two sides. Guru Hargobind's army fought the consequent battle at Kartarpur against Kale Khan, the governor of Peshawar, with much confidence. In the fighting that ensued, Sikh forces, which included the Guru's sons Baba Gurditta and Guru Tegh Bahadur, managed to evade the Mughal attacks.

Soon after, the Guru left for Kiratpur. Mughal forces led by Ahmed Khan attacked the group on their journey. Despite securing the win, the Sikhs lost many warriors in this battle.

In brief

1606
Guru Hargobind succeeds Guru Arjan

1606
The Akal Takht is constructed in Amritsar

1609
Emperor Jehangir imprisons Guru Hargobind

1621
Guru Hargobind's troops fight the Battle of Rohilla, the first against Mughals

1627
Shah Jahan becomes the Mughal emperor

1635
Sikhs and Mughals clash in the Battle of Kartarpur

1635
Guru Hargobind moves to Kiratpur

► A painting depicting **Guru Hargobind** with one of the two swords that he carried to symbolize the *miri* and *piri*.

Guru Hargobind

Guru Hargobind carved his distinct legacy by establishing the Akal Takht, the highest seat of temporal authority, at Harmandir Sahib in Amritsar, and by preparing his followers militarily to face challenges from Mughal and other forces.

By the time he was 11 years old, Guru Hargobind Singh had received extensive training in martial arts by Baba Buddha, a respected Sikh elder. He had also mastered the Sikh religious tenets, taught by Bhai Gurdas, one of the scribes of the Adi Granth.

In 1606, the brutal execution of his father, Guru Arjan, by Emperor Jehangir (see pp.80–81) led to his initiation as the sixth Sikh Guru. The new Guru faced the challenge of Mughal interference and rival claims to his spiritual authority.

Guru Hargobind found the answer to these problems in a shift from the practices of his predecessors toward martial activity. He donned the twin swords of *miri* and *piri* to assert his position (see pp.84–85). He was eager to arm his community so that they could defend themselves. He commissioned the construction of a high platform, which came to be known as Akal Takht (the immortal throne), opposite the Harmandir Sahib in Amritsar. He would address the community from here on the sanctity of violence enacted to uphold faith. The Lohgarh Fort was constructed under his leadership for defense. He also wrote *hukamnamas* or holy orders inviting followers to render offerings of arms and horses, and to join his army.

A devout Sikh

The emphasis on military training and strategy impressed the value of martial actions, martyrdom, and heroism on the Sikh psyche, giving the community a novel disposition. Guru Hargobind continued to propagate the spiritual tenets of his predecessors, stressing on the role of worship, meditation, and service in the emancipation of the soul. The only difference was that now a martial hue was also emphasized.

Sikh accounts tell of how he woke up three hours before sunrise each day to contemplate the Divine and recite verses from the Guru Granth Sahib. He spent the rest of the day in training and overseeing the administration.

> "After Arjan Mal, **Hargobind** also made a claim to succession and sat in his father's seat . . . He encountered **many difficulties**. One was [i.e. arose from the fact] that he adopted the style of **soldiers**, and, contrary to his father's practice, **girded the sword**, employed servants and took to hunting."

DABISTAN-I MAZAHIB, *SIKH HISTORY FROM PERSIAN SOURCES*
[EDITED BY J. S. GREWAL AND IRFAN HABIB]

Adversary of the Mughals

Guru Hargobind's growing force irked Jehangir, who ordered his imprisonment, under the pretense of non-payment of fines levied against his father (see pp.80–81). Sikh legends suggest that Guru Hargobind's popularity was such that his devotees regularly went to the fort requesting a presence with the Guru. While it is not known how long he was imprisoned, it is believed that he secured the emancipation of 52 prisoners along with his release, earning him the title of *Bandi Chhor*, literally meaning "release of prisoner." *Bandi Chhor Divas* (The Day of Liberation), when Guru Hargobind returned to lead his faith, is still celebrated today.

The later years

While Jehangir chose conciliation with Guru Hargobind after his release, there were several Mughal incursions after Shah Jahan's succession as the Mughal Emperor in 1628. On all occasions of hostility, Guru Hargobind was pragmatic, encouraging his followers to take up military action or withdraw as and when required. In 1634, he shifted his religious center to Kiratpur, a hill town he established on the banks of River Sutlej, where he stayed until his death in 1644.

▼ **An oil on canvas,** depicting a young Guru Hargobind being handed a sword by Baba Buddha.

At Aurangzeb's court

Amid growing pressures from within the Sikh community, Guru Har Rai, the seventh Sikh Guru, sought to unify his followers as they faced many challenges. Meanwhile, the succession of Emperor Aurangzeb to the Mughal throne brought with it fresh troubles.

> "He sent his son Ram Rai instead, enjoining him to **fix** his **thoughts** on **God**, and everything would prove **successful**."

PATWANT SINGH, *THE SIKHS*, 1999

◀ **Guru Har Rai is depicted on a walk in this portrait, with an attendant** raising an enormous parasol over the Guru's head, signifying his exalted status.

Guru Hargobind passed on the seat of spiritual authority to his grandson, Guru Har Rai, in 1644. Besides the *gurgaddi* (Guru's seat), Guru Har Rai also inherited 2,000 armed retainers and a large force of horses. Unlike the previous Gurus, however, he did not face the violent aggression of the Mughals.

Guru Har Rai is believed to have initiated three important missions called *bakshishes* for the purpose of preaching Guru Nanak's message. He traveled widely himself, and dispatched several of his followers to preach in different places, including far-flung cities such as Kabul, Dhaka, and Multan. At his center, Guru Har Rai held daily audiences with devotees, encouraged *langar*, and recited the verses of his predecessors.

Period of isolation

Initially, Guru Har Rai continued the use of the center established by his grandfather Guru Hargobind, at Kiratpur. Nevertheless, within a few months, he was compelled to move to another isolated location further in the hills. There was fear of Mughal attacks as Kiratpur was in the territory of the Raja of Bilaspur, who was embroiled in a bitter conflict with the Emperor. Over the next few years, Guru Har Rai lived in relative seclusion in the village of Thapal, in the territory of Sirmur, which became his new religious center. However, this move reportedly hampered his ability to directly supervise the administration in other centers, such as Khadur, Amritsar, Goindwal, Kiratpur, and Kartarpur.

The Guru's absence from the main centers also led to disruption in the *masand* system of appointing representatives to oversee the affairs of a local Sikh congregation. This allowed Guru Har Rai's brother, Dhir Mal, and Harji, the son of Prithi Chand, to make claims to guruship.

Cognizant of the fragmentation of the community, the Guru set out on a tour across the country to revive the community and bring more members into its fold.

A thorny friendship

In 1658, Aurangzeb, Emperor Shah Jahan's third son, ascended the Mughal throne after defeating his brother Dara Shikoh in battle. His reign was marked by aggressive social policy, such as the reimplementation of *jizya* (a tax levied on non-Muslim subjects of a state), after more than a century of its abolition by Emperor Akbar.

Guru Har Rai moved back to Kiratpur almost at the same time as Aurangzeb's ascension. A fleeing Dara Shikoh reached Punjab and asked the Guru for assistance, who obliged as he would for anyone. According to historical accounts, state officials gave an amplified version of the Guru helping the fugitive prince to the Emperor. This invoked Aurangzeb's ire and he called for an audience with the Guru at his court in Delhi to explain his conduct. The Guru sent his elder son, Ram Rai, in his stead.

It is believed that Ram Rai conducted himself obsequiously at the Mughal court. He readily agreed to change a verse in the sacred Adi Granth, which pleased Aurangzeb. The Emperor even patronized him and encouraged him to Guruship by granting him a piece of land to establish his religious center. Sources suggest that this relationship fostered tensions between Ram Rai and Guru Har Rai, as it pained the Guru deeply that his son lacked conviction and courage and he had compromised the purity of the holy scripture. The Guru reportedly banished Ram Rai and consequently chose his younger son, Harkrishan as the eighth Guru.

▶ **An early 18th-century watercolor painting by court** artist Bhavanidas depicts Aurangzeb on a gilded palanquin along with his hunting party.

KIRATPUR

Kiratpur was a township that was established on the banks of the Sutlej River by Guru Hargobind's eldest son, Bhai Gurditta, on the Guru's orders. After the Mughal onslaught, Guru Hargobind was forced to evacuate his center at Amritsar and stationed his seat at Kiratpur, a location that was relatively isolated from Mughal access because of the terrain. The Guru lived within the Gurdwara Shish Mahal complex and held his sermons at the Gurdwara Takht Kot Sahib, where Guru Har Rai was anointed. Kiratpur became the seat of all succeeding Gurus until Guru Tegh Bahadur, who founded a new center at Anandpur.

A 17th-century painting of Dara Shikoh, the heir to the Mughal throne, in full battle regalia atop an elephant with his army. In the struggle for the throne, his brother Aurangzeb defeated and executed him in 1658.

The Guru and a troubled prince

Not only did Guru Har Rai heal Dara Shikoh, he also gave him protection at Goindwal. The Guru's support of the rival claimant to the Mughal throne further burdened the relationship between the Sikhs and the Mughal Empire.

In the late 1650s, trouble was brewing in the Mughal court. Emperor Shah Jahan's illness gave rise to a war of succession between the princes. The heir apparent, Dara Shikoh, was a tolerant man with an affinity for religions and philosophy. However, his bigoted younger brother Aurangzeb also coveted the Mughal throne.

During this time, the relationship between the Mughals and the Sikhs was tenuous at best. Guru Arjan had been executed by Emperor Jehangir, Guru Hargobind had faced many attacks from Emperor Shah Jahan, and even Guru Har Rai had to move out of Kiratpur. Eventually, the Guru and the Mughals' relations improved once the former treated the Emperor's son, Dara Shikoh, for poisoning. However, this dynamic changed once again when Dara Shikoh sought Guru Har Rai's blessings in 1658.

Healing the enemy

In 1658, rumors of Shah Jahan's death led to the princes declaring sovereignty in their own provinces. Dara Shikoh sent several generals from his army to quell the rebellion, but Aurangzeb colluded with their younger brother Murad Baksh to defeat his forces. This led to Dara Shikoh himself leading an army against his brothers. He lost the battle, about 10 miles (16 km) south of the River Yamuna at Samugarh. Barely managing to escape, he fled northward to Punjab and requested an audience with the seventh Sikh Guru, Guru Har Rai in Goindwal. Sikh accounts suggest that many years earlier when Aurangzeb had poisoned Dara Shikoh, Guru Har Rai sent a remedy of rare herbs to cure him. The Sikh leader had explained this act of doing good to even those who were offenders. He had said that if a flower was plucked with one hand and given away with the other, both the doer and the giver received the fragrance. This incident as well as Sufi saint Mian Mir's praises of the Guru led Dara Shikoh to seek Guru Har Rai.

A helping hand

Historians and Sikh sources often depict the relationship between Guru Har Rai and Dara Shikoh as one of respect, an easy friendship between two intellectual, spiritual leaders. Dara took deep interest in understanding different religions, especially the tenets of the Sufi faith, which he was most drawn to. To this effect, he had even composed religious doctrines, biographies, and translations, including those from Sanskrit to Persian. The Guru is believed to have appreciated his spiritual knowledge, and to have instructed him in the Sikh religion.

The Guru allowed Dara Shikoh safe passage through Punjab, and also gave him armed protection. Sikh historian Sarup Das Bhalla, in *Mahima Prakash*, suggests that the Guru sent his own troops to delay Aurangzeb's forces from capturing fugitive Dara Shikoh.

Nevertheless, Dara Shikoh was captured in Gujarat and executed in Delhi in 1659, owing to his political conduct and heterodox opinions. Guru Har Rai's aid irked Aurangzeb as he had issued a decree that anyone helping his brother would face his wrath. Aurangzeb began to perceive Guru Har Rai as a further threat after he heard rumors circulated by his courtiers and others that exaggerated the relationship between the Guru and Dara Shikoh. The Emperor summoned the Guru to meet him in Delhi and explain his conduct.

As per Sikh tradition, Guru Har Rai sent an emissary, his eldest son Ram Rai, in his stead to Aurangzeb's court in 1661 (see p.89), which ultimately influenced the choice of the future successor.

> "Akbar's great grandson **Dara Shikoh**… through his own writing as well as his translations… **championed** the view that **true wisdom** was **not related** to a **single religious** tradition."

SIGNE COHEN, "DARA SHIKOH AND THE FIRST TRANSLATION OF THE UPANISADS," *THE UPANISADS: A COMPLETE GUIDE*, 2017

A young Guru

The Sikh tradition's youngest Guru had a humble attitude and a sharp mind. In his brief term, he demonstrated great political acumen, a deep commitment to the faith, and miraculous healing powers.

Guru Harkrishan was barely five years old when his father Guru Har Rai chose him as his successor. British scholar Max Arthur Macauliffe in his work *The Sikh Religion* notes that even at a young age, Harkrishan instructed the community, addressed their doubts, and led them on the path toward redemption. His father saw him as an extraordinary child, one with a divine vision, and hence, preferred him over his older son, Ram Rai, for Guruship.

Between two brothers

Ram Rai felt betrayed at not being named the Guru despite his time at Aurangzeb's court (see pp.88–89). He had traveled from Kiratpur to Delhi at his father's command. At Delhi, he won the favor of the Mughal Emperor, who showered Ram Rai with wealth. His sycophancy at the Mughal court, along with his willingness to change a verse in the Adi Granth, is said to have turned his father against him.

Linguist and philologist Ernest Trumpp in his work *The Adi Granth, or the Holy Scriptures of the Sikhs* postulates that Guru Har Rai could have ruled out Ram Rai from Guruship as, "the Guru was displeased with his eldest son because he made disciples of his own and worked miracles." However, most scholars agree that Guru Har Rai decided to give the Guruship to his younger son soon after Ram Rai's stay in Delhi. Ram Rai retaliated by claiming to be the eighth Guru and established a center on land granted to him by the Emperor in

the modern-day district of Dehra Dun in the Himalayas. Aurangzeb continued to offer his patronage to Ram Rai on the assumption that Ram Rai was the heir apparent, and could be manipulated into bringing the Sikhs under Mughal control.

After Guru Harkrishan took up the mantle, Emperor Aurangzeb summoned him to his court by sending word through Raja Jai Singh of Amber (see box). As his final order before his death, Guru Har Rai had instructed the young Guru to never appear before the Emperor. Guru Harkrishan knew that if he chose to do so, he would be breaking a pledge he made to his father.

According to Macauliffe, Ram Rai orchestrated this meeting in order to reengineer the Guruship in his favor. However, author Khushwant Singh writes that Ram Rai, who was just fifteen years old at the time, is unlikely to have pursued the succession issue on his own. He supposes that Raja Jai Singh convinced the Guru that he would not have to see the Emperor personally. So, after considerable thought, Guru Harkrishan left Kiratpur for Delhi.

Performing miracles

Pandit Tara Singh, a nineteenth-century Punjabi scholar, narrates an interesting story about the Guru's journey to Delhi, in his work *Gur Tirath Sangrah*. He relates that while camping in the village of Panjokhara, now in Haryana, a Hindu priest challenged Guru Harkrishan to read passages from the Bhagavad Gita. The Guru

> "According to the Hindu proverb the nature and ultimate size of a tree can be judged by its sprouting leaves, so this **child** ... gave early **indications** of being **worthy** to succeed to the **high dignity** of his time."

MAX ARTHUR MACAULIFFE, *THE SIKH RELIGION: ITS GURUS, SACRED WRITINGS AND AUTHORS, VOL. IV*, 1909

confounded the priest by having a local man discuss the verses on his behalf. Legend has it that this man, identified as Chajju in some sources, could not speak or hear prior to this, attesting to Guru Harkrishan's healing powers.

The great healer

In 1661, after covering a distance of 200 miles (320 km), Guru Harkrishan reached Delhi, the Mughal capital, where he stayed at Raja Jai Singh's house. On his way, he is said to have healed several individuals who were maimed and suffered from leprosy, simply by touching them. At the time of his visit, the city was struck by the cholera epidemic. As news of his arrival spread, hundreds of patients took refuge at the Raja's residence pleading with him to free them of the disease. The Guru placed his hand upon them and offered them holy water. Legend has it that the patients were cured after drinking this water and perceived it to be *charanamrit*, or nectar. Later, when the smallpox outbreak engulfed the children of Delhi, mothers flocked in thousands seeking the Guru. He is believed to have healed them the same way.

Subsequently, when the Guru himself caught the disease, devout followers attributed it to him imbibing the sufferings of his followers into his own person.

Guru Harkrishan passed away in 1664 before Aurangzeb could meet him. Raja Jai Singh of Amber dedicated his bungalow in Delhi, the brief residence of the Guru, in memory of Guru Harkrishan and it soon became the site for the popular Gurdwara Bangla Sahib.

RAJA JAI SINGH OF AMBER

Jai Singh I was the king of Amber (now Jaipur in Rajasthan) and a Mughal military general. During Shah Jahan's reign, he ascended the ranks and also played an important part in the fight against Central Asian and Persian invasions. Shah Jahan bestowed the title "Mirza" on him. However, he later supported Aurangzeb, going against Shah Jahan, who wanted Dara Shikoh as his successor. Under Aurangzeb, Jai Singh waged a victorious campaign against Maratha ruler Shivaji, compelling him to sign the Treaty of Purandar, which laid down the terms of Shivaji's relationship with the Mughals.

A matter of faith

Guru Tegh Bahadur's leadership spanned over a decade. During this time, he traveled across the country, preaching the teachings of Guru Nanak as well as defending the religion against the orthodox Mughal state.

The youngest son of Guru Hargobind, Tegh Bahadur moved from Kiratpur to the village of Bakala, near Amritsar, in 1644 and lived there with his wife and mother after the death of his father, the sixth Guru. Here, he became absorbed in meditative contemplation even though he lived the life of a householder. In 1664, an ailing Guru Harkrishan named "Baba Bakala" his successor, revealing that the ninth Guru would be found in Bakala.

The Guru's journeys

According to contemporary Sikh records such as the *Bhatt Vahi Talauda Pargana Jind*, Tegh Bahadur was anointed the ninth Guru in 1664.

As Guru, he traveled the length and breadth of the subcontinent, visiting many scattered Sikh congregations.

One of the first journeys he undertook as the Guru was to Harmandir Sahib in Amritsar. When the schismatic caretakers refused to allow him entry, he went to Kiratpur, the town settled by his father. However, faced with the hostility of his nephews and brothers there, the Guru set up a new religious center on a hillock in the village of Makhowal, near Kiratpur. Called Chakk Nanaki, it was later renamed Anandpur, which means haven of bliss. By 1665, he journeyed across Punjab and the Gangetic plains in order to establish contacts with Sikh

▼ **This painting depicts** Guru Tegh Bahadur meeting Kashmiri Brahmins who approached him in 1675 to intervene on their behalf with Emperor Aurangzeb.

congregations, consolidate them into the fold, and restore a measure of confidence in the community. Wherever he went, he was met with veneration. When he reached the area of Delhi, Ram Rai, Guru Har Rai's son and Guru Harkrishan's brother, who was still at the Mughal court, had him imprisoned on the charges of disruption and being an imposter. The Guru was released only by the intervention of Raja Ram Singh of Amber.

Afterward, Guru Tegh Bahadur went to Mathura, Agra, Prayagraj, Varanasi, Sahsaram, Gaya, and Patna. Later, Patna (in modern-day Bihar), became one of the five great centers of Sikhism with the establishment of Takht Sri Harmandir Sahib, which marks the site of the birth of his son, Guru Gobind Singh in 1666. After a brief stay in Patna, he traveled further east. Across the Brahmaputra River, he visited Sikh centers in Sylhet, Chittagong, Sondip, and Dhaka, in response to the wishes of Sikh *sangats* in Assam and Bengal (including parts of modern-day Bangladesh). Sikh sources indicate that none of his predecessors had visited

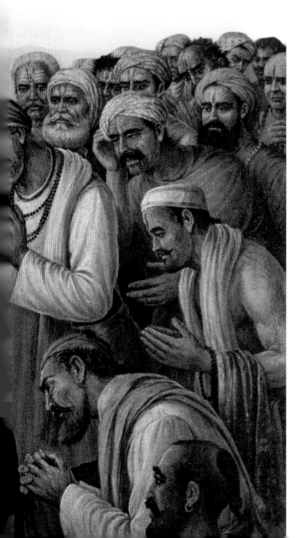

> ## "One who is not perturbed by misfortune, who is beyond comfort, attachment and fear, who considers gold as dust ... In such a person resides God."

GURU TEGH BAHADUR, GURU GRANTH SAHIB

these congregations since Guru Nanak, almost 160 years earlier. Historian J.S. Grewal asserts in his book, *The Sikhs of Punjab*, "In the first five or six years of his pontificate Guru Tegh Bahadur traveled more than any of his predecessors after Guru Nanak. If his idea was to reassure the far-flung congregations *(sangats)* of the Guru's concern for them, he was amply successful."

Guru Tegh Bahadur's later years
He returned to Punjab in 1671, where he encountered the effects of the Mughal policy of religious persecution. Indian historian Sir Jadu Nath Sarkar gives an account of repressive measures taken by the state against non-Muslim subjects in his book, *History of Aurangzeb.* Sarkar notes that the Emperor had ordered the demolition of temples, the expulsion of Sikh *masands* (agents) from cities and offerings collected by them to be sent to the Mughal treasury, forced conversions, and levying of taxes on non-Muslims.

In the face of the Mughal persecution of Sikhs and Hindus, Guru Tegh Bahadur worked toward reassuring the people with his message of tolerance. He traveled widely across the region, now falling in the states of Punjab and Haryana, moving from village to village to emphasize the importance of righteousness. Everywhere he went, he was received by enormous crowds.

In 1675, a group of Brahmins from the Kashmir Valley approached Guru Tegh Bahadur in Anandpur with grievances of systematic religious oppression and conversion by the Mughal governor, asking him to intervene. He reassured them and appealed them to stand firm on their faith (see pp.96–97) and took it upon himself to oppose the regime. This act of public opposition to the Mughal state was met with disapproval and he was summoned to Delhi.

In November 1675, Aurangzeb's soldiers detained Guru Tegh Bahadur. Unable to shake his belief or coerce the Guru, the Mughals executed him in Delhi.

In brief

1664
Guru Tegh Bahadur is anointed the ninth Sikh Guru

1665
Left Makhowal to establish contact with some of the Sikh confederations

1665
Guru Tegh Bahadur's arrest by Aurangzeb and three-day detention at the Mughal court

1671
Move back to Makhowal

1673
Aurangzeb's policy of religious persecution reaches a high point

1675
Guru Tegh Bahadur's execution at Chandni Chowk, Delhi

The execution of Guru Tegh Bahadur

The ninth Guru's execution immortalized him in history for his secular sacrifice, while defending the freedom of another faith. It also laid bare the Mughal state's apprehension at the growing strength of the Sikh community, which led to the conflicts that took place under Guru Gobind Singh.

In May 1675, a group of distraught Kashmiri Brahmins made their way to Anandpur, seeking Guru Tegh Bahadur's help. At the time, a Mughal governor overseeing the Kashmir Valley had resorted to forcible conversions following Emperor Aurangzeb's policies of religious intolerance. The Brahmins disclosed that they were being threatened with execution for their refusal to give up their religion.

A decisive step

Guru Tegh Bahadur was a staunch believer in the right of an individual to follow a religion of his own choice. Determined to restrain the Mughal state's bigotry, the Guru decided to sacrifice himself for the cause of standing against religious oppression. He asked the Kashmiri Brahmins to make an arrangement with Aurangzeb. They would agree to convert without resistance, but only if the Emperor could convince the Guru to change his religion. Author Arvind-Pal Singh Mandair asserts in his book, *Sikhism: A Guide for the Perplexed*, "The

Guru's stance was a ... challenge, not to the sovereignty of the Mughal state, but to the state's policy..." This decision, as expected by the Guru, resulted in the ire of the Emperor. Soon, Mughal forces arrested Guru Tegh Bahadur in the Ropar region and kept him imprisoned in Sirhind for four months. They later moved him to Delhi in November 1675, where the Guru and his three disciples appeared before the Emperor.

In defence of faith

Here, they defended their faith and refused to convert to Islam. Bhatt Sarup Singh Kaushish's *Guru Kian Sakhian* states that Aurangzeb gave the Guru three choices: to convert, perform a miracle, or choose to die. The Guru chose death.

Sikh texts indicate that his disciples were tortured before him and then put to death. Shortly after, the Guru was beheaded in Chandni Chowk in Delhi, in November 1675, immortalizing him in history for his sacrifice to defend the freedom to practice any faith. Reportedly, his head was taken

> "These **care-free souls** of Punjab
> **Jest** with **death**,
> **Unafraid** of dying
> They become slaves if loved,
> **Sacrifice** and give away their lives,
> But **do not submit** to anyone's arrogance,
> Standing up with clubs raised on shoulders.
> **Stubborn**, full of **abandon**,
> from the beginning."

"JAWAN PUNJAB DE," PURAN SINGH

▲ **A *talwar* or sword with its scabbard,** possibly from around 1600, features an inscription in Arabic and Persian along the back edge of the blade. The Persian inscription mentions Aurangzeb while the Arabic words praise Allah. The parasol engraved close to the handle shows its possible provenance as the Emperor's sword.

to Anandpur in Punjab by Bhai Jaita and ceremonially cremated. His body was taken by Lakhi Shah, another Sikh, who cremated the body using his house as a funeral pyre. Today, the Gurdwara Sis Ganj Sahib (*sis* meaning head) in Delhi marks the site of the Guru's brutal execution and Gurdwara Rakab Ganj Sahib marks where his body was cremated.

Sikh historian J.S. Grewal notes how Guru Gobind Singh greatly admired his father's "unique sacrifice … not only of his own faith but also in the cause of freedom of conscience." Guru Gobind Singh wrote of his father's execution extensively in the *Bachitar Natak* (as noted by author Purnima Dhavan in *When Sparrows Became Hawks*):

"He protected the *tilak* (vermilion mark) and the *juneo* (sacred thread) and enacted a great sacrifice,

For the saintly he accomplished this, he gave up his head without a complaint,

This sacrifice he performed to protect *dharam*, he gave up his head (*sir*), but not his spiritual knowledge (*sirr*)."

The meaning

There are several interpretations of the Guru's martyrdom. Some historians view it as a retaliation by the Mughal state against the growing politico-religious strength of the Sikh community. Persian historian Muhsin Fani's *Dabistan*, for instance, records Guru Tegh Bahadur's use of religious and political symbols to fight Mughal power. He embodied the title *sacha padshah* (meaning true king, which originated with Guru Arjan). Grewal regards him as a "Prophet of Assurance" for his successful efforts in reinstating the community's confidence in the Sikh faith.

However, there is no doubt that the Guru's martyrdom is a prominent event in the history of human rights. Guru Tegh Bahadur's sacrifice was a protest against bigotry, orthodoxy, and religious persecution.

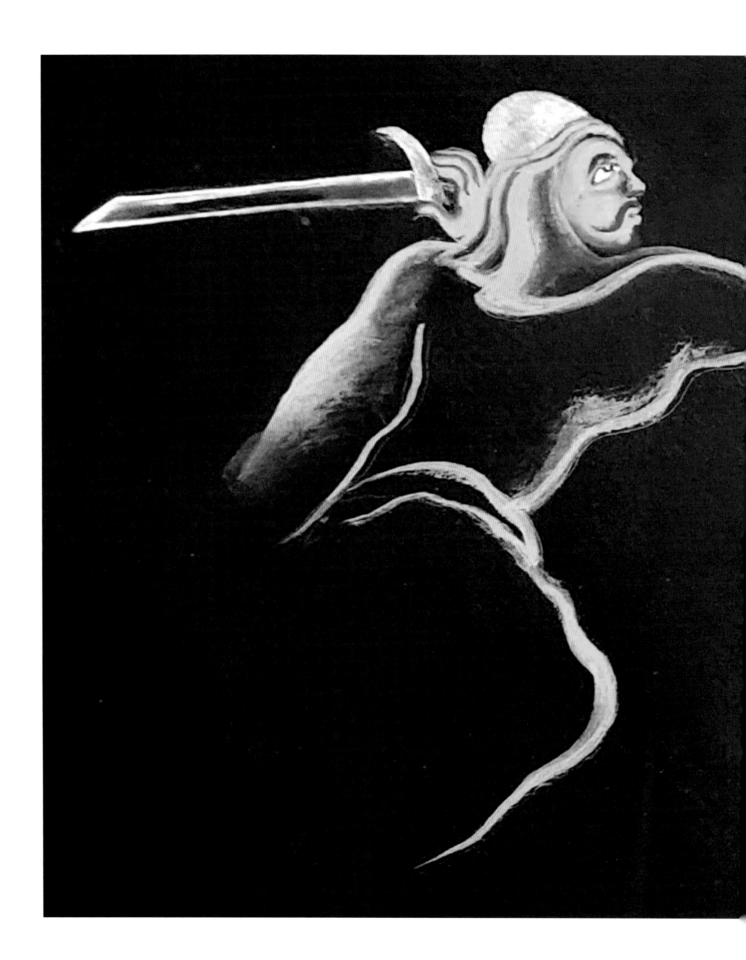

Titled *Chandni Chowk*, this 2021 gouache painting by contemporary painter and graphic artist Arpana Caur depicts a Mughal executioner raising his sword to behead Guru Tegh Bahadur. The Guru was martyred on November 24, 1675, upon Mughal orders at Chandni Chowk in Delhi. Today, Gurdwara Sis Ganj Sahib stands where the Guru was executed.

▶ **This early 19th-century painting** from Guler, Punjab Hills, depicts Guru Tegh Bahadur sitting under a canopy, engaging with a devotee.

Guru Tegh Bahadur

The ninth Guru enjoyed great popularity at a time when the Mughal Emperor Aurangzeb was trying to brutally suppress the Sikh community. His fearless attitude and devotion to the faith only served to increase his followers.

It was a period of great unrest and anxiety for the community. Mughal Emperor Aurangzeb had started taking an active and aggressive interest in Sikh affairs. It was in the midst of this fraught environment that Guru Tegh Bahadur took over the seat of spiritual power. The transition to becoming the ninth Guru was not smooth. He faced hostility not just from the Mughals, but from other contenders to his guruship. Soon after Guru Tegh Bahadur was anointed, he left Punjab, and traveled to Sikh centers in northern and eastern India.

The journey took him through the Gangetic Plains and across the Brahmaputra river into, what is today, Assam and Dhaka in present-day Bangladesh. The people accepted him in every town and Sikh center he visited. For them, he was a source of comfort and solace; he was their Guru.

The power of the Divine

For Guru Tegh Bahadur, the Divine was the source of all authority and he believed in the transience of power. So, even though he had a rightful claim to the position of the Guru, he never actively vied for it, unlike the other claimants (see pp.94–95). This very detachment from authority and material indulgences also garnered him the support of locals. He adhered to the ideals of forgiveness, harboring no resentment or vengeance toward those who attempted to depose him or dispute his guruship.

The shield of justice

He adopted a similar approach in the face of Aurangzeb's antagonistic policies. During his travels, he spread a message of hope to different Sikh congregations, offering assurance, and alleviating their concerns regarding the Empire's rising theocratic orthodoxy. He nurtured contact with his followers, emphasizing the importance of remembering God's name—the only eternal one in a world where human existence is fleeting.

The Sikh community completely embraced their Guru wherever he went. Historians note how they

▲ **Sikh priests at the Golden Temple, Amritsar, carry the Guru Granth Sahib** to mark the 394th birth anniversary of Guru Tegh Bahadur in 2015.

gathered in large groups to listen to Guru Tegh Bahadur speak even during festivals, brought offerings by way of fine cloth and money, looked after him when he visited their town, and even celebrated his son's birthday. He returned to Punjab from his travels in 1671, but made a journey to Delhi again in 1673 to reassure and speak to the peasants and landowners who had been affected by Aurangzeb's harsh policies. With such defiant displays of leadership and an increasing cadre of followers, it is only natural that the Guru attracted the displeasure of the Mughal Empire. For his acts of resistance, he is often called "*Hind-Di-Chadar*," or the shield of India.

In 1675, Kashmiri Brahmins facing religious persecution from the Mughals asked the Guru for aid (see pp.96–97). Guru Tegh Bahadur decided to confront the Mughal state. He was arrested and executed on Aurangzeb's orders and attained the status of a martyr, the second in Sikh history after Guru Arjan.

Today, Guru Tegh Bahadur is revered for showing fearlessness in the face of injustice and sacrificing his life to protect the religious freedom of others.

> "One who enshrines the **Lord's Name** in his heart night and day—even for an instant—has his fear of Death eradicated. O Nanak, his life is **approved** and **fulfilled**."
>
> GURU TEGH BAHADUR, GURU GRANTH SAHIB
> (TRANSLATION BY DR. SANT SINGH KHALSA)

Portraits of martyrdom

The popular visual culture of the Sikh Panth, *shahadat tasveeran*, art depicting martyrdom, has always held an important place within the community. These paintings and lithographs, which honored the road paved by Sikh martyrs by recognizing their hardships and sacrifices, rejuvenated the Sikh consciousness.

Contemporary portraits of later Sikh Gurus and objets d'art from their households, such as the decorated chariot of Guru Ram Das or the armor of Guru Gobind Singh with inscriptions from *gurbani*, are early and significant examples of Sikh art.

The stability brought in during the reign of Maharaja Ranjit Singh and the rulers of the Phulkian states allowed for court patronage, and created an environment in which art flourished. During the 18th century, Sikh art resembled and followed the stylistic pattern of Mughal portraits. The incorporation and patronization of the Kangra (hill) style of painting also came about. Western techniques of realism and oil painting came next. The arrival of the printing press led to mass production and circulation, which further popularized Sikh art.

Shahidi and art

The Sikh religious ethos reveres both divinity and valor. Thus, the art of the Sikhs often evokes two images: of saints and of warriors. The latter motif includes themes such as bravery, sacrifice, courage, and martyrdom or *shahidi*. Scenes from Sikh history depicting the tyranny of the Mughals, the *shahadat* (martyrdom) of the Gurus, and the massacre of courageous Sikhs have always been popular, and are still commissioned by gurdwaras, institutes, and private patrons.

The emergence of Sikh calendar art in the 20th century further revolutionized the artistic sphere and the spirit of the community. Artists such as Sobha Singh, Kirpal Singh, and Amolak Singh painted (and printed) heartrending images of the martyrdom of the *sahibzadas*, the sons of Guru Gobind Singh—the older two, at seventeen and fourteen years of age, in battle against the Mughal army and the younger two, who were nine and seven years old when they were executed. Other key events, such as Vadda Ghallughara, the massacre by the Afghan army of Ahmed Shah Durrani in 1762; the Chhota Ghallughara, the smaller massacre of 1746; the execution of Bhai Mati Dass; and the mutilation of Bhai Mani Singh were also popular themes. One of the most well-known prints of Sikh martyrs is that of Baba Deep Singh by artist G.S. Sohan Singh. According to Sikh lore, upon hearing of the desecration of the Harmandir Sahib in Amritsar by the Afghans in 1757, the seventy-five-year-old scholar and warrior Baba Deep Singh led a force to ward off the invaders. In the battle that followed, he was wounded and nearly decapitated, but held on to his head with his left hand while wielding his sword with the right, striking terror in the hearts of the Afghans.

The stirring imagery used to depict such scenes serves to underline the unwavering valor and devotion of a Sikh. Many such images can be found on display in *langar* halls and gurdwara museums. They are also produced on banners, posters, calendars, book illustrations, and online forums. Ajaibghar or the Central Sikh Museum within the Golden Temple houses many such prints depicting scenes of Sikh history, such as tales of martyrdoms and heroism from the Mughal, post-Mughal, British colonial, and even post-colonial times.

An evocation of shared memories

Jaswant Singh's celebrated painting of the massacre at the Jallianwala Bagh Martyrs' Gallery in Amritsar is another example of *shahadat tasveeran*. Also included in the genre are the portraits of Bhagat Singh, an unparalleled secular hero who challenged colonial rule. They emerged in circulation soon after his martyrdom in 1931. The symbolism employed in Sikh paintings was later evoked in various instances forming a key part of shared Sikh memory and history. Perhaps, as Louis Fenech and other scholars have argued, the advocation and emphasis upon the rhetoric of martyrdom was for political, cultural, and religious advances. It enabled the notion of an imagined community and helped establish an external identity for the Sikhs. It inculcated within the community a sense of pride and an expectation of such absolute devotion.

This sculpture from Gurdwara Mehdiana Sahib in Punjab depicts the Mughal soldiers torturing the warrior-disciple of Guru Gobind Singh, Banda Singh Bahadur. He was executed in Delhi in 1716.

Hill rajas and the Sikhs

Guru Gobind Singh had a tumultuous relationship with the hill rajas of Punjab, which came to a head with the Battle of Bhangani in 1686. However, a common enemy in the Mughals led to a shaky alliance that saw them combine forces to fight in the Battle of Nadaun in 1691.

Guru Tegh Bahadur's execution showed Guru Gobind Singh that there was an urgent need to resist injustice actively and protect the community from religious persecution. His philosophy is represented in a quote from the *Bachitar Natak*, attributed to him: "The only reason I took birth was to see that righteousness may flourish, that the good may live and tyrants be torn out by their roots." The Guru continued to emphasize martial training while upholding the Sikh faith's openness to all. As more lower-caste Hindus joined the Panth, the Hindu rulers began seeing the Sikh Guru as a crusader against puritanical Brahmanism and its caste-based structure of social stratification.

Regional discontent

Anandpur, where the tenth Guru lived, was located in the kingdom of Raja Bhim Chand of Kahlur (now Bilaspur). The hill rajas belonged to a Hindu-warrior community called the Rajputs. The town of Anandpur was built upon land purchased by the previous Sikh Guru and not governed by the raja.

Bhim Chand, much like the other hill chiefs, looked at the growing military prowess of the Sikhs with great concern. Though they had initially committed to supporting the Guru against the Mughals, they now began to see him as a threat.

BACHITAR NATAK

Bachitar (or *Vichitra*) *Natak*, which translates to "wondrous play," is a lyrical poem included in the Dasam Granth (see pp.120–121). The work begins with a eulogy to the Divine Being, and covers the first thirty-two years of Guru Gobind Singh's life, including his early challenges, and the battles at Bhangani and Nadaun. The poem is split into fourteen chapters or *adhyays*, but stops abruptly after chronicling events from 1696. It concludes just before the Amrit Sanchar ceremony (see pp.108–109) and the foundation of the Khalsa at the end of the 1700s.

This sentiment gained traction after the Sikh community built a *nagara* or a war drum. Until now, such an instrument was only used by the hill chiefs. In another incident, the Guru refused to lend Raja Bhim Chand an elephant gifted by a follower, believing that he would not get it back. This displeased the king as he wanted the Guru to recognize him as his sovereign. Sikh accounts state that eventually, upon the invitation of Raja Mat Prakash of Sirmur, the Guru relocated to Paonta, although the reason is not specified.

Battle of Bhangani

Sikh accounts offer differing reasons behind the clashes between the Guru's and the Raja's forces. Some sources note that Paonta was located on disputed land between the Sirmur and Garhwal kingdoms, and its use by the Guru prompted retaliation from Garhwal. Other sources, such as the *Bachitar Natak*, attribute the battle to Guru Gobind's refusal to give worthy offerings to Bhim Chand on the event of his son's marriage, such as a beautiful canopy. Fearing an attack, the Guru also did not allow anyone other than the groom and his attendants to cross through Paonta to reach Garhwal's capital for the wedding, which forced Bhim Chand to take a longer route. However, contemporary Sikh sources believe that the dispute between the hill Rajas and the Sikhs was largely political.

This bad blood culminated in a battle at Bhangani, located 6 miles (9.7 km) away from Paonta. Though it only lasted less than a day, Indian author Khushwant Singh calls this the Guru's "first baptism of steel." Sikh forces emerged victorious, and the Guru eventually returned to Anandpur in 1689.

◀ **This painting by artist G.S. Sohan Singh** shows Guru Gobind Singh with an adorned elephant, said to be a gift from a follower.

◀ **A photograph by Bhai Sewa Singh and Bhai Jawahar Singh** displays weapons reputed to be the personal arms of Guru Gobind Singh, held at Takht Keshgarh Sahib in Punjab, c. 1925. The weapons include the *khanda*, double-edged sword, and *karpa barsha*, cobra spear.

Altered political relations

By the 1680s, the Mughal military campaigns in the Deccan plateau had reduced funds in the royal treasury. They decided to collect revenue from the hill states that were behind on annual tributes. Upon nonpayment, Mian Khan, the *faujdar* or viceroy of Jammu, dispatched an army to punish the hill chiefs. This compelled Raja Bhim Chand to seek Guru Gobind Singh's help in resisting the Mughal army.

The Guru, who was against the idea of paying the Mughals an annual tribute, expounded his philosophy of fighting tyranny and injustice with force, and offered his support to Bhim Chand and the other rajas. The joint forces of the Sikhs and the hill Rajas fought the Mughals in the Battle of Nadaun in 1691. In the ensuing clash, the Sikh forces secured an early victory. Even though this gave them the advantage, the hill chiefs agreed to settle with the Mughals. However, Guru Gobind Singh refused to do so and withdrew his troops.

In brief

1675
Guru Gobind Singh is anointed

1680–1707
Deccan Wars fought between the Mughals and the Marathas

1685
The Guru moves to Paonta

1686
Sikhs fight the Battle of Bhangani against hill Rajas

1689
The Guru returns to Anandpur

1691
Sikhs fight the Battle of Nadaun with hill chiefs against the Mughals

"Pay **no tribute** to the Turks [Mughals], if thou pay it today, there will be **another demand** on thee tomorrow. But if thou **fight** and **cause the Turks** [Mughals] **to retreat**, then shall no one molest thee."

GURU GOBIND SINGH [TRANSLATION BY MAX ARTHUR MCAULIFFE, *THE SIKH RELIGION: ITS GURUS, SACRED WRITINGS AND AUTHORS*]

Reformation

From the abolishment of the *masand* system to the establishment of the Khalsa Panth, Guru Gobind Singh's reforms consolidated the vision of his predecessors into an organization that cemented the Sikhs as a social and religious community.

Sustained Mughal persecution in the years after the death of Emperor Akbar and the subsequent martyrdom of Guru Arjan had led to crucial changes in the organization of the Sikh community under Guru Hargobind. There was a greater focus on military training and more encounters on the battlefield as the Sikhs sought to protect their way of life. However, during Guru Gobind Singh's time the faith's considerable evolution became more conspicuous.

The tenth and the last Sikh Guru was at the helm of some crucial changes, which came about as a reaction to challenges. In some cases, these were external, such as disagreements with the hill kings in whose territories many of the Sikh centers had been previously established. In others, it was from within, such as the corruption of the *masand* system.

Internal challenges

Masands were officials tasked with preaching the Sikh faith, collecting contributions, and ensuring the well-being of the community (see pp.56–57). However, by the time Guru Gobind Singh was anointed, the community regularly complained of theft, coercion, and misappropriation of funds by the *masands*.

Some *masands* deviated from the Panth and set themselves up as pretenders in faraway Sikh centers, preaching their own version of the faith, and naming successors. So, Guru Gobind issued a proclamation that revoked their position. To counter the damage they had caused, he also excommunicated several officials along with their followers from the Panth.

Birth of a new order

Guru Gobind strongly believed in the right of the Sikhs to defend themselves against the religious tyranny of the Mughals. In the face of oppression, force was to be adopted when other means had been exhausted. So, he furthered the development of the Sikh army.

The community's military character evolved further with the initiation of the Khalsa Panth in 1699. The Khalsa was a functional institution that had far-reaching implications. Its origins, of course, need be contextualized within the atmosphere of the late-seventeenth century, as well as the core of Guru Gobind Singh's mission and the tenets of Sikh philosophy.

This initiation took place in 1699 at Anandpur Sahib on the day of Baisakhi. Guru Gobind Singh christened five loyal followers as the *panj pyare*, or the cherished five (see pp.108–109). They became the first five "pure" Sikhs, free of any prejudice of class and caste, and symbols of a renewed Sikh ethos that celebrated valor and justice along with equality and service.

Guru Gobind Singh also settled another internal threat to the Sikh community: the debates over succession. He dissolved the lineage of gurus. Instead, he vested spiritual powers on the Guru Granth Sahib and temporal powers on the Khalsa collectively.

> "**When all** has been **tried**, yet **Justice** is not in **sight** It is then **right to pick** up the **sword**, It is then **right to fight**."
>
> GURU GOBIND SINGH, *ZAFARNAMA* (TRANSLATION BY NAVTEJ SARNA)

Understanding the changes

Over the years, historians have tried to ascribe different personal and political reasons for the establishment of the Khalsa Panth by the tenth Guru. Scholars such as Ernest Trumpp believe that he carried out this change in order to avenge his father's execution. Yet others associate the event with the need to disrupt the corrupt functioning of the existing *masand* system. The *Bachitar Natak*, a chapter in the Dasam Granth (see pp.120–121) posits that Guru Gobind Singh intended to instil values such as self-respect, spiritual awakening, and strength in those suffering under an unjust regime. Guru Gobind believed that authority emanated from God. Any power he wielded was only on behalf of the Divine and was in accordance with his mission of good triumphing over evil.

Sikh historian and author Mandanjit Kaur notes that the tenth Guru was a "creative genius" who set out on a project to create an organized community of saint-warriors who would stand as vanguards of righteousness.

▼ **A 19th-century gouache painting on cloth** depicts Guru Gobind Singh on horseback. He is accompanied by five devotees who hold Sikh insignias including the battle flag, a parasol, and a fly whisk.

The five beloved ones

During a harvest festival, Guru Gobind Singh asked his followers for a "great sacrifice." Among those gathered, only five men stepped forward. They were met not with a beheading, but with *amrit* (nectar) and an initiation into the Khalsa Panth, and came to be known as the Panj Pyare.

On the day of the spring harvest festival of Baisakhi in 1699, devotees gathered to celebrate at the flourishing town of Anandpur Sahib in the foothills of the Shivalik range in northern India. This was where Guru Gobind Singh lived. During the festivities, the tenth Guru emerged from a tent, sword in hand. He looked at the gathered devotees and asked for a volunteer for a sacrifice. It had to be someone who followed all his duties and undertook spiritual responsibilities with faith and interest.

Five men came forward and pledged to sacrifice their lives for the faith. They were from different professions, and many had been lower-caste Hindus in the past. Yet, each demonstrated unwavering loyalty and faith in their Guru. Daya Ram was a Khatri from Lahore; Dharam Das a Jat from Delhi; Mohkam Chand had been a tailor; Himmat Chand, a cook; and Sahib Chand, a barber from Bidar in central India.

The Guru took them into a tent, away from the gathering. Here, instead of the sacrifice they were expecting, the men underwent an initiation into the Khalsa fold. The ceremony, which came to be known as Amrit Sanchar, took place in front of the Guru Granth Sahib. The tent had an iron dish with sugar crystals that were mixed with holy water in an iron bowl. The Guru stirred this

> "Grant me **protection**, **merciful** Lord, prostrate here at your door; Guard me and keep me, **Friend** of the humble, weary from wandering far. You love the **devout** and recover the sinful; to you alone I **address this prayer**: Take me and hold me, merciful Lord, **carry me safely to joy**."

GURU ARJAN, *"VAR JAITASARI,"* ADI GRANTH
[TRANSLATION BY W.H. MCLEOD, 1984]

nectar, or *amrit*, with a *khanda*, a double-edged dagger or sword, as the five men sang Sikh hymns. In the Sikh penal code Tankhanama, Bhai Nand Lal, a devotee and contemporary of Guru Gobind Singh, wrote that this double-edged sword was now necessary to attain the goal of justice.

As part of the initiation, each volunteer kneeled on the ground in the Bir Asan, a posture where the right knee touches the ground and the left knee remains folded. The *panj pyare*, or the cherished five, received five handfuls of *amrit* in their palms while chanting the composition, "Wahe Guru ji ka Khalsa, Wahe Guru ji ki Fateh." This emphasized that the Khalsa belonged to God and so did the victory. The volunteers took sips of the remaining nectar from the same bowl reiterating the Sikh doctrine of a society without caste, and establishing it as a cornerstone of the Khalsa organization.

Codes of conduct

After the initiation, Guru Gobind Singh presented the five men before the gathering, announcing the birth of the Khalsa Panth. The men received the appellation of "Singh," which translates to "lion." They took formal vows to wear the *panj kakar*, or five Ks (see pp.110-111): *kesh* (unshorn hair), *kirpan* (sword), *kangha* (comb), *kachera* (short breeches or boxers), and *kara* (steel bracelet). They were also required to follow the four core norms of behavior or *rahit maryada*, which spelled out sartorial, behavioral, liturgical, and dietary restrictions and obligations they were to follow also.

The Khalsa order was now open to Sikhs. Anyone who underwent the initiation earned the name *Amritdhari*. Those who chose not to undergo the ritual, but continued to follow Guru Nanak's doctrines, were known as *Sahajdhari* Sikhs. If any members of the Khalsa failed to comply with any of the pledges, they were referred to as *tankhaiyas*, or defaulters. Defaulters would be punished, even excommunicated, and only readmitted to the Khalsa after they performed an appropriate penance. This was the unyielding formal order of the Khalsa.

◄ **This intricately embroidered silk cloth** or *Rumalla Sahib* depicts Guru Gobind Singh and the Panj Pyare. A *Rumalla Sahib* is a piece of fine cloth used to cover the Guru Granth Sahib in a gurdwara when it is not being read.

Kes or uncut hair worn under the customary turban

Kirpan or sword, often worn over clothes

A *kanga* or comb to keep hair tidy

Kara or iron bangle, worn on the right forearm

Kachera or a pair of breeches or shorts

This *granthi* (a priest) from Fatehgarh Sahib, Punjab, bears all the symbols of identity. He is seen in a turban and a long, unshorn beard. The visible black strap holds the *kirpan*.

> "These baptismal forms, with the accompanying **commitment** of **purity**, love and **service**, have aided them [Sikhs] in **keeping** themselves **united** …"

BHAYEE SIKANDAR SINGH AND ROOPINDER SINGH,
SIKH HERITAGE ETHOS & RELICS, 2011

The five emblems
Visual symbols of Khalsa identity

The *panj kakar* (5 Ks) is a sacred obligation of all Sikhs initiated into the Khalsa order, forming a part of their external appearance, and giving them a distinct identity. When introduced, these five objects of faith had the combined function of erasing the markers of caste identity, emphasizing the faith's unwavering belief in equality, as well as preparing the Khalsa for a life of fierce dedication to their religion. An *Amritdhari* Sikh dons all of these symbols.

Kes
The *kes*, or unshorn hair, is the most distinguishable trait of a Sikh. When vowing to keep the hair untrimmed, the Khalsas embrace the notion of a life beyond bodily fixations, respecting the natural will of the Divine. It is a symbol of saintliness and spiritual devotion.

Kanga
The *kanga*, or comb, used to keep the hair tidy, represents cleanliness. *Amritdharis* are instructed to comb their hair twice daily and wrap it in a turban to symbolize order and hygiene. Some Sikh scholars extend this cleanliness to the sphere of spirituality, with the comb being a metaphor for purity and spiritual discipline.

Kirpan
A *kirpan*, meaning sword, is derived from the terms 'kripa' (compassion) and 'an' (honor). A manifestation of the martial spirit of the Khalsa, it preserves Guru Gobind Singh's message of fearlessness in the face of injustice. The *kirpan* is only to be used to maintain righteousness.

Kara
Kara, or the iron bangle worn by Sikhs in their right hand, represents self-discipline and self-restraint. It reminds the bearer to constantly pursue the holy path of God. So, every time a Sikh raises a *kara*-adorned hand bearing a sword, the bangle acts as a reminder that it is only to be used in the cause of righteousness supported by God. The circular shape of the *kara* also stands for wholeness (without beginning or end) and the everlasting spirit of the One eternal being.

Kachera
Kachera or *Kachha*, meaning a pair of shorts, is a sartorial emblem of moral restraint and a reminder of the restriction against adultery. These shorts are also worn as clothes of simplicity, which assure briskness and action in the face of a confrontation to uphold justice.

**Thousands of members of the Sikh community walk toward the
City Hall in Toronto**, Canada, to mark the annual event of Khalsa Day in a
parade in 2018. The day coincides with the Sikh New Year or Baisakhi. This is
a key festival in Canada, which is home to nearly two percent of the world's
Sikh population, the third largest concentration after India and the US.

Impact of Guru Gobind Singh's reforms

The tenth Guru's reforms led to the rise of Jat peasants as a community of significance, even as the influence of the wealthy Khatris receded into the background. The rising militancy of the Sikhs also posed a threat to the neighboring chieftains and the Mughals.

Guru Gobind Singh's inauguration of the Khalsa in 1699 caused an immediate stir within the Sikh community. With its creation, the Guru had abolished all-pervading social divisions as was fundamental to the teachings of Guru Nanak. With the Khalsa, he also changed the constitution of the Sikh Panth. In this new order, the rich, the influential, the poor, and downtrodden would all be considered equals and drink *amrit* (see p.109) from the same vessel.

Reactions to the Khalsa

From the very beginning, the Sikh Panth drew its largest number of followers from the upper-caste Khatris, the community of traders, artisans, and landowners. While about 20,000 followers embraced the new order of the Khalsa (see pp.108–109), many others did not.

This was especially the case with the Khatri community, where some members embraced the reforms and underwent initiation to the new order, becoming *Amritdhari* Sikhs (those who underwent the *Amrit Sanchar* ceremony). At the same time, others chose not to join and continued to exist as *Sahajdhari* Sikhs (those who believe in Sikhism but have not been inducted or have shorn their hair). These members, belonging to the Brahmin and Khatri communities, rejected the Khalsa Panth and chose not to follow its teachings, as they believed that it questioned the legitimacy of Hindu Vedas and other scriptures delineating a code of conduct, which had been passed down to them by their ancestors. Author Khushwant Singh, in his book *A History of the Sikhs: Volume 1: 1469–1838*, asserts that, "They had been quite willing to pay lip service to the ideal of a casteless society preached by Nanak, but they were not willing to soil their lips by drinking amrit out of the same bowl [as lower-castes], as Gobind wanted them to do."

Rise of the Jats

Within a few days of the initiation ceremony at Anandpur (see pp.108–109), the number of converts had risen to more than 50,000. A majority of these were peasants from the Jat community, from the central districts

▼ A sketch made by Sani "the Draftman", c. 1860, depicts Jat women listening to a Sikh man read from the Guru Granth Sahib.

KURAHITS

Every Khalsa Sikh must pledge to obey four codes of conduct (*rahit*), and a violation of any of them is considered a cardinal sin (*kurahit*). These include showing disrespect to one's hair by chopping or cutting it, smoking tobacco or consuming other intoxicants such as smoking a hookah, touching or ingesting *kuttha* (halal or kosher) meat, and committing adultery. Any Khalsa Sikh who commits these *kurahits* can be reinitiated only if he seeks forgiveness from the Panth and performs the penance imposed on him.

A watercolor print demonstrating *kurahits* such as violence, drunkenness, and debauchery.

of Punjab, who were on the lower rungs of caste hierarchy. They were attracted to the faith for the same reasons that the others had moved away—their elevation in social status. When the *masand* system was abolished, the local Khalsa *sangats* took over the position, and their decisions were binding on the members.

Emergence of an army

Sikh accounts state that the baptism of Sikhs at Anandpur led to mass initiations into the Khalsa order all over northern India. Within a few months, there was a large community of warrior-saints in the hills surrounding Anandpur, ready to combat evil.

Guru Gobind Singh's rising power and influence in their region presented a threat to the neighboring chiefs, which ultimately led to attacks from the hill tribes and the Mughals.

"**He** [Guru Gobind Singh] **made** nationalism the religion of the **Khalsa**, and the **Sikhs** emerged as a **nation**."

BHAYEE SIKANDAR SINGH AND ROOPINDER SINGH, *SIKH HERITAGE ETHOS & RELICS*, 2011

Against the joint forces

As the 17th century drew to a close, the Khalsa fold multiplied as thousands joined their Guru in Anandpur. The nervous chieftains of small Hindu kingdoms surrounding the hilly citadel soon rallied with the Mughals against Guru Gobind Singh and his followers.

Between 1700 and 1704, the hill Rajahs harassed and provoked the Guru by engaging him in battles and putting up blockades to restrict the supply of resources into Anandpur. These attacks proved unsuccessful in driving the Sikhs out of the region. Desperate, the chiefs then appealed to Emperor Aurangzeb for help by portraying the militarized congregation as a threat to the Mughal state's religious and political sovereignty, while underplaying their self-interest in the matter.

Battles and losses

Mughal contingents of thousands of soldiers from Lahore and Sirhind along with the hill armies laid siege to Anandpur in May 1705. The siege lasted for seven months under the command of Wazir Khan, the governor of Sirhind. Even though food and supplies were running out, the Guru and his army managed to withstand the protracted attacks.

In December 1705, the Mughal commanders promised the Guru safe passage if he and his followers agreed to withdraw from Anandpur.

▼ **This manuscript of the Zafarnama**, a letter of victory, written by the Guru to Emperor Aurangzeb following the siege of Anandpur, is kept in Takht Hazur Sahib in Nanded, Maharashtra.

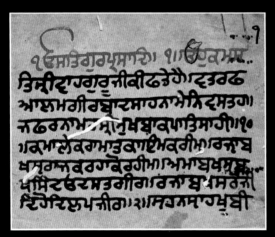

> "'What **use** is it to put out a **few sparks** when you raise a **mighty flame** instead?' **he** [Guru Gobind Singh] **wrote.**"

KHUSHWANT SINGH, *A HISTORY OF THE SIKHS, VOLUME 1: 1469–1838*

The assurance was issued in the name of Emperor Aurangzeb and solemnized by an oath made on the holy Quran. The Guru evacuated the fort at Anandpur along with his family and followers. As they were crossing Sirsa River, near Ropar, a large Mughal army attacked them. As the Guru and his retinue tried to evade the attackers, he was separated from his wife, mother, and younger two sons.

Guru Gobind Singh traveled farther south to confront the treacherous troops in Chamkaur. The mighty Sikh army was now reduced to a mere forty soldiers and faced a far bigger enemy. The valor of these Sikh soldiers in the Battle of Chamkaur is recorded in Sikh oral traditions and etched in the community's collective memory. Many valiant Sikhs, including Guru Gobind's elder sons Ajit Singh and Jujhar Singh, gave up their lives fighting the enemy.

Guru Gobind Singh survived and went to Machhiwara jungle. Author Khushwant Singh notes in his book *A History of the Sikhs*, "The Pathans put Gobind in a curtained palanquin and passed the Mughal sentries with the explanation that they were carrying their *pir* [saint]."

The Guru finally reached Jatpura, where he received a warm welcome from Muslim chief, Rai Kalha. Here, he learned of the brutal execution of his younger sons, Zorawar and Fateh Singh, at the hands of Wazir Khan for their refusal to give up their faith and convert to Islam, as well as the passing of his mother from shock in Sirhind. Sikh accounts state that the boys were mercilessly bricked alive.

In brief

1699
Establishment of the Khalsa Panth

1704
The siege of Anandpur and its evacuation by Guru Gobind Singh, followed by the Battle of Chamkaur

1705
The Battle of Muktsar

1707
After Aurangzeb's death, Bahadur Shah becomes the next emperor

ORIGIN OF THE WORD "KHALSA"

Scholars debate about the origin of the word "Khalsa." Ernest Trumpp, German missionary and translator of the Adi Granth, claims that the phrase implies "guru's own estate." However, according to *History of the Sikhs* author Joseph Cunningham, it has an Arabic origin meaning pure or special. So, "Khalsa" can refer to either the kingdom of Guru Gobind Singh or the chosen people who are solely answerable to Waheguru (God). The latter is widely accepted.

Trying times

The Guru moved southwest and tried to restore contact with Sikh congregations east of Sutlej, including regions near modern-day Bhatinda, in order to raise a force. Soon, Wazir Khan launched another attack in the nearby village of Khidrana, but was repulsed. This was also where forty men of the Majha district, who had earlier deserted the Sikh army during the siege of Anandpur, fought by the Guru's side. This village was later renamed Muktsar (pool of redemption) to honor these men who had laid down their lives. A period of relative peace prevailed and after almost a year, the Guru relocated to Talwandi Sabo. Here, he immersed himself in spiritual meditation and the compilation of the Adi Granth with his disciple Bhai Mani Singh, who later prepared the manuscript of Dasam Granth (see pp.120–121).

An attempt at peace

Emperor Aurangzeb decided to reconcile with Guru Gobind Singh and invited him to the Mughal court. However, on his way, the Guru learned of the Emperor's death in March 1707. Later, he formally visited the new monarch, Bahadur Shah, in Agra. The Guru stayed in Agra for four months, but the promised action against Wazir Khan remained delayed as the Emperor was embroiled in a bitter succession dispute. Guru Gobind then decided to accompany the Mughal camp on their way to the Deccan to suppress the rebellion of Kam Baksh, Bahadur Shah's younger brother.

▶ **This 19th-century folk painting** by an unknown artist depicts Mai Bhago (top right), a Sikh woman, fighting alongside the Guru in the battle of Muktsar. She was responsible for motivating forty deserters to rejoin the Guru at Muktsar.

The Zafarnama

The tenth Guru's heartbreak at losing his family and anger at the Mughal Emperor for orchestrating the attack in Chamkaur in 1705 are evocatively captured within the *Zafarnama*, in this poignant letter addressed to Aurangzeb.

Within the compositions of the Dasam Granth (see pp.120–121) lies a moving letter that Guru Gobind Singh wrote to Emperor Aurangzeb. Titled the *Zafarnama*, the word is a compound of the Arabic "zafar" meaning victory, and Persian "namah" meaning letter, thus translating to a letter or epistle of victory. It was written in exquisite Persian in 1705 or 1706, as the Guru passed through the Majha region after fleeing the Mughal onslaught on Anandpur, his headquarters.

A treacherous attack

The combined forces of the Mughals and the hills chiefs had laid siege on Anandpur in May 1704. It was during this time that the Guru received a written assurance of safe passage for himself and his followers from Aurangzeb and his representatives. This was only if he vacated Anandpur. The promise held great value as it was written on a copy of the Quran. This was a standard practice of the time and such a token gave legitimacy to the promise.

As per the agreement, the Guru and his retinue left Anandpur. However, they hadn't gone too far when the imperial forces descended on the party. This deceitful attack on a small number of Sikhs by an army of thousands led to the death of the Guru's two elder sons. The Guru managed to escape to Jatpura, a village in the Ludhiana district of Punjab. It is here that he learnt of the cruel execution of his two other sons at the hands of the Mughals and of the death of his mother.

A Guru laid bare

Guru Gobind Singh wrote the *Zafarnama* after this breach of faith by Aurangzeb. The letter begins with a customary invocation of the gracious, merciful, and omnipresent Divine. The address to the Emperor follows in a section named *Dastaan* (the tale). Here, the Guru emphasizes the supremacy of morality in the affairs of the state as well as the conduct of individuals. With utmost honesty, the Guru rebukes the Emperor for his immorality and the wicked attack. For the Guru, the responsibility of monitoring his officials fell upon the Emperor. He calls upon Aurangzeb to practice truth and justice in God's name.

The poem also mentions the vindictive role played by the hill chiefs who had incited the attacks with their opinions to the Emperor about the position of the Guru. An outraged Guru Gobind Singh even forewarns the end of the Empire, as it has lost its sanctity.

He declares that the one who puts his faith in the Emperor's oath is a ruined man. He chastises Aurangzeb for his false promise of peace. Then, he laments how a meager party of 40 Sikhs could counter the imperial army of thousands. In later verses, the Guru narrates how the war led to casualties on both ends, such that "chopped heads and hacked limbs lay piled on the battlefield" (verse 38).

In his book *A History of the Sikhs: Volume 1*, author Khushwant Singh writes that Guru Gobind Singh justifies the need to embrace violence for self-defense by citing the following lines from the *Zafarnama*, "When all other means have failed … it is permissible to draw the sword."

The letter also shows the Guru in a gracious light for being willing to meet with Aurangzeb to resolve the issue, despite having lost faith in his promises.

The Mughal reception

Sikh accounts narrate that following the letter, a remorseful Aurangzeb invited the Guru to meet him in the Deccan. However, before the two could get together, Aurangzeb died in 1707. Khushwant Singh contends that the letter could not have touched the Emperor's heart due to its reproachful material. Singh adds by saying, "The epistle that the Guru sent must have been in a different tone, because Aurangzeb was in fact induced by it to invite the Guru to meet him."

Character of the Zafarnama

The 111 stanzas in the letter follow a distinct one-meter style of Persian poetry. It is generally clubbed with 12 Persian parables called the *Hikayats* in the Dasam Granth, either because they were dispatched along with the letter as lessons on righteousness, or because of the common language of composition.

The Sikh canon includes the *Zafarnama*, one of the only Persian texts to be given the status of a Sikh scripture. Its verses are sung on special occasions as well.

▼ **Guru Gobind Singh wrote** the *Zafarnama* in 1705 as depicted below. The scribe of this illuminated manuscript is unknown.

This illustrated frontispiece of the **Dasam Granth** is from a manuscript dated 1825–1850. The text in the center is written in the Gurmukhi script.

Dasam Granth

The Dasam Granth, also known as the Dasven Padshah ka Granth (the scripture of the tenth leader), is a voluminous collection of writings associated with Guru Gobind Singh. This magnificent anthology includes eighteen works in around 1,428 pages and is written primarily in the Braj language, with a few sections in Punjabi and Persian.

The Dasam Granth was compiled, for the most part, at Anandpur, the childhood home of the tenth Guru. The scripture was put together at the request of Mata Sundari, Guru Gobind Singh's widow, and the task to collect the Guru's *bani* fell to his companion and disciple Bhai Mani Singh. It took him nine years to accomplish this mammoth charge, during which he traveled widely and even acquired copies of Guru Gobind Singh's works from his other disciples.

Most scholars agree that the Dasam Granth's works can be divided into three categories— philosophical, mythical, and autobiographical. Some of the compositions have been used in Sikh ceremonies and prayers since the time of the tenth Guru.

Philosophical and mythical compositions

Among the philosophical and devotional texts of the Dasam Granth are hymns from the *Jaap Sahib, Akal Purakh,* and *Gian Probodh*. These compositions, while philosophical in nature, use several mythical references. The *Jaap Sahib* has 199 verses exalting the Divine Being as omnipotent, all-powerful, and omniscient. It is considered to be a meditative text. The *Akal Purakh*, meaning "praise of the timeless one," on the other hand uses references from several texts that have myths to state that the primal being assumes numerous forms, but in reality is one. Starting with praises of the Divine and dialogues between the soul and the Almighty, the *Gian Prabodh* (which means guide to enlightenment) poems discuss emotions, the four eras—*Satyug, Treta, Dwapur,* and *Kalyug*—and the four facets of dharma—*Bhog, Raaj, Dhaan, and Mokh*.

Autobiographical texts

There are some personal details in a few of the texts that were compiled as the Dasam Granth. These details, such as dates and locations, help reconstruct Guru Gobind Singh's life and activities. These autobiographical compositions include the *Bachitar Natak* and the *Zafarnama* (see pp.118–119).

Bachitar Natak, meaning the "wondrous drama," traces Guru Gobind Singh's lineage back to the Hindu deities, Ram and Sita. This work also includes passages about his past life as *Dusht Daman*, the destroyer of evil, during which he meditated at Mount Hemkund (see pp.126-129) until he was summoned by God.

The *Zafarnama*, meaning a letter of victory, meanwhile is a poetic epistle in Persian addressed to Emperor Aurangzeb. A poignant piece of writing, it sheds light on the Guru's opposition to the Mughal regime's tyranny and fanaticism.

Other compositions

The Dasam Granth also contains some martial pieces; this increases its significance for religious groups such as the Nihangs. The scripture has 1,300 verses praising different *shastras*, or weapons, characterizing them as a representation of God's might. Some portions of the scripture speak of Hindu gods and goddesses as well. However, some historians posit that though the Dasam Granth tells the stories of Hindu mythological figures, it does not advocate their worship.

> "**Eternal God,** Thou art our shield. The dagger, knife, the **sword we wield,** to us **protector** there is given ... but chiefly Thou, protector brave, **All steel, wilt Thine own servant save.**"

AKAL USTAT, DASAM GRANTH (TRANSLATION BY MAX ARTHUR MACAULIFFE)

► **Guru Gobind Singh, seated on an elephant** with two armed companions, rides into battle in this painting from the 18th century.

Guru Gobind Singh

The tenth and last Sikh guru, Guru Gobind Singh, is remembered as a heroic figure who reshaped the community by establishing the Khalsa Panth and for bestowing guruship on the Guru Granth Sahib.

When Gobind Rai was nine years old, his father, Guru Tegh Bahadur, agreed to intervene on behalf of a group of Kashmiri Brahmins, oppressed under Mughal state's policies of religious persecution. He knew that only the sacrifice of someone noble would give them the right to practice their religion freely (see pp.96–97). Young Gobind Rai told his father that he did not know of anyone more noble than the Guru.

Gobind Rai's maturity and keen understanding of Sikh philosophy at a young age pleased his father, who named him his successor and left for Delhi. Thus began the pontificate of the tenth Guru, which saw significant reorganization and reformation, and gave the faith the core symbols and practices that have lasted to this day.

Shaping a guru

Guru Gobind was born in Patna in December 1666, where he learnt the local Braj language. By the age of five, he had joined his father in Anandpur, continuing his education and learning languages, including Persian.

After his anointment as the tenth Guru, he established the town of Paonta in the state of Sirmaur. Here, he learnt hunting and archery, and prepared to carry forward Guru Nanak's divine mission, as the Gurus before him.

There is no doubt that Guru Gobind was a mystic and a spiritual leader with a farsighted political vision, but he was also a poet and scholar beyond compare. In the book *Sikh Heritage: Ethos & Relics*, authors Bhayee Sikandar Singh and Roopinder Singh note that the Guru's compositions were "marked by sublimity of style, mystic ardor, and vibrant dynamism of thought and action." Not only did he compose the Dasam Granth, but his compilation of the Guru Granth Sahib is integral to the faith.

The righteous sword

A lot of the Guru's work carries the symbolism of the sword, which he posited to be akin to the Divine itself. This deification and usage of the sword should not be misinterpreted as his belief in force and violence; rather, this divinely imbued symbol was to be utilized solely as a defender of righteousness and justice.

It is also an apt metaphor for Guru Gobind's leadership: he coalesced the idea of the spiritual and the martial as the way forward. The incidents that transpired during his guruship added to his desire to instil this martial spirit. Various fissures and corrupt tendencies within the community, along with external threats from hill chiefs and the Mughal state, prompted the Guru to establish the Khalsa Panth (see pp.106–107). It was during this event that he took on the appellation "Singh" (lion).

The Guru's life, however, exemplified the compassionate aspect of the Sikh legacy. Having taken up arms against tyranny and injustice, his philosophy was an acclamation for a better and more humanistic world.

Leadership ethos

Guru Nanak's ideal of togetherness was crucially opposed to the caste system. Guru Gobind reinforced this notion by promoting brotherhood among the Khalsa on the basis of loyalty and benevolence. His act of codifying commensality (sipping water from the same iron bowl) as a symbol of initiation into the Khalsa was the ultimate marker of this shared love which regarded all people as equal.

His leadership was guided by divine purpose as per Sikh philosophy, which viewed authority as flowing from God. It is perhaps in continuation of this belief that he declared the end of the Guru lineage. Guru Gobind's last act was to bestow guruship upon the sacred text, the Guru Granth Sahib, which is considered the divine guide and embodiment of teachings from the Gurus.

▼ **Guru Gobind giving his wife Mata Sahib Kaur** five weapons which belonged to Guru Hargobind before sending her from Abchal Nagar to Delhi.

"Grant me this **boon**, O God, from Thy Greatness
May I never refrain from **righteous** acts;
May I fight without fear
All foes in life's battle,
With **confident** courage claiming the **victory**!"

GURU GOBIND SINGH, CHANDI CHARITRA 1, *DASAM GRANTH* (TRANSLATION IN *SELECTIONS FROM THE SACRED WRITINGS OF THE SIKHS*, 2000)

A *khanda* (double-edged sword) with stylistic engravings. It was given to Baba Ram and Baba Taloka of Patiala by Guru Gobind Singh. They had taken *amrit* from the Guru's hands in 1706

A *katar* or punch dagger, with its blade decorated with a hunting scene

Guru's weapons
Martial accessories

With the annexation of Punjab in 1856, the East India Company took possession of Maharaja Ranjit Singh's *toshkhana*, or treasury, and its contents were either auctioned, donated to the Queen, or chosen for inclusion in the East India Company's collection. Of particular interest to Lord Dalhousie, the Governor General of India, was a collection of artifacts, specifically weapons, which reportedly belonged to Guru Gobind Singh. These weapons were later found in the custody of his great-granddaughter, Lady Lindsay. They were eventually returned to India and placed on display in Anandpur Sahib's inner

Important piece of history
Among the weapons preserved in the Patiala State collection are several pieces of armor, such as the *Char Aaina*, which the Guru wore during the Battle of Bhangani. It was mounted on a leather belt. Inscribed on it are four quotations from the Guru Granth Sahib and the Dasam Granth. The family also has, in their possession, a Nishan Sahib (see pp.164–165)—the cloth wrapped around it still intact, which Guru Gobind Singh gave to their ancestors when they received *amrit*.

The Guru's *khandas* (double-edged swords) are also part of the collection. One of them is

The opening stanza of *Akaal Ustat* of the Guru Granth Sahib is engraved on the

A panel of the armor worn by the Guru during the Battle of Bhangani. Known as a *Char Aaina*, it was mounted on the chest with leather straps

Some of Guru Gobind Singh's weapons have been lost to time, while others are preserved and exhibited at gurdwaras as religious relics.

Hemkunt Sahib

Set in the lap of the Himalayas, Hemkunt Sahib (also known as Hemkund Sahib) is an important symbol of faith for the Sikhs: a pilgrimage site, as well as a source of immense natural beauty. The Dasam Granth asserts that Guru Gobind Singh, the tenth Sikh Guru, meditated here for several years.

In the midst of the mountains

Every year, hundreds of Sikhs make a perilous journey over hilly slopes and dizzying heights in order to reach Hemkunt Sahib in the Chamoli district of Uttarakhand. The gurdwara's unusual pentagon roof is shaped like an inverted lotus, and it easily sheds snow during the colder months. The Hemkunt Lake (Lake of Snow) is a pristine body of glacial water, adjacent to the temple. Traditionally, pilgrims take a dip in this sacred pool before entering the shrine. Inside, the enormous hall has elaborately decorated tapestries as well as walls adorned with images of Sikh Gurus. In the center, a *chandwa* (umbrella-shaped canopy) is suspended from the ceiling over the Guru Granth Sahib.

▲ **Late 20th-century photograph depicting the roof of the** Hemkunt Sahib under construction.

The Hemkunt Sahib is a fabled Sikh shrine set in the Himalayas on the Hemkunt Lake. It is the only gurdwara in India to be built at an elevation of around 15,000 ft (4,329 m) above sea level.

Scriptural origins

Sikh accounts maintain that the gurdwara's establishment can be traced to a serendipitous attempt by Sant Santok Singh, a priest who read the Dasam Granth, to locate the meditation spot of Guru Gobind Singh in his incarnated form. The geographical parallels with the text in this nook of the Himalayas were simply astounding.

The initial building of the gurdwara was completed in 1935 and Bhai Vir Singh, renowned Indian poet and scholar, installed the holy book, the Guru Granth Sahib in the shrine. However, the facade changed over time due to expansion and renovations made for ease of access. Construction of the present gurdwara began in the 1960s and was accomplished in 1993. The establishment of Hemkunt Sahib based on its connection with the Guru's incarnated existence rather than his pontificate makes it a unique site.

1. Pilgrims taking a dip in Hemkunt Lake; **2.** Worshipper at Gurdwara Gobind Ghat, the starting point of Hemkunt Sahib pilgrimage; **3.** Visitors at the gurdwara in winter; **4.** Pilgrims trekking through snow to reach the gurdwara; **5.** Festive celebration; **6.** View of Valley of Flowers National Park, a popular trek close to Hemkunt Sahib; **7.** Devotees outside the temple; **8.** Pilgrims riding mules to reach Hemkunt Sahib.

Sikh men attend a reading of the Guru Granth Sahib in the city of
Benalla in Victoria, Australia, on December 16, 1920. The holy text was
procured for the occasion by the local Australian Sikh community
from India. However, many in the community believe that a copy of
the text first reached the country even earlier than 1920.

The eternal Guru

Regarded as the eleventh and immortal Guru of the Sikhs, the Guru Granth Sahib was hundreds of years in the making. Within its nearly 1,400 pages are the teachings of the ten Gurus and saints, in hymns, that lay out the Sikh way of life.

The Guru Granth Sahib contains the spiritual and mystical poetry that delivers the divine message from the Guru's mouth. The book enjoys an exalted status due to its hymns being referred to as *dhur ki bani*, or original hymns. This understanding of revelation is based on the doctrine of the *shabad*, the experience of Divine Truth in verbal form, which serves as a conduit of communication between the eternal and formless God, the *Akal Purakh* and an awakened soul. The idea of "revelation" is significant in determining the sacred text's absolute authority and its divine origin.

Guru Gobind Singh, the tenth Guru, bestowed spiritual authority on the Guru Granth Sahib in 1708, and declared it the bearer of the "true and ultimate word" of the faith. Since then, it has been revered and worshipped as the repository of godly speech. It is believed to be the personification of the essence and philosophy of each of the Gurus.

Symbolic reverence

The irrevocable belief in the sacredness of the text is also seen in the way it is displayed. The consecrated book is the presiding presence in all Sikh *sangats*, or congregations, and is placed on a *takht* or raised platform at the center of the prayer hall under a rich canopy. It is treated as a "scared, infallible being," fanned with a *Chaur Sahib*, or a ceremonial, feathered whisk, as one would fan a human Guru. Ceremonies are performed and many *kirtans*, or devotional songs, are recited around it throughout the day. At night, it is carried to a sanctified space for rest. The daily *ardas*, or the morning and evening prayer, closes with an exhortation to uphold the purity of the text: "*Sab sikhan ko hukam hai, Guru maneyo Granth,*" which translates to "all Sikhs are commanded to behold the (holy) book as the Guru."

> "The influence of **Sikh scripture** on **Sikh life** has been **all-pervasive**, ranging all the way from **art** to **weaponry**. While the Sikh **scribes** spared no pains in creating illuminated and calligraphically elegant **manuscripts** of Sikh scripture, eighteenth-century Sikh blacksmiths inscribed its **hymns** on **swords** and **shields**."

GURINDER SINGH MANN, *THE MAKING OF SIKH SCRIPTURE*, 2001

This shared belief in the Guru Granth Sahib as a "living Guru" is nurtured through various allegorical and ceremonial practices. These include a sense of personal attachment evoked through the memorized oral recitation of *banis* (hymns) and the practice of *vak laina* or *hukam laina*, which means to receive the Guru's command from the Guru Granth Sahib, after prayer. Ceremonies such as marriages, initiations, naming of children, and birth and death anniversaries are all done in the presence of the holy book and are blessed by reading hymns from its pages.

One can also witness the enormous reverence bestowed upon the scripture by attending the daily morning practice, *praksh karna*, or the installation of the Granth at the Golden Temple in Amritsar. The Guru Granth Sahib is carried in a gilded palanquin followed by a procession of thousands of devotees. Thus, as an embodiment of the Sikh faith, the holy book has authority that transcends its text and is revered in the same way as the ten Sikh Gurus.

◀ **Sikh soldiers used a miniature edition of the Guru Granth Sahib during WW1.**
They carried it in their turbans and it could be read using a magnifying glass.

A 2013 photograph shows the Guru Granth Sahib being taken on a neighborhood procession from its resting place in a London *gurdwara*. The holy book is carried on the head as a mark of respect while another priest follows with a whisk.

4

The Rise and Fall of the Sikh Empire

1710–1849

As the faith became more organized, prominent leaders emerged who fought the oppressors and the invaders during the 18th century. They empowered the people and created the environment that saw the rise of the mighty Sikh Empire, under the rule of Ranjit Singh, which was both feared and coveted by the British in India.

The rise of a new leader

An encounter with Guru Gobind Singh led to the rise of a man, once an ascetic, who would gather a peasant army, lead it to countless victories, and change the course of Sikh history in the 18th century. This man, Banda Singh Bahadur, emerged as the new face of the Sikhs amid growing animosity with the Mughal state.

In 1707, Guru Gobind Singh was accompanying Mughal Emperor Bahadur Shah on his way to the Deccan to suppress a rebellion for succession when they halted at Nanded, a city in Maharashtra on the banks of the Godavari River. During his time with Bahadur Shah, the Guru had informed him about the atrocities committed against him, his family, and his followers in Punjab (see p.117). He made repeated suggestions for the punishment of the wrongdoer—Wazir Khan, the Viceroy of Sirhind. However, the Emperor's evasive replies prompted Guru Gobind Singh to take charge of the situation and bring the tyrant to justice on his own. He left the Mughal base and settled outside the city.

THE AGRARIAN SYSTEM IN THE 18TH CENTURY

In the agrarian system in Mughal India in the 18th century, the *zamindars* occupied the highest position in the social hierarchy, and peasants or landless laborers were at the lowest rungs. The *zamindars* were a class of landed proprietors who employed cultivators on their land. They derived their status from their high caste and the money and power that came with their role as revenue collectors on behalf of the Mughal state. In the late 18th century, not only the peasants but also the *zamindars* revolted against the Mughal state for its unjust policies.

An engraving depicting a farmer irrigating his land.

Meeting Banda Singh Bahadur

Sikh accounts state that Guru Gobind Singh visited the monastery of Madho Das Bairagi in 1708. An ascetic, Madho Das had established a base for himself at Nanded and mastered the *tantric* arts. In Das's absence, the Guru occupied the hermit's seat and commandeered his camp. Troubled by this, Madho Das tried to humiliate the Guru by showing his *tantric* prowess. However, at the end of it, he submitted to the authority of the Guru, became a follower, and earned the name Banda Singh Bahadur.

Guru Gobind saw in Banda Bahadur the capability to be a warrior for justice and righteousness. It is possible that Banda Bahadur trained with the Khalsa before his appointment as the Guru's military commander. Determined to hold Wazir Khan accountable, the Guru deputed Banda Bahadur to Punjab to raise an army against the Viceroy. Why he chose Banda Bahadur is not historically evident as the Guru had only known him a few weeks, but it likely resulted from a demonstration of his ability and loyalty during training.

Banda Bahadur set out northward, armed with five arrows and a drum that the Guru had bestowed upon him as emblems of temporal authority and a pledge of victory. He also took with him some of the Guru's followers and his *hukamnamas* (holy orders), calling Sikhs to action. The news of the Guru's tragic demise reached him in the vicinity of Delhi.

A mighty leader

Cautious of Bahadur Shah's hostility, Banda Bahadur traveled in disguise or took longer routes. On his year-long journey to Punjab from Maharashtra via Rajasthan, he visited many towns and villages, encouraging people to join him and his cause. Over time, his leadership acquired a spiritual temper as well. Author Khushwant Singh notes in his book, *A History of the Sikhs*: "Although the Guru had specifically restricted his role to that of military commander of a punitive expedition, Banda widened it to embrace a spiritual ministry as well… He preached sermons and gave benedictions." Banda Bahadur gave away offerings made to him, and the talk of his generosity brought even more followers and donations to his camp.

He promised protection to the people, from thieves to despots. Such a declaration ignited locals—chiefly the agricultural classes who had strong objections to Mughal policies—into action, and they joined him on his mission.

Another disaffected community was that of the *zamindars*. They had also been resisting Mughal authority in the Punjab region since the reign of Aurangzeb. Now, many of them readily accepted Bahadur as their leader. They supplied his army with weapons and provisions, though this did not mean that they took to Sikhism.

Banda Bahadur's army consisted of seasoned Khalsa warriors looking to undermine the Mughal enemy, and a number of peasants, ready to support him without giving up their own religion. He also had assistance from some of the hill tribes as well as merchants from Punjab who were drawn to the egalitarian nature of the Khalsa, and the common goal to overthrow the Mughals. It was this support base and his military competency that enabled Banda Singh Bahadur to forge an agrarian uprising against the Mughal rule.

▼ **A painting from a gurdwara in Maharashtra** showing one of Banda Singh Bahadur's journeys. This depiction with weapons and battle gear is common to artworks relating to him.

Show of strength

The years 1709 to 1715 saw a series of conquests under the Khalsa commander, Banda Singh Bahadur. Though his army largely consisted of agrarian groups, they demonstrated the ability of the Sikhs to consolidate politically and threaten the sovereignty of the Mughal state.

Soon after Guru Gobind Singh appointed Banda Singh Bahadur as his military commander, he instructed him to end the persecution of Sikhs in Punjab. By 1708, the warrior had marched across the Deccan and had Delhi, the capital of the Mughal Empire, in his sights. With him was a council of five Sikhs whose task was to assure those in Punjab that Banda Bahadur was carrying out the Guru Gobind Singh's orders. Though he only had a small group of soldiers accompanying him, the warrior carried important *hukamnamas* (holy orders) that the Guru had given him. These summons asked the Sikhs to join the campaign against an unjust Mughal rule. Camped in the region of present-day Hissar, Haryana, about

▼ **A painting from 1978 by** artist Kirpal Singh depicts Bhai Fateh Singh in blue beheading the Mughal governor of Sirhind, Wazir Khan, during the Battle of Chappar Chiri.

> "Coin struck through each of the **two worlds** (spiritual and temporal) by the grace of the **True Lord**. Of the victory of **Guru Gobind Singh**, King of Kings, **Nanak's sword** is the provider."

INSCRIPTION ON A COIN MINTED IN BANDA SINGH BAHADUR'S NAME, 1710

62 miles (100 km) from Delhi, Banda Bahadur began gathering an army and collecting weapons to wage a war against the Mughals. Once he was ready, he began to march northward, on the Grand Trunk Road, to Sonepat. Here, the army raided the state treasury and distributed the loot among Banda's followers before capturing the town of Kaithal.

Victory at Samana

The first big blow to the Mughal Empire came at the wealthy Punjab town of Samana. Infamous as the home of professional executioners who served under the Mughals, this was a place of significance for the Sikh army and Banda Bahadur. The town was home to the killers of Guru Tegh Bahadur and Guru Gobind Singh's two sons. Banda's army, now stronger by several thousand peasant-soldiers, stormed Samana on November 26, 1709. They faced a highly trained and well-equipped Mughal army, which was defeated in a battle that lasted three days. Banda Bahadur's army ravaged and burnt the town in the fervor of revenge. The fall of Samana set off alarm bells for Wazir Khan, the Mughal governor of Sirhind, as Banda Bahadur had now become a real threat to the region.

The battle at Chappar Chiri

Banda Bahadur crossed Malwa on his way to Sirhind, one of the Mughal Empire's largest and strongest fortified cities. Along the way he raided villages, such as Ghuram and Thaska, inhabited by Ranghars, a community of Rajputs that had converted to Islam, and Damla, inhabited by Pathans who had withdrawn their support for Guru Gobind Singh in a previous battle.

He also focused on expanding and strengthening his army. Many warriors of the Sikh army wished to avenge the deaths that had taken place during the battle in Chamkaur, Sirhind, in 1704. Others wanted to punish the persecutors of their faith, while a part of the army consisted of Gujjars, Jats, and Rajputs who aligned themselves with Banda Bahadur for their own motivations. Made up of many agrarian groups, and reinforced with weaponry, much of it through donations, this motley army set out toward Sirhind city.

Wazir Khan understood Banda Bahadur's intentions. His fears were further heightened with news of groups of peasants moving toward

Sirhind from across Punjab. He sent messages to the Mughal Emperor Bahadur Shah and imposed blockades to stop the army of supporters coming from the north of the Sutlej River. He also got the Muslim landowners to join his forces.

The two armies collided in Chappar Chiri, a village just outside Sirhind, on May 12, 1710. The Mughal forces had heavy artillery and thousands of elephants, leaving the Sikh troops at a disadvantage. Banda Bahadur stepped onto the battlefield and roused the soldiers to fight with new vigor.

The battle culminated with the death of Wazir Khan at the hands of Bhai Fateh Singh. After their win, the Sikh forces laid siege to Sirhind, burning its buildings, punishing Wazir Khan's supporters, and looting the treasury. It was with this victory that Banda Bahadur came to rule all 28 parganas (administrative subdivisions) of the province of Sirhind between the Yamuna and Sutlej rivers. He abolished the *zamindari* system, replaced administrators with his own people, and established a capital at the Mukhlisgarh fort, which he renamed Lohgarh, meaning "iron fort."

Further acquisitions

Banda Bahadur's victory over Wazir Khan's forces inspired other groups in the region to rise up against unjust administrators, including the Gujjar herdsmen who fought the oppressive local rulers and *zamindars* in Saharanpur. Styling themselves as Nanakprasth (Guru Nanak's followers), they joined Banda Bahadur's army to plunder Behat, Ambheta, and Nanauta.

Banda Bahadur continued amassing territory through the summer of 1710, but returned to Punjab when the monsoons began. The peasants from the Jalandhar Doab area, troubled by Shams Khan, the commander of Rahon, pleaded for his help. The Sikh army fought and won this battle and seized Jalandhar and Hoshiapur soon after. By the autumn of 1710, the entire doab between

THE SEAL OF BANDA SINGH BAHADUR
Banda Singh Bahadur issued a seal for *hukamnamas* and letters. It bore the inscription *"Deg-o-tegh-o fateh-o nusrat bidirang, Yaft az Nanak Guru Gobind Singh."* The mention of Guru Nanak and Guru Gobind Singh symbolized the holiness of the orders, while *"degh tegh fateh"* announced the intention of following the Khalsa code. *Degh* (the cauldron) symbolized a commitment to *langar*, *tegh* (the sword) symbolized the power of the Khalsa, and *fateh* meant victory to both.

Sutlej and Beas had become Sikh territory. The Mughal state grew anxious as Banda Bahadur showed no signs of stopping. His army took Amritsar, Batala, Kalanaur, and Pathankot, leaving Lahore and Kasur as the Mughal authority centers in the region. At this point, the Emperor Bahadur Shah ordered Firoz Khan, his trusted aide, to launch a campaign against Banda Bahadur.

By the end of the year, the Sikh army was outnumbered as the Mughals took back control of Malwa plains. On December 11, 1710 the forces raided Lohgarh, but Banda Bahadur managed to escape into the Shivalik hills, where he received help from local tribal chiefs.

In brief

1708 Banda Singh Bahadur sets off on his mission	1710 Battle of Sirhind	1710 Mughal forces under Firoz Khan strike back	1712 Bahadur Shah is succeeded by Jahandar Shah as Emperor	1715 Abd us-Samad Khan lays siege to Gurdas Nangal and captures Banda Singh Bahadur	1716 Execution of Banda Singh Bahadur
1709 Conquest of Samana	1710 Sikhs take control over most of the region between the Sutlej and Beas rivers	1710 Mughal forces storm Lohgarh fort	1713 Farrukh Siyar succeeds Jahandar Shah as Emperor		1716 Sikh prisoners are brought to Delhi for execution

The end

In early 1711, Banda Bahadur sent *hukumnamas* asking Sikhs to join him at Kiratpur. Though he seized control of many towns in the hills and plains by the spring, it was only after Bahadur Shah's death, when the Mughal Empire plunged into battles of succession, that he was able to take back Lohgarh. The subsequent emperors were unable to capture him and he went into hiding until early 1715.

Banda Bahadur now faced dwindling support from the Sikh community. They began opposing the excesses committed during the raids. He had also made changes to the Khalsa order, such as adopting red garments instead of blue, creating a new salutation, and requiring soldiers to be vegetarian. Many felt it went against the code. The differences eventually paved the way for a two-faction split in the Khalsa into the Bandai and the Tat Khalsa.

The Mughal viceroy for Punjab Abd us-Samad Khan managed to lay an eight-month siege to the fort of Gurdas Nangal (near present-day Gurdaspur), where Banda Bahadur was. The Sikh warrior and his followers finally surrendered in December 1715.

They were all taken to Delhi, where they were paraded on the streets along with thousands of Mughal soldiers carrying the heads of Sikhs on spears. The first set of executions began on March 5. Banda Bahadur was kept in prison and tortured for two more months before he was finally beheaded in June at Mehrauli.

▼ **A 20th-century** painting by Kirpal Singh depicts a captive Banda Singh Bahadur in a cage atop an elephant being paraded through the streets of Delhi. Soldiers carrying spears with severed heads of Sikh soldiers lead the procession.

The Sikh identity

The need for self-determination and self-preservation within the Sikh community had its basis in repeated persecutions that resulted in the violent deaths of two Gurus. Another factor was the festering animosity tied to the long-running fight for sovereignty between the Mughals and the Sikhs.

Until the sudden and violent death of Guru Arjan (see pp.80–81), the community was characterized by its faith and spirituality. The death of the beloved leader who had shaped a distinct Sikh consciousness through the construction of the Harmandir Sahib in Amritsar and the compilation of the Adi Granth shocked the Sikh community. This was only compounded by the execution of Guru Tegh Bahadur nearly seventy years later. These events as well as attempts by successors Guru Hargobind and Guru Gobind Singh to defend the faith sowed the seeds for the community's future trajectory.

Beginnings

When Guru Hargobind was anointed the Guru in 1606 after the torture and execution of his father Guru Arjan, he realized the pressing need to revive the strength of the community in the face of repeated Mughal aggression. By this time, the Sikhs had their own scripture, customs, and traditions, and lived on lands they governed. Guru Hargobind recognized that this assertion of unique spirituality by the community had led to their persecution at the hands of the Mughal Empire. However, he realized, their rivals would find it difficult to succeed if the Guru held temporal authority too.

Donning the *miri-piri* swords, Guru Hargobind positioned himself as the supreme figure of authority for the community. In this

role, he was conscious of his mission to preserve the religious freedom of those ruled by the Mughals.

Antagonism and militarization

The path Guru Hargobind chose in order to protect the community was a martial one. Along with creating a strong military force, he also made other changes to this effect, such as the construction of the Akal Takht (see pp.84–85).

The Sikhs now demarcated themselves as separate from Hindus and Muslims. This was a turning point in Sikh history, as it changed the very nature of the Sikh community, which

▲ **A painting depicts Banda Singh Bahadur** and his army surrounding the Sirhind governor Wazir Khan, to avenge the killing of Guru Gobind's young sons (seen in the foreground behind a brick wall).

In brief

1606
Guru Arjan's death and Guru Hargobind's anointment

1620s–1630s
Guru Hargobind travels to Kashmir and elsewhere to spread the faith

1675
Execution of Guru Tegh Bahadur by Emperor Aurangzeb

1699
Creation of the Khalsa Panth by Guru Gobind Singh

1708
Declaration of the Guru Granth Sahib as the Sikh spiritual authority by Guru Gobind Singh

1799
Formation of the Sikh Empire under Maharaja Ranjit Singh

1709
Banda Singh Bahadur's military conquests begin with the siege of Samana

had been focused on spirituality. The reforms by Guru Hargobind strengthened the core of the Panth which had united as it coped with Guru Arjan's death.

By 1699, Guru Gobind Singh had established the Khalsa Panth as a distinct community (see pp.106–107), by instituting a process of initiation. On the one hand, it marked the uniqueness of the community, while on the other, it created a means to protect and preserve the people through the declaration of the Khalsa's duty to take up arms. This idea was strengthened by the campaigns of Banda Singh Bahadur in the 1700s, where he roused the peasantry to fight the Mughals (see pp.144–145). However, this caused fissures among the Sikhs as they saw wins in the form of violence, in this case largely toward Muslims, and towns laid to waste. Things started to change after the violent persecutions carried out by the Mughal generals who oversaw the Lahore region. These ignited a desire for carving out a space where Sikhs would be free from oppression by external forces.

A distinct community

The claim to sovereignty among the Sikhs was significantly tied to their desire for self-determination. The establishment of rigid boundaries around the faith that began to differentiate itself from other religions can be seen in Sikh texts dating as far back as the 18th century. While the various *gurbilas* were hagiographic accounts that chronicled the Gurus' work, the Sikh *Rahit Maryada* set out guidelines, or a code of conduct for all members to follow.

With these, the essence of the faith evolved further. The need for self-preservation eventually manifested into the desire for a self-governed kingdom, the process for which had begun with Banda Bahadur's campaigns where the Sikhs governed the territories they won. This aspiration gave birth to the idea of a space that was visualized as Punjab, the birthplace of Guru Nanak, and thereby of the Sikh faith.

A quest for identity, which essentially grew out of an instinct for survival, prompted all further developments in the 18th century. It ultimately led to the formation of an independent Sikh Empire in 1799, consolidated by its first ruler, Maharaja Ranjit Singh (see pp.170–171).

"Though differences seem to mark and distinguish, all men in reality are the same. **Gods and demons**, celestial beings, men called **Muslims** and others called **Hindus**—such differences are trivial, inconsequential, the outward results of locality and dress."

"AKAL USTAT," *DASAM GRANTH* (TRANSLATION BY W.H. MCLEOD)

▶ This steel *chakkar* or *chakram* (quoit) with *koftgari* (gold work) from the 19th century is inscribed with a verse in Gurmukhi and was likely carried by Sikh warriors.

▶ **An actor portraying the** Sikh warrior Banda Singh Bahadur (in blue) is seen in a play performed on the 300th anniversary of his martyrdom in 2016, in New Delhi, India.

Banda Singh Bahadur

The former hermit Banda Singh Bahadur altered the geography of 18th-century Punjab, forging a legacy of rebellion to be followed by those that came after him. In doing so, he managed to bring into question the might and sanctity of the Mughal state, unsettling it to its core.

For a figure so central to Sikh history, there is surprisingly very little historical knowledge about Banda Singh Bahadur's early life, which can only be partially reconstructed using Sikh accounts. Most historians agree that Banda was born as Lachman Das on October 27, 1670, to a Bhardwaj Rajput family at Rajouri in Jammu, and that he grew up learning the skills of horse riding, hunting, duelling, and archery.

Turn towards asceticism

It is believed that Banda once hunted a pregnant deer, and the sight of it turned him toward a life of asceticism. He found his teacher in the Bairagi saint Janaki Prasad, who gave him the name Madho Das and introduced him to the tenets of Vaishnavism, the Hindu tradition of worshipping the god Vishnu. He later received the tutelage of several other hermits, including Tantric yogi Augur Nath, from whom he learnt the occult sciences. He set up a hermitage at a site next to the Godavari river, where he built a body of disciples through his teachings of Bairagi philosophy and Tantrism.

According to Sikh narratives, Banda prided himself on his occult skills, but was humbled when he was unable to humiliate Guru Gobind Singh, the tenth Guru, with his magic. Thus Banda, former disciple of a Bairagi saint, transformed into a disciple of Guru Gobind Singh, and became a member of the Khalsa, the Sikh order founded by the Guru in 1699.

Crafting sovereignty, igniting a legacy

In fulfilling Guru Gobind Singh's orders, Banda Bahadur forged his own kingdom in Punjab through raids and warfare. He soon came to symbolize the military might of the Khalsa. After consolidating a significant amount of territory, Banda styled himself like other emperors of his time: he acquired a fort, demarcated a capital, issued a distinct coin, crafted his own seal, and even drafted his own calendar dating back to the capture of Sirhind (see pp.139–140)

as the year of accession. He had the names of Guru Nanak and Guru Gobind Singh inscribed on the seal (see p.140), signifying his allegiance to the Sikh lineage and justifying his choice of nomenclature as *banda*, or a slave to the Guru. These actions became characteristic markers of the Sikh sovereignty that Banda fostered, and which other Sikh leaders later emulated.

In his conquests across Punjab, he abolished the Mughal *zamindari* system, whereby rich landowners would hire peasants to work for them. This displaced customary land proprietors and allowed cultivators to become owners of their lands, thus aiding in the creation of sovereignty. Sikh historian Rattan Singh Bhangu notes in his book *Sri Gur Panth Prakash* that in this, Banda Singh Bahadur was most likely influenced by Guru Gobind Singh's firm belief that every individual has sovereign power and is their own ruler. Beyond showing his military

▲ **The two sides of a coin** minted during Banda Singh Bahadur's time, c. 1712. While the obverse mentions Guru Nanak and Guru Gobind Singh, the reverse gives the year of its minting.

and political prowess, Banda Singh Bahadur's rebellions left behind a legacy of social disorder in Punjab, which played out through anti-Mughal revolts by various local communities after 1715.

Within the Sikh community as well, Banda Bahadur came to be seen as someone who splintered the organization of the Khalsa (see pp. 108–109), sparking debates about the true nature and obligations of the Panth. It is these facets taken together that ultimately make Banda Singh Bahadur a commanding figure, crucial in understanding the discourse of contemporary Sikhism.

"There is a **parasitical creeper** that ruins a tree from the top… known by the name of 'Bando'… **Band Singh** should become a similar **poisonous creeper**… squeeze, sap, and destroy the **oppressive Mughal Empire**."

RATTAN SINGH BHANGU, *SRI GUR PANTH PRAKASH* (TRANSLATION BY KULWANT SINGH)

Emergence of a collective

Banda Singh Bahadur's consolidation of territory was one of many rebellions that threatened Mughal sovereignty in the 18th century. While his execution caused a void in the Sikh leadership, it ultimately led to a new Khalsa that helped shape the Sikh faith and community in myriad ways.

The Mughal persecution of the Sikh community continued even after Banda Singh Bahadur's execution in 1716. This was most evident in the edict that Abd us-Samad Khan, the Mughal *subedar* or viceroy of Punjab, received. In it, Emperor Farrukhsiyar ordered Khan to imprison or kill on resistance all members of the Khalsa, easily recognizable because of their turbans and long beards.

The brutality continued through 1726, when Abd us-Samad's son Zakarya Khan became the governor of Lahore and unleashed his armies on the community. Rewards were also offered for the head of every Sikh brought to Lahore. This onslaught of persecution forced some members of the Khalsa to seek refuge in the hills from where they raided state treasuries and the homes of the wealthy. Many Sikhs were *Sahajdharis*, literally slow adopters, or those that did not have the visible symbols of the Khalsa. Their ranks swelled.

There were two key developments within the community during this time. These helped in the consolidation of the community and the emergence of collective leadership.

> "Although **Bhai Mani Singh's** head got severed … he kept his faith intact… The people … **mourned his death** … Sikhs felt … victorious and proud at his **sacrifice**."

RATAN SINGH BHANGU, *SRI GUR PANTH PRAKASH, VOLUME 2*

▼ **A 2020 painting by artist Sumeet Aurora** depicts the twelve Sikh *misl* chiefs including Kapur Singh and Jassa Singh Ahluwalia (first row), with Banda Singh Bahadur (top) as their leader.

Role of the Sarbat Khalsa

Even as the Sikhs tried to survive the onslaught of Mughal forces, a new tradition emerged, almost as a way to fill the void of a leader following Banda Singh Bahadur's execution. Every year, members of the community began to gather in Amritsar on the occasions of Baisakhi and Diwali. This assembly came to be known as the Sarbat Khalsa, and it began to decide matters, notes Sikh historian Harbans Singh in *The Encyclopedia of Sikhism*, "by common counsel." These were either to resolve differences within the community; decide matters of state policy with groups, such as with the Marathas; or develop strategies to tackle Mughal forces. These decisions, or Gurmatas, were the decrees of the Guru, so-called as they were made in the presence of the holy book, the Guru Granth Sahib.

Internal conflicts

Meanwhile, disputes tore into the community. Unrest among Banda Bahadur's followers led to the creation of two factions: the Bandai and the Tat Khalsa. While the Bandai followed Banda Bahadur's changes to the order, the Tat Khalsa stayed true to the tenets instituted by the Gurus. This friction mushroomed with time, culminating in a conflict over the control of the Harmandir Sahib in Amritsar.

The severity of the conflict needed an intervention, and Mata Sundari stepped in to help resolve it. Guru Gobind Singh's widows, Mata Sundari and Mata Sahib Devan still retained considerable influence within the community. Their residence in Delhi, where they lived under the care of Bhai Mani Singh, was often a site of homage for the Sikhs.

It is why, in 1721, Mata Sundari deputed Bhai Mani Singh to take charge of Harmandir Sahib. He settled the dispute by vote. Much later, the Bandai Khalsa joined the Tat Khalsa, leading to a unified collective leadership under the order.

Fighting back

The resolution of this conflict allowed the Sarbat Khalsa to assert its authority in a more effective manner. As the Sikhs continued to hold their

own against the Mughals, Zakarya Khan reached out to the Khalsa on Baisakhi in 1733 to offer them three cities as *jagirs*, or revenue estates. Kapur Singh, a renowned warrior, was nominated the leader and *jagirdar* of the cities. He requested all those who had fled their homes following Mughal persecution to return and also instituted the Dal Khalsa, an army.

There were two wings in the army, Budha Dal, or the veteran fighters, and Taruna Dal, the youth. The Dal Khalsa was organized into *misls* or small confederacies based on kinship under a military chief to support Kapur Singh's governance of the Sikh kingdom. Much to Zakarya Khan's displeasure, the Taruna Dal seized revenue paid to the Mughal state in Haryana, and the Budha Dal tried to take control of Malwa.

In 1738, Bhai Mani Singh asked Zakarya Khan for permission to use Harmandir Sahib for a Diwali fair. He was instructed to pay a tax of 5,000 rupees, which he expected to come from pilgrim donations. Sikh accounts indicate that this was a ruse on Khan's part to gather members of the Sikh community in one place. Suspicious, the pilgrims failed to gather in Amritsar and Bhai Mani Singh was unable to pay the fee. As a result, he was arrested and taken to Lahore. When he refused to convert to Islam, he was tortured and executed in December 1738. The Sikh community was furious, but revenge had to wait in the face of the Persian invasion.

▲ **This hand-drawn map** by French cartographer Christopher Rigobert Bonne is believed to be the first map to recognize Sikh *misl* territories in Punjab.

In brief

1716
Execution of Banda Singh Bahadur

1721
Bhai Mani Singh takes control of Harmandir Sahib upon Mata Sundari's request

1726
Zakarya Khan succeeds Abd us-Samad Khan as governor of Punjab

1733
Sarbat Khalsa meets to deliberate Zakarya Khan's offer of *jagir*

1738
Beginning of the Persian invasion of Mughal India

Death of Bhai Mani Singh

The Rise and Fall of the Sikh Empire

▶ **Mata Sundri, the wife of Guru Gobind Singh**, is depicted in this painting. She was a far-sighted guide of the Sikh community.

Mata Sundari

Guru Gobind Singh's widow was an influential figure, who could even temper the authority of the Sikh military leader Banda Bahadur. She may have never been a guru or military leader, yet her contribution to the Sikh ethos is undeniable.

Very little is known about Mata Sundari beyond her identity as the wife of the tenth Sikh Guru, and her role in shaping the order of the Khalsa. Some historians indicate that she may have been born in the Hoshiarpur district of Punjab. However, no one has yet reconstructed the early years leading up to her marriage to Guru Gobind Singh in 1684.

After the onslaught of the Mughals and hill chiefs at Anandpur (see pp.110–111), Mata Sundari escaped to Delhi with the help of Sikh scholar Bhai Mani Singh (see pp.146–147).

Sikh accounts state that her son, Ajit Singh, lost his life in the battle of Chamkaur (see pp.116–117). These sources further mention a son Mata Sundari adopted, also named Ajit Singh, whom she supposedly took in for his resemblance to her martyred son. The Mughal Emperor Bahadur Shah assumed that this adopted child would be the tenth Guru's heir and so honored him while bestowing him with riches. However, this made him arrogant toward the Sikh code of conduct and Mata Sundari ultimately disowned him.

A force to reckon with

After Guru Gobind Singh passed away, Mata Sundari became a source of solace for many Sikhs in Dilli (modern-day

> "So whatever **orders** were sent to Khalsa Panth by the **Guru mother**, The same were **accepted** by the Khalsa Panth in the letter and spirit, Since Banda Singh used to be stingy towards the Khalsa Singhs, They felt **elated** after Guru mother's instructions (for a **separation**)."

RATAN SINGH BHANGU, *PRACHIN PANTH PRAKASH VOL 2*

Delhi). She kept a close watch on the developments at Amritsar. Some Sikh followers had begun to congregate around Banda Singh Bahadur (see pp.144–145) as the next leader. However, she was one of the first people to speak up against his adjustments of the Khalsa code and penned a *hukamnama*, a holy order where she censured his actions. Her sharp criticism was immediately hailed by her followers and became a venerated symbol of justification for many who formed the *Tat Khalsa* (see p.46). This faction

led by close associates of the Guru and Mata Sundari, had remained loyal to the original Khalsa principles. So, her *hukamnamas* were valued by the Panth alongside the Guru's.

Through orders to Bhai Mani Singh, such as managing the gurdwaras in Amritsar, Mata Sundari was able to resolve the internal issues within the Khalsa after Banda Bahadur's execution, and compile the dictates of the Guru to keep the Khalsa true to its origin. She also wrote and circulated several other *hukamnamas* between 1717 and 1730, signifying her position and her authority in the Sikh community.

According to Sikh traditions, Guru Gobind Singh was carrying his literary compositions with him when he, his family, and followers were forced to leave Anandpur in 1704, and they were lost while on the move. After Guru Gobind Singh passed away, Mata Sundari instructed Bhai Mani Singh to collect and bind his works in one volume. It took Mani Singh nine years to collect the scattered compositions before putting them together in the form of the Dasam Granth in 1734.

◄ **A 2011 painting by Devender Singh** imagines Ajit Singh, the elder son of Guru Gobind Singh, being bestowed a sword by his father before the Battle of Chamkaur in 1704.

A Persian invasion

In 1738, the Shah of Persia set out to invade North India, disrupting the administration in Punjab and striking a strong blow to the Mughal Empire. It was during this invasion that the Sikhs rose and displayed their valor and fighting spirit. This only served to invite further onslaught from the Mughals after the Persian armies had left the region.

After the conquest of Kandahar, in present-day Afghanistan, in 1738, Persian ruler Nadir Shah set his sights on the Mughal throne. The Empire had been gradually crumbling under the many regional revolts across the subcontinent and Shah considered it ripe for the picking.

Nadir Shah's army entered from the northwest and made quick work of Kabul. They marched into the Punjab region where they forced Lahore governor Zakarya Khan to surrender after a brief battle. Meanwhile, the Sikhs had retreated into the foothills. Nadir Shah allowed Zakarya Khan to retain his governorship and proceeded to the capital of Delhi. Along the way, his army continued their raids, seizing money and elephants.

The fall of Delhi

Mughal Emperor Muhammad Shah started preparing for the invaders, accumulating troops, but faced defeat at the Battle of Karnal in February 1739. Nadir Shah pushed further in and looted whatever he could lay his hands on, his ransom in exchange for the throne. Around this time, a rumor of the Persian ruler's death broke out in the bazaars.

The people of Delhi started attacking and killing the Persians. Shah retaliated by killing and enslaving thousands of the city's residents. The massacre stopped only after the Emperor appealed to Nadir Shah for mercy and promised him more riches. In the aftermath, the Mughal state lost several valuables from its treasury,

◄ **This Mughal-style tempera painting** from c. 1605–1658 shows the Mughal ruler Shah Jahan seated on the Peacock Throne, the seat of the Mughal Empire.

including the Peacock Throne, which went on to become a symbol of Persian might. The diamonds Koh-i-Noor and Darya-i-Noor were also seized.

By May 1739, a victorious Nadir Shah and his forces set out to return to Persia, choosing to traverse through the Himalayan foothills.

Encounters with the Khalsa

It was on his journey back that Nadir Shah encountered an unexpected force—the Sikhs. They had withdrawn to the mountains in the north during the Persian invasion and had now become well acquainted with the region. This gave them an advantage against the enemy. Nadir Shah entered Punjab with his long

MARTYRDOM AT SAHIDGANJ

Zakarya Khan responded to the Khalsa's activity after Nadir Shah's invasion with great vigor. He blew up the Sikh fort at Dallewal and offered rewards to villagers to capture Sikhs. Meanwhile, his forces imprisoned several Sikhs, who were then beheaded at the Lahore horse market. The site would be repeatedly used for other Sikh massacres as well. The market was later renamed Sahidganj in honor of the martyred.

In brief

1738
In a span of seven months, Nadir Shah invades many towns and cities, such as Ghazni, Kabul, Jalalabad, and Peshawar

1739
On February 13, Nadir Shah's troops defeat the Mughal army at the Battle of Karnal

1739
On March 22, Nadir Shah massacres a large population of Delhi after riots the day before

1739
In May, the Khalsa strategically plunders Nadir Shah's army and rescues prisoners

caravan of loot and the Sikhs attacked almost immediately. They avoided a direct confrontation with the invaders. Instead, they chose stealth and set upon the Persian camp in the dead of the night, making away with the riches.

The Sikhs had organized themselves into light cavalry bands, unlike Nadir Shah's army. Burdened with looted items and faced with burning heat, they struggled to make their way through the difficult terrain. The Sikh bands followed closely, plundering the army at every available chance. In this manner, they were successful in taking over a substantial amount of the Persian spoils of war and managed to free the people, including women, enslaved by Nadir Shah during his invasion of Punjab and Delhi.

Foreshadowing of power

Seething with anger over the loss of his loot, Nadir Shah looked into the identity of the looters. Records indicate that Mughal governor Zakarya Khan, seemed to have called the Sikhs "fakirs who bathed in the Guru's tank" and "whose homes were their saddles." Persian court scholar Ahmed Shah Batalvi's account indicates that Nadir Shah responded to this by auguring, "Take care, the day is not far distant when these rebels will take possession of your country."

The plunder of Nadir Shah and the restoring of women prisoners to their families likely cemented the Sikhs' power further among the people of Punjab, who probably drew a contrast to Zakarya Khan, the puppet of the Persian Shah during the invasion.

With renewed support, the Khalsa returned to the plains, built a mud fort at Dallewal, and restarted their pilgrimage to Amritsar. Zakarya Khan (See box) and his successors responded

to this triumph of the Sikhs with further violence. The Khalsa, however, remained resilient and reorganized itself to brace against the persecution, and subsequently the stronger Afghan enemy that would emerge in 1752.

▲ **This 19th-century Persian rug** depicts the fierce battle between Nadir Shah's forces and Muhammad Shah's army at Karnal. While it incorporates the block-printing technique for the border, the central design is hand-drawn and painted.

Afghan invasions

The Afghan ruler Ahmad Shah Durrani (formerly Abdali) set his sights on India, but he did not account for the Sikhs, who became a force to be reckoned with. They presented a strong opposition to incursions in their region, as did some other local armies. The result of these battles was that, after nine invasions, the Afghans returned to Kabul weary and unsuccessful.

"As **Nadir Shah** had come to be known as **Delhi's destroyer**, So had **Ahmed Shah** come to be known as **Nadir Shah's destroyer**, So had **Khalsa panth** come to be known as **Ahmed Shah's destroyer, Who had forced** (the mighty) Ahmad Shah Abdali to flee."

RATTAN SINGH BHANGU, EPISODE 158, *SRI GUR PANTH PRAKASH*, VOL 2

◀ **Portrait of Ahmad Shah Durrani**, the founder of the Afghan Empire.

A power struggle between the sons of the Mughal governor Zakarya Khan, after his death in 1745, formed the backdrop for the Afghan invasions. While Yahya Khan, the first son, became the new governor of Lahore, Shah Nawaz Khan, the other son, became the governor of Multan. The latter deposed his brother in 1747. However, eager to retain his victorious position, Shah Nawaz Khan invited the Afghan emperor Ahmad Shah Durrani, also known as Ahmad Shah Durrani, to Punjab.

The Afghan had been keen to plunder the riches of his neighbor and took this invitation as the perfect opportunity. He entered the territory in January 1748 with his army and displaced Shah Nawaz Khan, who by now had undergone a change of heart. Durrani proceeded toward Delhi, but was forced to retreat when his army faced Mughal resistance at the Battle of Manupur in 1748. Mir Mannu, the son of the slain Mughal commander, emerged a hero in this fight.

The Dal Khalsa unites

About a decade before Zakarya Khan's death, the coming of the Afghans, and after the establishment of the Sarbat Khalsa (see pp.146–147), there was a slight dissonance within the collective unity of the Sikhs. Several chiefs had already emerged across Punjab, and as their numbers grew, loyalty decreased in the face of personal ambition.

Kapur Singh, who had become the head of the Sarbat Khalsa in 1733, along with other senior leaders, convinced the chiefs to unite for the larger cause of the Sikhs. Jassa Singh Ahluwalia, a confidante of Kapur Singh, would lead this newly united military force.

Meanwhile, the conflict with the Mughals had made the Khalsa a resilient force, with years of training in the martial arts and warfare. The army, called the Dal Khalsa, was divided into eleven *misls* or confederacies (see pp.160–161), each under a Sikh leader, or *misldar*, for the protection of the area under its control.

1746
Chhota
Ghallughara

1748
Battle of Manupur

1752
The province of
Punjab is ceded
to the Afghans

1753
Death of
Mir Mannu

1758
Marathas defeat the
Afghans at Peshawar

1762
Wadha
Ghallughara

1766
Durrani offers
subedari of Lahore
to the Khalsa

The memory of persecution

Through the 1740s, the Sikhs raided a large number of cities in Punjab. Finally, in 1745, on the eve of the first Afghan incursion, they launched an attack on Lahore. In the subsequent incursion with the Mughal army, Jaspat Rai, brother of the revenue minister, or *diwan*, of Punjab, Lakhpat Rai, was killed. This drew vengeance from the imperial seat.

On orders from Yahya Khan, the Sikhs living in Lahore were executed at Sahidganj. Meanwhile he and Lakhpat Rai breached an aggression on the Khalsa army, forcing it into retreat. Many Sikhs were captured and beheaded at Sahidganj in June 1746, an event remembered as Chhota Ghallughara, or the lesser holocaust.

The persecution they faced at the hands of the Mughals further motivated them to strengthen the Khalsa. By the time Ahmad Shah Durrani had been driven away from Delhi, Sikhs under Jassa Singh Ahluwalia were preparing to take advantage of the political vacuum in Punjab. They kept up the anti-Afghan momentum by breaking up into more than sixty smaller bands to drive Durrani's forces up to the Indus River, where his army was stranded without provisions.

▼ **Jassa Singh Ahluwalia** engaged in battle, depicted in a painting by Devender Singh, a contemporary artist from Punjab.

The subsequent invasions

When Durrani launched a second invasion in December 1748, Mir Mannu was the governor of Punjab. His preoccupation with the Afghans allowed the Sikhs to take control of Lahore for a short period. Instead of fighting, Mannu attempted to appease Durrani by granting him enormous territory, thus becoming his subordinate in rebellion to the Mughal minister, or *wazir,* Safdar Jung, who wanted to depose him. The third invasion took place because Mir Mannu failed to pay revenue to the Afghans. Kaura Mal, a respected Sikh officer under the Mughals (see box), died in the resultant war. Mir Mannu was forced to pass Lahore and Multan into the hands of Durrani.

With Kaura Mal's death, the Sikhs lost their link to the governor and set out to capture the whole territory of Punjab. When Mir Mannu returned from the war with the Afghans, he found

▼ **A drawing from c. 1770** depicting the Third Battle of Panipat, with Ahmad Shah Durrani riding a brown horse.

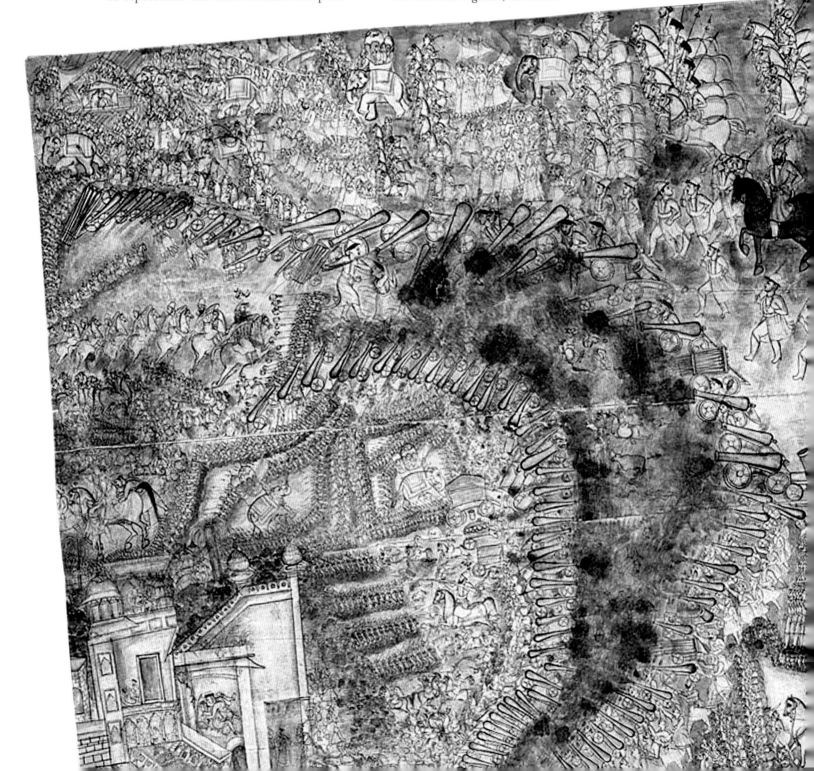

his territory in Sikh hands. This incited an onslaught on the Sikhs which continued until his death in 1753. Following the death of Mir Mannu, the Sikhs made use of this political vacuum by pushing forward as the self-proclaimed rulers of Punjab. As the Dal Khalsa acquired the reins of administration too, they forged a rule built upon the *rakhi* system, whereby villages and towns were protected by the Sikhs in exchange for one-fifth of the produce. This ensured a regular flow of revenue without the need for any raiding. This system was established in four out of the five doabs of Punjab, symbolizing the influence of the Khalsa state.

The Afghans return

In 1756, Durrani turned his attention to Punjab yet again, this time sending his son, Timur Shah, to govern the region. Jahan Khan was sent with him as the military commander. This time, standing in opposition to the Afghans were the forces of the Mughal official Adina Beg Khan, the Sikhs, and the Marathas, a confederacy formed by Shivaji against the Deccan Sultanate, who were now on a quest of expansion. The Marathas swiftly defeated Durrani, but thereafter left Punjab in the hands of Adina Beg Khan.

However, the death of Adina Beg Khan a few months later allowed the Sikhs to consolidate even more power. The Afghans retaliated by defeating the Marathas at Panipat in 1761 and placing Khwaja Obed as the governor of Lahore. However, the Sikhs ensured that he too was soon deposed. According to some accounts, the Sikhs are said to have minted their own coins using the Mughal mint in Lahore after conquering the region.

It wasn't until his sixth invasion in early 1762, however, that Durrani wreaked vengeance on the Sikhs. His army stormed a congregation of around 50,000 Sikhs at Kup in Punjab, taking them by surprise. The Afghan forces had covered about 150 miles (240 km) in less than two days. Unable to use their characteristic hit-and-run technique, the Sikhs resorted to combat, but the Afghans swiftly slaughtered both combatants and noncombatants in an event remembered as the Wadha Ghallughara, also known as the great holocaust.

The triumph of the Sikhs

The *Jangnama* (see pp.156–157), a historical war poem penned by Afghan historian Qazi Nur Muhammad, gives a detailed summary of the next confrontation that took place between the Afghans and Sikhs in 1765, during Durrani's seventh invasion. The Sikhs repeatedly evaded the Afghan army using their characteristic hit-and-run strategy. This exhausted Durrani who eventually left Punjab, paving the way for Sikh control over Lahore and thereafter the entire territory between Sirhind and Derajat.

Durrani returned to Lahore in December 1766 for one final confrontation with the Sikhs, but the appeals of the residents persuaded him to initially offer a hand of conciliation in the form of the grant of the *subedari* or governance of Lahore to the Khalsa under the umbrella of Afghan rule. The Sikhs refused the offer, which prompted him to head to Sirhind, but his departure created the space necessary for the Sikhs to recapture Lahore, forcing Durrani to return. Meanwhile, the Afghan troops entered Amritsar, inviting heavy attacks from the Sikh forces.

Durrani eventually returned to Kabul after failing to achieve victory over the ceaseless attacks of the Sikhs. By the second half of 1767, the Sikhs had amassed the entirety of Punjab under their control again. Though they faced some resistance from the Mughal commander Mirza Najaf Khan, they ultimately succeeded. The rule of the Sikhs in the region through the twin elements of the *misls* and *rakhi* eventually led to Ranjit Singh building upon it, and carving out a Sikh kingdom by the end of the century.

HARMONY UNDER KAURA MAL

A *sahajdhari* Sikh, Kaura Mal was chosen by the governor Shah Nawaz Khan to become the diwan, or revenue minister, of Punjab. His appointment ushered in a period of peace after twelve years of conflict. Kaura Mal was reinstated as the *diwan* and the deputy governor of Punjab under Mir Mannu after the exit of the Afghans in 1748. He built the Gurdwara Bal Leela and cleaned the pool at Harmandir Sahib desecrated by Lakhpat Rai, earning the sobriquet Mittha Mal from the Sikh community (*mittha* in Punjabi means sweet).

Jangnama

A versified history of Ahmed Shah Durrani's seventh invasion of India, the *Jangnama*, tells the story of the Afghan crusade against the Sikhs, who challenged the Afghans' political supremacy in the northwestern region.

The Sikhs had made major inroads into Punjab following the Afghan invasion of 1762, recapturing territories across the region. Among these was Kasur, the largest Afghan pocket, which fell to the Bhangi *misl* led by Hari Singh. By 1764, the Sikhs had also seized Sirhind, attacked Lahore, and raided the provinces in the Ganga–Yamuna Doab twice.

Seeking vengeance for the 1762 massacre and the desecration of the sacred shrine, and the desecration of the sacred shrine, the Sikh forces took Afghan soldiers captive and made them clean the Harmandir Sahib as punishment. When the news reached Ahmed Shah Durrani (or Abdali, as he was also known), he gave a call to arms, announcing a war against the Sikhs.

Durrani led an army of 18,000 Afghan soldiers and invited the Baluchi sultan, Nasir Khan, to join him. Nasir Khan met him at Eminabad with a troop of 12,000 men. The tale of their encounters with the Sikhs has been immortalized in the *Jangnama* by Afghan historian Qazi Nur Muhammad, who accompanied Durrani during the invasion.

An Afghan chronicle

The *Jangnama*, written in 1765, is a vivid Persian chronicle of Ahmed Shah Durrani's foray into Punjab in 1764–1765. An eyewitness narrative, it sketches the events leading up to the invasion, the religious impulses of both sides, the war tactics they employed, the heroic zeal of the Sikhs to defend their faith, and the mission of the Afghans to crush their enemies.

The Sikhs' first encounter was with a Baluchi force, during which they retreated into the Lakhi Jungle and used their technique of persistent guerrilla warfare to hound the invading soldiers.

In *A History of the Sikhs*, author Khushwant Singh translates a line from the *Jangnama* that describes the combat strategies of the Sikhs: "They enter secretly like thieves and attack like wolves." The Sikh forces, Nur Muhammad states, granted no rest to their enemies.

The *Jangnama* details the Shah's journey to Amritsar and the destruction of the land of the Sikhs. It describes the battle of Amritsar as a fight between the superior Afghans and the outnumbered Sikhs.

He recounts how a band of thirty Sikh warriors led by the heroic Gurbaksh Singh, a warrior from Amritsar, faced 30,000 Afghans and sacrificed their lives for their faith.

According to Punjabi historian Ganda Singh's translation in *Qazi Nur Muhammad's Jang Namah*, Nur Muhammad states, "A few of them had remained in an enclosure so that they might spill their own blood. And they sacrificed their lives for the Guru."

Sikh bravery and Afghan wrath

Qazi Nur Muhammad imbues his work with the superiority of his own faith and praises of the Shah, Ahmed Shah Durrani, and Nasir Khan, who he deems to be the true destroyer of the infidel. However, Muhammad also lauds the valor of the Sikh warriors against a much larger Afghan army and the weapons they wield. According to one translation, he writes how "singh" means a lion in Hindustani. "In battle they are veritable lions and in peace they excel Hatim," he writes.

Nur Muhammad goes on to praise the high moral standards of the Sikhs in the *Jangnama*. He even notes that they never assaulted women, children, the weak, or the defenseless; and furthermore, none of the Sikhs were thieves, plunderers, or adulterers.

> "They were **only thirty** in number. But they had **not** a **grain of fear** about them. They had **neither** the **fear** of **slaughter** nor the **dread of death**."
>
> QAZI NUR MUHAMMAD, JANGNAMA
> (TRANSLATION BY GANDA SINGH, *QAZI NUR MUHAMMAD'S JANG NAMAH*, 1939)

This 19th-century painting by
Patiala artist Sheikh Basharat Ullah
depicts a bloody battle between Sikh
warriors and invaders.

An annual Sikh festival, Hola Mohalla was first established by Guru Gobind Singh, the tenth Sikh Guru, in 1699 at Gurdwara Anandpur Sahib. A grand, three-day event, it features mock battles, weaponry displays, and feats of bravery such as bareback horse riding. This photograph from Anandpur shows a performance with a traditional *vadda chakkar,* a circular weapon.

This painting of Nawab Kapur Singh, who established the Singhpura *misl*, shows him on horseback and in the full regalia of a Sikh warrior, including the blue robes of the Khalsa, a turban, and a sword.

Misls

The Sikhs needed a strong fighting force to expand their authority in Punjab. Tasked with the objective to carve out an independent Sikh territory and to protect it from invaders, small independent armies of trained warriors, also known as *misls*, were formed. A local military commander, or *misldar* led each *misl*.

Contingents of trained warriors emerged in the 1720s. Under the leadership of their *misldar*, they provided protection to farmers against invaders and took over more territories. While the *misls* did effectively expand and protect their regions, there was conflict among them. To address this issue, Kapur Singh, the leader of the Sikhs, announced the creation of eleven *misls*—each with its own leader—entrusted with different territories within Punjab. This *misldari* system strengthened the Sikhs and stopped internal conflict. Kapur Singh also stressed their ultimate loyalty to the Dal Khalsa (see p.147) to override any personal ambitions of the leaders.

Organizational framework

All Sikhs capable of combat had to join a *misl*, which ensure a good strength of fighters for the Khalsa. They could choose a *misl* of their choice, to whose *sardar*, or leader, they would maintain their allegiance. Once a territory was acquired, it was customary for the leader to divide it among the members of his *misl*. The same was done even if the Sikhs only got access to the tribute from villagers after taking control of an area. It was not uncommon for members to occupy territories on their own, but they were required to remain loyal to their leader.

The organization and spatial spread of the *misls* allowed the Sikhs to rapidly mobilize and disperse while employing their hit-and-run tactics, putting them at an advantage against the army of the Afghan ruler Ahmed Shah Durrani during his invasions. Their organization into small contingents also helped execute the *rakhi* system, where the Sikhs offered protection in return for one-fifth of the produce from villagers.

The eleven misls

Each of the eleven *misls* was organized under dynamic leaders who are remembered in the tomes of Sikh history for their militaristic abilities. Unsurprisingly, the *misls* were named after the leader or his hometown. Kapur Singh and Jassa Singh Ahluwalia led the Singhpura and Ahluwalia *misls*, respectively, in the areas on either bank of the Sutlej River. Hari Singh and Naudh Singh were leaders of the Bhangi and Sukerchakia *misls* in the Chaj and Rachna Doab. Dasaunda Singh and Gulab Singh led the Nishanwalia and Dallewalia *misls* at Amritsar. In the districts to the north of Amritsar,

> "We may see some **ambitious (misl) chief**, led on by his **genius** ... display from the ruins of ... commonwealth, the **standard of monarchy**."
>
> GEORGE FORSTER, *A JOURNEY FROM BENGAL TO ENGLAND*, 1783

Jai Singh and Nand Singh formed the Kanhaiya and the Ramgarhia *misls*. Hira Singh set up his *misl* Nakkai to the southwest of Lahore, while Deep Singh and Karora Singh established their Shaheed and Karora Singhia *misls* to the east of the Yamuna River. There was a twelfth *misl*, Phoolkia, but it was not part of the Dal Khalsa.

Misl states

The retreat of the Afghans from Punjab and the weakening condition of the Mughal state left the region between the Indus and Yamuna open for Sikh conquest. Without a common enemy to fight, the *misls* divided the areas among themselves. In the 1770s, they occasionally united to fight the Mughal commander Najaf Khan, the Marathas, or the Rohillas, but without a common goal, the *misldars* turned on each other, fighting to expand their own territory and riches. New territories were conquered by the *sardars*. The existing administrators of those areas were made Sikh tributaries and they paid *rakhi* for protection. Most of the *misls* did not amass enough power to become full-fledged states, but they kept the spirit for centralization alive by making multiple efforts to protect their territory and claims to revenue.

The Ahluwalias and Sukerchakias, however, eventually gained enough prestige to establish their own small kingdoms within Punjab. Under Jassa Singh Ahluwalia, the Ahluwalias formed the Kapurthala state, whose ruling family was made up of his descendants. Naudh Singh's son, Charhat Singh of the Sukerchakia *misl*, constructed a fortress at Gujranwala. His grandson Ranjit Singh would go on to inherit this territory and later expand it to form the Sikh Empire at the end of the 18th century.

Valiant warriors

Eighteenth-century Sikh warriors are figures of familiarity even today. They are known for their exploits, fierce leadership, and courage. Usually memorialized in iconography as riding a horse with a sword in one hand, these are the leaders, men and women, who were behind the expansion of the Sikh Empire.

The tenor of the Sikh faith changed when Guru Hargobind Singh declared that he would accept weapons and horses as offerings. In later years, it became imperative for the Sikhs to have a fighting force so that they could combat the declining Mughal authority, foreign invasions, and local rebellions. The establishment of the Khalsa (see p.106) and later the *misls*, gave rise to powerful warriors who are still remembered to this day.

Among them was Jassa Singh Ramgarhia, leader of the Ramgarhia *misl* and one of the most well-known Sikh *misldars*. It is believed that he came from a family that was once in service of the tenth Guru. The governor of Punjab, Adina Beg Khan, inducted Ramgarhia into his army at first. However, he switched sides after witnessing the persecution of his community under Beg Khan. From 1748, Ramgarhia

and his *misl* were behind many raids against the enemies of the Sikhs in Punjab, occasionally even collaborating with other *misls* to fight a bigger force. He carved out a territory in the Majha region, with his headquarters at Ramgarh Fort. He ruled until his death in 1800, often through sensible alliances with other communities. Ramgarhia did not strictly adhere to Khalsa norms, sometimes drawing the ire of Jassa Singh Ahluwalia, leader of the Ahluwalia *misl*.

Padshah of Kapurthala

Mentored by Kapur Singh, Jassa Singh Ahluwalia became the commander of the Dal Khalsa, or the grand army, in 1748. He held a great antipathy for all anti-Sikh forces, who he exterminated, keeping with the *Rahit namas*, or Sikh code of conduct. Much of the Sikh military prowess

Mai Bhago (center), a devout follower of
Guru Gobind Singh, is shown here in the
Battle of Muktsar fought in 1705. She played
a key role in convincing forty Sikh deserters to
return to the Guru's side and fight the Mughals.

> "[Mai Bhago] either **disguised** [herself] **as a man** or was given **special permission** to wear male-specific garb by Guru Gobind Singh."

DORIS R. JAKOBSH, "GENDER IN SIKH TRADITIONS,"
THE OXFORD HANDBOOK OF SIKH STUDIES, 2014

was due to the excellent leadership of brave warriors such
as Ahluwalia. He won many battles and his administrative
abilities led him to build a sovereign state in Kapurthala.

Female military figures

The active involvement of women in Sikh armed forces does
not get its due in history. This inclusion was one of the main
reasons that the military could sustain its numbers. One such
warrior was Mai Bhago. Trained by her father, she fought beside
Guru Gobind Singh at the battle in Muktsar in 1705. Often
disguised as a man during combat, Mai Bhago followed the
Guru to Nanded after the battle and settled near Bidar in 1708.
For her contributions, her hut was converted into a gurdwara.

Mai Sukhan was another warrior of great repute. The wife
and widow of *misldar* Gulab Singh Bhangi, Mai Sukhan was
a respected authority in the *misl*. She ran several military
campaigns, including one in 1805 against Ranjit Singh. It was
during this campaign that she encountered the army of Sada
Kaur, another female warrior who had a significant role to
play in the rise of Ranjit Singh.

A nawab and a sardar

Nawab Kapur Singh and Baba Baghel Singh played a key role
in the spread of Sikh power in Punjab. In 1733, Kapur Singh
was chosen as the *jagirdar* (administrator), in charge of the
jagir (feudal land grant) gifted to the Sikhs by governor
Zakarya Khan. This earned him the title of nawab, deputy.
He also became the head of the Sarbat Khalsa and the Buddha
Dal, a wing of the Dal Khalsa army. His role in the birth of
the *misldari* system was pivotal and helped set up a strong
Sikh force. He took charge of the Fyzullapuria *misl* and
staged several attacks on the Mughal army as well as the
Persian and Afghan invaders.

Sardar Baghel Singh, another important Sikh military
general, defeated the Rohillas and Mughals and expanded his
territories beyond the Yamuna. In 1783, he stormed the Red
Fort in Delhi, coercing the Emperor into paying him a part
of the tax annually, and gaining permission to build eight
gurdwaras at places of historic importance to the Sikhs.

"Over the course of the 18th century, the **gurdwaras**, Guru, sangat, karah prasad, langar, and the **nishan sahib** became institutions tethered to **Khalsa identity** and **faith**."

MICHAEL HAWLEY, "SIKH INSTITUTIONS," *THE OXFORD HANDBOOK OF SIKH STUDIES*, 2014

Nishan Sahib
The Sikh flag

Gently fluttering in the sky, the Nishan Sahib, a triangular saffron flag with a navy blue insignia, called *khanda*, can be seen outside all gurdwaras. Used to signal the presence of a Sikh temple, the flag proclaims the lasting authority of the Gurus as well as the history of martyrdom that has been crucial in shaping the Sikh community.

A developing tradition

According to Sikh studies scholar Michael Hawley in *The Oxford Handbook of Sikh Studies,* the earliest references to a Sikh flag date back to Guru Angad, the second Guru, who spoke of a "banner of honor," and Guru Amar Das, the third Guru, who spoke of a "banner of patience." The latter's flag was white without an emblem, while Guru Angad's featured the inscription *Ik Onkar* (see pp.44–45). It was Guru Hargobind, the sixth Guru, who changed the color from white to saffron, possibly as a symbol of martyrdom and self-sacrifice, and added a figure of two swords (see pp.84–85) representing *miri* (worldly power) and *piri* (spiritual authority). It is believed that he also proposed a second flag where the symbol for *miri* was placed lower than *piri*, implying the latter's superiority.

A mark of the community

Guru Gobind Singh, the tenth Guru, introduced a different, blue Nishan Sahib. It featured the symbols of *kattar* (dagger), *dhal* (shield), and *kirpan* (sabre). Standing for the everlasting authority of the Guru, the flag became a symbol for the Khalsa when soldiers began to carry it on their missions in the 18th century. Later, a sword, a cauldron, and a dagger were added. These were the symbols of *"degh, tegh, fateh"*—a commitment to communal service, war, and victory.

The modern *khanda* came to adorn the Nishan Sahib in the early 20th century, which linked the concepts of victory and *miri-piri.* The emblem includes a double-edged sword, flanked by two *kirpans*, and a *chakram* (circular throwing weapon) in the center. This iteration signified both the Guru and the military might of the community, commanding utmost respect.

A 19th-century line engraving depicting Ranjit Singh, the leader of the Sukerchakia *misl* and founder of the Sikh Empire, on horseback. An attendant, dressed in finery and holding an umbrella, is shown beside the Maharaja.

The rise of Ranjit Singh

Ranjit Singh's military flair, evidenced by his success in besting rebellious *misls*, led to his rise as a strong leader, who solved the internal disputes among *misls* and combated the threat of invasions that loomed over the Sikhs in the late 18th century.

The years after the 1760s saw an increase in friction among the Sikh *misls*. Individual attempts to govern more territory around the Punjab region brought them into contention with one another. By the last decade of the century, the *misldari* arrangement (see pp.160–161) was showing all signs of disintegration. The instability had laid bare the lack of a united Sikh front and there now emerged the threat of yet another Afghan ruler, Shah Zaman, keen to conquer Punjab. There was a need for a strong leader who could unite the Sikhs. Ranjit Singh, chief of the Sukerchakia *misl* and the descendant of one of the first *Amritdhari* Sikhs, proved himself more than competent for this role.

Misls in the late 18th century

In the period after the return of Ahmed Shah Durrani to Kabul (see p.155), the Sikh *misls'* attempts to capture territory in and around Punjab were met with little resistance from the Mughal commander Najaf Khan. After the commander's death in 1782, individual *misls* consolidated their control in the Punjab and Shiwalik regions, and pushed eastward to conquer the Jamuna–Ganga Doab, where they were stopped by the Marathas, a warrior community from the Deccan plateau. In the Majha and Malwa Sikh strongholds, tensions had been intensifying among the *misls* since the 1770s. In the former, this related to the succession in Jammu, with the Kanhaiya and Sukerchakia *misls* forming an alliance against the Bhangis. This dynamic shifted twice, first by 1775, and then again by the next decade.

SHAH ZAMAN, RANJIT SINGH, AND THE BRITISH

After returning to Kabul in 1798, the Afghan ruler Shah Zaman sent gifts of good faith to Ranjit Singh. The act spurred rumors of a conspiracy between the Afghans and the Bhangi *misl* to launch another attack. This caused panic among the British who entreated Ranjit Singh to cut all ties with the Afghan ruler. While Shah Zaman had been preparing an army, the attack never occurred as he had to turn his attention to Kabul due to a revolt by his brother.

> "... were it not for... **Ranjit Singh** the whole of the **Punjab** would... have become a **desert waste** since... the grass never grows where their [the Afghans'] horses have... trodden."

LETTER FROM JOHN ULRICH COLLINS,
BRITISH RESIDENT AT THE MUGHAL COURT, 1800

Securing authority

Ranjit Singh was born in 1780 to the chief of the Sukerchakia *misl*. By the time he took over as leader in 1792, the infighting among the *misls* had led to most becoming silent and ineffectual, leaving only a few dominant ones. Ranjit Singh had made a few marriages of political importance which gave him ties to two prominent *misls*, the Kanhaiya and Nakkai. With their support, he launched an attack on the Bhangi *misl* stronghold in western Punjab and sought to suppress other *misls*.

By the end of the 18th century, Ranjit Singh had made a name as a formidable opponent, amassing rival *misl* territory and building his kingdom. Around this time, Ahmed Shah Durrani's grandson Shah Zaman had made multiple attempts to seize territory in Punjab. Supported by Sada Kaur of the Kanhaiya *misl* (see pp.168–169), Ranjit Singh persuaded the *misl* chiefs to unite in the fight against the Afghans.

This Sikh army led by Ranjit Singh fought the Afghan force outside Amritsar and pushed them to the Lahore border. Troubles in Kabul forced the Afghans to turn back from there. Once the *misl* chiefs returned victorious, Ranjit Singh took the opportunity to set out with his army. He captured Lahore, then took over *misls* in Bhasin, both provinces in Punjab, ultimately conquering the Jammu region. The victories cemented his reputation as the fearsome overlord of Punjab, paving the path for the subsequent creation of an empire of Sikhs under his leadership.

In brief

1782
Death of Mughal commander Najaf Khan

1792
Ranjit Singh becomes the Sukerchakia leader

1796
Shah Zaman's first two invasions

1797
Ranjit Singh persuades the *misls* to fight Shah Zaman

1798
Shah Zaman's final invasion and defeat

The guide to the leader

Politically and militarily capable, Sada Kaur helped Ranjit Singh forge the Sikh Empire. Her role as a mentor, mother-figure, and commander has left an indelible mark on Sikh history.

Born in 1762 amid the chaos of Ahmed Shah Durrani's invasions, Sada Kaur grew up with a resentment for the Afghans. At the age of six, her father arranged her marriage to Gurbaksh Singh, the son of Jai Singh Kanhaiya, the first Kanhaiya *misl* chief. The marriage pulled her into a world of disputes, and she learnt the skills to run an organization.

Her husband was killed in the Battle of Batala with the Sukerchakia *misl*, after which she secured her daughter's betrothal to Ranjit Singh. By the time of their wedding, Sada Kaur had taken over leadership of the *misl*. She had enough knowledge and authority to handle administrative and military matters and was intent on keeping the power. She found the means in Ranjit Singh.

Conquering Punjab

After Ranjit Singh's succession as the leader of the Sukerchakia *misl*, she urged him to make a name for himself in Punjab by persuading the Khalsa to stand and fight Shah Zaman Durrani in 1796. At the Sarbat Khalsa after the second Afghan invasion (see pp.152–154), she inspired the Sikh leaders into joining them in the fight. Ranjit Singh's role in defeating the Afghans won him immense prestige. But it was his mother-in-law Sada Kaur's wise counsel and support that had helped him claim power and emerge as a leader in a time of crisis.

Over the years, Sada Kaur became Ranjit Singh's trusted aide and mentor, offering advice on political matters. Her influence over Ranjit Singh was recognized by many: a British messenger appointed to warn Ranjit Singh about the possible return of Shah Zaman Durrani also met with Sada Kaur. In 1799, when the people of Lahore called on Ranjit Singh to liberate them, he turned to her for advice on battling its Bhangi *misl* rulers.

Her support came not only by way of strategy but also as military aid. She led a Kahnhaiya army of 25,000 warriors to help in the fight.

He annexed Lahore, then the capital of Punjab, and became the head of the region. An alliance of rival Sikh misls battled him for the seat in 1800, but Sada Kaur's aid once again ensured Ranjit Singh's victory. She helped him conquer Jammu, take Amritsar from the Bhangis, subdue the Pathans at Kasur, and capture Chiniot.

Rift in partnership

Ranjit Singh's eventual split with Sada Kaur had its roots in his hostile relationship with her daughter, Mehtab Kaur. The friction intensified in 1801, when Datar Kaur, his favored second wife, gave birth to a son. Ranjit Singh became the Maharaja of Punjab and announced his son with Datar Kaur as his heir. Sada Kaur was supportive, but was aware of her daughter's weakened position.

The birth of Mehtab Kaur's twin boys restored some peace, but rumors soon spread of the children being foundlings brought in by Sada Kaur to keep her influence intact. She also became vocal about the king's new wife, Bibi Moran, a Muslim courtesan whom Ranjit Singh had married, much to her ire. As a result, Ranjit Singh exiled Sada Kaur to Batala.

▲ **Portrait of Mehtab Kaur, Sada Kaur's daughter.**

Meanwhile, British forces formed an alliance with her. Tensions escalated gradually for almost a decade before Ranjit Singh sequestered all her estates in 1821, and then apprehended her when she attempted to escape. Sada Kaur spent the last years of her life in incarceration in Lahore, until her death in 1832.

◀ **Sada Kaur leads her army** at the Shahi Fort, Lahore, in the battle against the Bhangi *misl* in this painting.

In Brief

1762 Birth of Sada Kaur	**1797** Sada Kaur's address at the Sarbat Khalsa	**1821** Sada Kaur jailed by Ranjit Singh
1795 Wedding of Mehtab Kaur and Ranjit Singh	**1799** Conquest of Lahore, aided by Sada Kaur	**1801** Ranjit Singh crowned Maharaja of Punjab
		1832 Sada Kaur's death in prison

BIBI SAHIB KAUR OF PATIALA (1771–1801)

Another strong political and military leader was the princess of Patiala, Bibi Sahib Kaur. She became the prime minister in 1793, when her younger brother, the third Maharaja of Patiala, Sahib Singh, sought her help to quell internal disputes. Early on in her political career, the fierce warrior rescued her husband, Jaimal Singh of the Kanhaiya clan, after his capture by a rival chief. Among Sahib Kaur's feats was an unlikely victory against the Marathas in 1794, even though her troops were outnumbered. In 1799, she launched an offensive against George Thomas, an Englishman who ruled over Hissar and Hansi, in retaliation for his attempts to encroach upon the kingdom's territory.

Rise of the Sikh Empire

The Sikh Empire emerged within the radical political shifts of the 18th century when the waning Mughal control was replaced by various regional entities. It attained its peak in the early 19th century with Maharaja Ranjit Singh's conquest of neighboring lands.

The Mughal Empire had already shown signs of rupture by the time Banda Singh Bahadur was established as a leader in the beginning of the 18th century. The following years saw the emergence of many regional sovereignties, all vying for power. This included Mughal governors who formed their own kingdoms in Bengal, Awadh, and Hyderabad.

Political shifts

Invasions by the Persians and Afghans further weakened the Mughal hold over their empire while inadvertently legitimizing the Sikh influence in northwest India. It was around this time that Maharaja Ranjit Singh consolidated power by resolving internal disagreements among the *misldars*, waging battles to expand his territory,

and unifying the Sikhs. He conquered territories across Punjab and its outlying regions, but ensured that he governed this territory through effective peasant-conciliatory policies. The Sikh Empire came into being only after he seized control of Lahore from the Mughals. Spanning 50 years, its four provinces grew to include Multan, Peshawar, and Kashmir.

Other new kingdoms also emerged across the subcontinent, including the Afghans who took control in Rohilkhand, the Nizamat in Arcot, and the Marathas in the Deccan. Other significant leaders were Tipu Sultan in Mysore and Martanda Varma in Travancore. Agrarian revolts such as by the Jats, who allied with the Sikhs, further supplemented this growing political autonomy.

A hostile ally

Similar to the Jats and Sikhs, the Marathas were another regional force that gained support from an agrarian base of peasants. They had been providing their military services to the Deccan sultanates until now, but they banded together in the 17th century as agriculturalists and peasants. The lineage cast by Shivaji Bhonsle, popularly referred to as Chhatrapati Shivaji, consistently resisted Mughal dominion, first pushing Aurangzeb out of the Deccan, and thereafter pushing into regions further north.

The relationship between the Sikhs and the Marathas was mostly adversarial, as they had been fighting over parts of Punjab. On occasion, they did turn allies. In 1757, a few months after capturing the Mughal seat in Delhi from the Rohilla Afghans, they combined forces to oust the Afghans' Durrani Empire out of Peshawar. In 1759, as well, an alliance of Sikhs and Marathas defeated the Afghans, following which the Sikhs re-established control and pushed the Marathas out of Punjab.

The emergence of the East India Company introduced a new dynamic in the 1770s that had an impact on all these relationships. As the Company was increasingly gaining control, it considered regional autonomies a threat. In 1785, it mediated a treaty between the Sikhs and Marathas to forge peace in the area around Delhi, but the alliance eventually failed. A lack of trust led to similar failures at maintaining agreements between states in the coming years.

The Marathas and the British fought three wars during the late 18th and the early 19th centuries. In the course of the second war (1803–1805), Marathas had to give up control of Delhi and the Maratha chieftain of Indore fled to Punjab seeking refuge. However, Ranjit Singh denied the request, cementing the Marathas' exit from Sikh territory, and marking the final interaction between the two regional powers.

In brief

1674
Beginning of Maratha rule under Shivaji Bhosle

1717
Murshid Quli Khan establishes control in Murshidabad in Bengal

1722
Sadat Khan becomes Nawab of Awadh

1724
Chin Qilich Khan becomes Nawab of Hyderabad

1729
Martanda Varma becomes ruler of Travancore

1757
Marathas take control of Delhi

1782
Tipu Sultan becomes ruler of Mysore

First treaty between Sikhs and Marathas

1803
Start of second Anglo-Maratha war

◄ **Hungarian painter August Schoefft imagined** Maharaja Ranjit Singh listening to the Guru Granth Sahib, overlooking the Golden Temple, in this mid-18th century painting.

A painting of Maharaja Ranjit Singh's lavish court by Imam Baksh Lahori c. 1825–1845, depicts the ruler, seated on the golden throne, surrounded by his generals.

The golden throne

A ceremonial seat of state, Maharaja Ranjit Singh's golden throne is one of the greatest treasures of the Sikh Empire. It became a symbol of his power and came to signify the magnificence of the Sikh kingdom.

After ambushing Afghan invasions in 1799, Lahore became the capital of the Sikh Empire. From his court here, styled as the Lahore Durbar, Maharaja Ranjit Singh ran his affairs in the Punjab. Historical accounts state that although the ruler was known for his modesty, the court was as splendid as possible, featuring a golden throne meant for state occasions.

An iconic symbol

British accounts of the time note that the ruler commissioned Hafez Muhammad Multani, a goldsmith from the city of Multan, now in Pakistan, to make the golden throne. Ranjit Singh's empire was a testament to the Sikh ideals of inclusion and equality, and the Muslim identity of the craftsman demonstrated its very hybrid nature.

Although not as grandiose as the thrones of past rulers of Lahore, the golden throne was a symbol of Ranjit Singh's power, wealth, and sovereignty. It was not embellished with materials such as precious stones, but enveloped in thick sheets of striking gold. Octagonal in shape, the structure was made of wood and resin, and handles were attached at the base to aid its mobility. The seat of the throne, fitted with cushions, had a solid back with supports on either side and engraved branches that once held golden orbs. The use of these materials made it very clear that the occupant was the king.

The base, uniquely shaped like a cup, had golden engravings shaped as lotus petals. In Sikh sacred literature, the motif of a lotus was frequently employed by Sikh Gurus as a symbol of purity and spirituality.

Courtly grandeur

Having established his seat in Lahore, Ranjit Singh deviated from the accepted norms of royal etiquette of the time. He refused to sit on the Mughal throne, dressed plainly, preferred to be addressed with a simple honorific, and even held court seated cross-legged in a chair and received guests in a casual setting, while reclining on cushions on a carpet. By having his own throne made, the Maharaja signified a shift in

> "All that the **imagination** can conceive of **human grandeur** … to portray the acme of **royal splendor** … was here embodied forth."
>
> HENRY STEINBACH, *THE PUNJAUB*, 1845

authority in Punjab. However, Ranjit Singh and other Sikh kings never assumed spiritual authority; the throne was a potent symbol of political, not religious, power. All of this pointed to his intentions of establishing a distinct identity, surpassing the legacy left behind by his Mughal predecessors in the region.

The golden throne fitted the grandeur of the court, and it was a reflection of the tangible wealth and might of Ranjit Singh. It was placed at the center of Musamman Burj pavilion, a chamber decorated with glittering glass mosaic in the Lahore Fort. The royal court (see pp.184–185) often hosted extravagant dance and music performances for the king, courtiers, and visitors. The facade was aimed to impress, in particular the European dignitaries who occasionally met with the Maharaja.

The fate of the throne

In 1849, within years of Ranjit Singh's death, British forces led by the Earl of Dalhousie, the Governor General of India at the time, annexed Punjab. Lahore's vast treasury, including the throne, was seized as spoils of war.

Interestingly, before shipping it off to the Indian Museum in London, Lord Dalhousie commissioned a replica of the throne to be made in mahogany. Perhaps, this in itself indicated the glory of the Sikh Empire and was a testament to the beauty of the fabled seat of Maharaja Ranjit Singh.

Military matters

The army under Maharaja Ranjit Singh was a marriage of traditional and modern systems. Over the course of his reign, he welcomed advisors, reorganized its structure, and invested in large-scale reforms that made his army one of the most prominent and efficient military systems in Asia.

In the early 19th century, Maharaja Ranjit Singh brought about a series of reforms to his army. Many historians believe that this desire to reorganize his military system came about after Ranjit Singh witnessed the efficient structure of the British troops during the second Anglo–Maratha War (1803–1805).

A changing militia

Ranjit Singh initially had an army made up of forces from his own *misl*, which continued to grow with his conquests in the first two decades of his rule. Later, the troops of his allies such as Sada Kaur, Fateh Singh Ahluwalia, and Jodh Singh Ramgarhia were also absorbed into the Sikh Empire's force.

This army, organized around a largely Sikh cavalry, followed traditional fighting methods which had seen success with swift raids on horseback in the past. Modifications to this order involved the recruitment of European mercenaries to the army, as well as training the soldiers to stand in closer ranks.

Ranjit Singh was keen to move away from the convention of independent chiefs ruling troops, characteristic of the *misldari* system, and toward a more professional arrangement, as he had seen in European troops. Other developments entailed a shift to regular wages, which was of major benefit as soldiers had hitherto been allocated a share of the revenue.

Historian J.S. Grewal notes, in his book *The Sikhs of the Punjab*, that Ranjit Singh, even before 1809, had a vast army of 1,500 soldiers and two batteries of artillery. The Maharaja replaced the dependence on a strong cavalry with a system that constituted ranks of infantry and artillery. He was eager to include Europeans, Muslims, and Marathas in the ranks. Though many people from other faiths signed up, the ruler had to work hard to convince Sikh soldiers to be part of the infantry, a role that they had once looked down upon. As a result, the artillery had more Muslim soldiers, and the infantry, Hindu.

However, once the new measures had been accepted, the new army proved to be a source of strength.

▶ **A painting of Ranjit Singh** on horseback, with attendants bearing an umbrella and a royal whisk. He is surrounded by his troops.

HARI SINGH NALWA

Hari Singh Nalwa was the commander-in-chief of the Sikh Khalsa Army in the Sikh Empire. Nalwa was renowned for his fervor in the battlefield, and for his extensive experience fighting for Ranjit Singh in major battles, including Kasur, Attock, Kashmir, Peshawar, and many others. He was also the administrator of the regions of Kashmir, Peshawar, and Hazara, and minted coins and erected buildings of note here. He met his end while fighting the Afghan ruler Dost Mohammad Khan at Jamrud on the Khyber Pass, now in Pakistan.

It undermined the tribes in the northwest districts of Punjab in 1831 and successfully resisted the invading Afghans in Peshawar six years later.

A growing army

The reorganization of the army had fiscal consequences. As the ranks in the army grew, Ranjit Singh was forced to increase the revenue to match the growing expenses of soldiers, animals, and arms. The new revenue system was similar to the survey arrangement conducted by the ruler's political predecessors, which aimed at arriving at the value of the crops cultivated in each plot of land. This, in turn, put more pressure on the cultivators in Punjab.

European influences

By the 1820s, Ranjit Singh had begun raising a cavalry unit along European lines. In 1822, Jean Francois Allard and Jean Baptiste Ventura, soldiers with impressive military expertise, joined the emperor's army. They had sought employment in Lahore after Napolean Bonaparte's army was disbanded in France. As a former member of a westernized army, Allard provided insight into how the Sikh soldiers could be efficiently trained. He was regarded as a loyal soldier to Ranjit Singh, having fought several wars for the Sikh Empire. Infantryman Ventura went on to become a general and then the Count of Mandi. Within a few years, there were various Europeans enlisted in the army and it grew rapidly in size. According to J.S. Grewal, "In 1831, there were 300 guns in the artillery and about 20,000 trained infantrymen in twenty-one battalions.... In terms of its striking power, the state of Ranjit Singh was stronger than many larger states in Asia."

▲ **The Howitzer gun from Ranjit Singh's artillery collection** (c. 1838) was presented to Sir Hugh Gough, a general in the British army, after the Anglo–Sikh Wars.

In brief

1799
Ranjit Singh establishes the Sikh Empire

1820
Westernization of Ranjit Singh's army commences

1822
Jean Francois Allard joins Ranjit Singh's army

1831
Ranjit Singh's reformed army is victorious in the northwest frontier

1837
Ranjit Singh's army undermines the Afghan rebellion in Peshawar

A Nihang Sikh wearing the customary turban, called *dastar banga*. The symbols and insignias on the turban hold either military or spiritual significance.

> "... it is the **custom** of their troops to **advance and retreat**, rally and return to the fight... a most **useful manoeuvre** it is... "

W BARR, *JOURNAL OF A MARCH FROM DELHI TO PESHAWUR* (1844)

Nihangs
The mighty Sikh warriors

The Nihangs likely originated at the time of Guru Gobind Singh, the tenth Sikh Guru, under whom they congregated, declaring their commitment to the Khalsa, a Sikh order that he founded in 1699. They differentiated themselves from other Sikhs with the claim that they followed the orders more stringently.

In the 18th and the 19th centuries, they were more commonly known as the Akalis. In warfare, Nihangs were most well-known for their hit-and-run tactic that won them many victories. After 1716, the Nihangs organized under their leader Akali Phula Singh, a figure of authority and Jathedar of the *Akal* Takht (see pp.278–279) in Amritsar. Later, they took part in the wars fought by Maharaja Ranjit Singh, choosing to maintain independence. In the first half of the 19th century, the Nihangs launched several attacks on British officials in Punjab. Perhaps this is why the group did not fare as well after the fall of the Sikh Empire when the British began ruling Punjab. The connection between the Nihangs and military action is demonstrated by the role these Sikhs have played in popularizing the Sikh martial art form, Gatka.

Striking ensemble

Nihangs are most popular for their distinct attire: loose deep blue clothes with an elongated turban. The Nihang turban is called the *dastar banga*, or the towering fortress. Common elements found on the turban are quoits symbolizing the values of the Khalsa; the dhal, or shield; the kirpan, a single-edged sword or knife, representing *miri-piri* (see p.169), the temporal power and spiritual authority; and others. Some have a *farla*, attached, signifying the bearer's position. According to sociologist Paramjit Singh Judge, the *Tat* Khalsa, the orthodox Sikh faction, likely borrowed elements of the Nihangs' dressing style to preserve the militaristic quality of the larger Sikh community.

In modern times

Modern Nihangs believe in the Dasam Granth and the Sarbloh Granth scriptures, which they attribute to Guru Gobind Singh. Their interpretation of the *Rahit nama*, or the code of conduct, differs from the one ordained by the Shiromani Gurdwara Parbandhak Committee (SGPC) in Amritsar.

A group of women performing Gatka with shields and swords in a martial art display in Manchester, England, during Baisakhi festivities. This Sikh *Shastar Vidiya* or martial art is mainly associated with the Nihang warriors who employed the techniques in battles. It is named after a wooden weapon often wielded by the warriors.

Expansion of the Sikh Empire

Ranjit Singh's forces captured Lahore in 1799. Over the next few years, he amassed territory all across Punjab. At its height, the Sikh Empire extended from the Khyber Pass in the north to the Sutlej River, including Ladakh and Kashmir, and even parts of western Tibet.

▲ **A remarkable painting,** c. 1845–1850, depicting a panoramic view of the walled city of Lahore. Inscriptions in Urdu and English identify different monuments such as the sprawling Lahore Fort.

Ranjit Singh crowned himself the Maharaja of Punjab in 1801. Over the course of the next forty years, he would conquer large parts of Punjab and beyond through a series of military campaigns. After Lahore, he was quick to take over Amritsar, and by 1809, had staked claim on all five doabs, regions between the rivers that run through Punjab—the Chenab, Jhelum, Ravi, Sutlej, and Beas. However, this was not without resistance.

By this time, the British East India Company controlled key areas of the Indian subcontinent. The Anglo-Maratha Wars had left them in charge of most of the region south of the Sutlej River, and they were keen to further their involvement.

The Treaty of Amritsar

As the Maharaja's army extended its campaigns beyond the Sutlej, the chiefs who had not taken to Ranjit Singh's activities well, appealed to the British East India Company to intervene. The

◀ **Map from 1839** showing Ranjit Singh's kingdom, or the *Raaj Sarkar-E-Khalsa,* around the five rivers of Punjab.

British called these principalities Cis-Sutlej states (Cis is Latin for "on this side (of)" the river). Primary among them were Jind, Nabha, Patiala, Faridkot, Malerkotla, and Kalsia.

Having seen the might of the Lahore Durbar in the late 18th century, the British were aware of their threatening presence in the region. To avoid conflict, the Treaty of Amritsar was signed in 1809, with the Company accepting Ranjit Singh's sovereignty and control in Punjab, while he agreed to limit his territory to the Sutlej River.

In the aftermath of the treaty, by 1818, Ranjit Singh's forces suppressed rival Sikh leaders in the north. He took over Multan first, and then wrested Peshawar from the Afghans, although he soon lost the region. By 1819, he had also undermined the hill chieftains in the Kashmir region.

Changing attitudes

The first signs of wariness between the Sikh Empire and the British became apparent in 1831, when Ranjit Singh met with the Company to discuss the ruling of Sindh. The Company was keen to hold on to the region and tried to dissuade the Maharaja from asserting control. He began doubting British intentions and turned his focus back to his expansion campaigns. In 1834, he took back control of Peshawar from the Afghans. He also deployed his allies, the Dogra brothers, to claim control over Ladakh on his behalf. While the relationship between the British and Ranjit Singh remained stable, he began to view them with a critical eye.

This suspicion, however, did not overpower the facade of goodwill between the two parties or their working relationship. In 1832, they signed a treaty to open the Indus River to facilitate trade.

The Sikh Empire also had other agreements with the British, as the Company was a good source of weapons to modernize their army. Another treaty was signed, in 1838, in which Ranjit Singh agreed to provide military support to Shah Shuja, second son of Emperor Shah Jahan, in staking a claim to the throne of Kabul.

After Ranjit Singh's death in 1839, the Sikh Empire lasted ten more years, although unrest and frequent successions weakened the state, giving the British the chance to annex it in 1846.

DOGRA BROTHERS OF KASHMIR

Ranjit Singh often found it hard to control Kashmir, then the stronghold of many local chieftains. Eventually, he relied on three brothers—Gulab Singh, Dhian Singh, and Suchet Singh, who forged the Dogra Dynasty. They joined the Sikh army, earning repute for their bravery along with the Maharaja's trust. In 1834, Gulab Singh led the Sikh Empire's army on an expedition to capture Ladakh.

Raja Dhian Singh, seen here on a white horse, became the prime minister of the Sikh Empire.

In brief

1799
Ranjit Singh takes control of Lahore

1805
Ranjit Singh captures Amritsar

1809
Ranjit Singh signs the Treaty of Amritsar with the British

1818
The Sikh Empire takes Multan and Peshawar

1819
Ranjit Singh completes the conquest of Kashmir

1834
Ranjit Singh reclaims Peshawar and takes Ladakh

► **An oil painting of Maharaja Ranjit Singh**, by Sobha Singh. The ruler has been depicted seated on a lion-crested silver throne, bearing the Khanda emblem.

Ranjit Singh

Immortalized as one of the greatest military commanders, Ranjit Singh was a forward-thinker who built a sovereign empire with ferocious might and combative acumen. There is much more to his person than martial presence, which softens in the face of his administrative ability, his patronage of the arts, and the celebrations at his court.

There are two words that come to mind when one envisions Ranjit Singh—warfare and splendor. He sculpted the extraordinary empire of the Sikhs, the borders of which spanned most of Punjab and extended into Kabul in Afghanistan and Tibet.

Rising flame

Heir to the Sukerchakia *misl*, Ranjit Singh was born into the fragmented landscape of Punjab in 1780. Slight of build and small of stature, a bout of smallpox in early years had left him blind in one eye. During his childhood, his time was taken up by military campaigns and he indulged in horse riding and swordsmanship among other pursuits.

Following his father's illness, Ranjit Singh took up the chieftain's mantle at a young age, but won the confidence of his *misl* with his courage and ability.

Conquests and administration

By the end of the 18th century, Ranjit Singh had successfully expelled the invading Afghans, acquired Lahore, and even consolidated all the *misls'* territories into his own, creating a unified and powerful state. With his superior military acumen, Ranjit Singh also raised a capable and modern army that held the British at bay for forty years. Ranjit Singh's rule was marked by his respect and inclusion of other faiths. In his administration, known as the Sarkar Khalsa (meaning "government of the honored Khalsa"), he appointed people belonging to different religions, who rose up in rank on the merit of their talents. His army, though its nucleus largely remained Sikh, had contingents of Muslims, Hindus, and others. British writer Sir Lepel Griffin reported in *Rulers of India*, "Ranjit Singh was not cruel or bloodthirsty. After a victory or the capture of a fortress he treated the vanquished with leniency and kindness however stout their resistance might have been, and there were at his court many chiefs despoiled of their estates but to whom he had given suitable employ."

All subjects were equal before law and had the same rights. He even paid respect to other religions institutions and participated in their festivals.

Historical accounts also note that cultivation, trade, and manufacturing grew rapidly during his rule.

Patronage and learning

Maharaja Ranjit Singh's courts attracted many artists from various regions. Several schools of miniature painting flourished under his patronage. Reportedly, he even commissioned a mural of Guru Gobind Singh to be made on the walls of the Harmandir Sahib, in addition to religious-themed murals painted in his palaces. It was also Ranjit Singh who had the temple encased in gold and marble, which led it to be called the Golden Temple. Other art forms that received his patronage were fine woodwork and textiles.

Indian author Khushwant Singh writes about the ruler's love for gardens and open spaces such as riverbanks.

This perhaps explains why he had many dilapidated buildings and gardens restored, including the Baradari (pavilion with twelve doors) of the Hazuri Bagh in Lahore.

Ranjit Singh knew Punjabi and wrote in Gurmukhi. He later learned Persian and sought the company of scholars. British linguist and traveler Gottlieb Wilhelm Leitner, author of *History of Indigenous Education in the Punjab*, asserts that Ranjit Singh endowed many centers of traditional learning, such as *madrasas* and *gurukuls* as well as secular schools, to spread literacy in the empire, even as he emphasized vocational training.

"He **revived prosperity** and **minimized oppression**. He **created opportunities** for members of several sections of the society to **improve** their **social position**."

J.S. GREWAL, *THE SIKHS OF THE PUNJAB*, 1990

The Lahore Durbar

Featuring luxurious furnishings, exquisite jewels, spoils from conquests, and offerings from supporters, the dazzling Lahore Durbar, itself an ornate showpiece, became an emblem of Maharaja Ranjit Singh's wealth, power, and prestige, and inspired awe from its bevy of guests.

Maharaja Ranjit Singh's seat of power was the royal court in the Lahore Fort, which his armies had conquered from the Mughals. This was also where he played host to foreign guests, from the British Governor General Lord William Bentick; British administrative and military officers such as Alexander Burnes, Henry Edward Fane, and W.H. Osborne; to English poet and novelist Emily Eden. All their accounts reveal a uniform awe at seeing the Lahore Durbar.

The flamboyance of the Durbar

The brick fort at Lahore had been a Mughal fortification from the 16th century, before the Sikhs conquered it and made it the political center under Maharaja Ranjit Singh. The octagonal tower known as Musamman Burj located to the northwest around a courtyard was chosen as the Maharaja's private and official quarters. The new regent purposely occupied the fort to usher in a change in authority and assert his strength over what was once Mughal property. Ranjit Singh was eager to showcase his power, and this translated into the splendor of the Lahore Durbar. Set within the fort, it was a reflection of the array of riches from the treasury, which was brimming with spoils from conquests and offerings from supporters.

Decked with extravagant wall fabrics, carpets, and luxurious curtains embroidered with gold, the pavilion became a symbol of Ranjit Singh's sovereignty. The flamboyance was replicated even when the Durbar was held outside the fort, under pitched tents or in garden houses to sustain the image of the Maharaja's might.

The wealth of the fabrics on the walls and floor of the Musamman Burj was matched by other riches such as the gold chair-throne (see pp.172–173) of the Maharaja crafted to distinguish his ruling style from his predecessors. The *toshkhana* or treasury held precious items, from *khilats* or ceremonial robes and carpets to valuable coins and jewels, including the Koh-i-Noor (see pp.188–189), which were occasionally displayed or gifted.

Tours and performances

The Durbar was open to local and foreign dignitaries who were taken on tours around the rooms in the Musamman Burj. Inevitably, they were left awestruck at its magnificence. The invitees were given an elaborate reception with food and drink, and walks around the courtyard with adorned tents displaying various items of gold in the Maharaja's possession. Honorary guests were invited to attend the proceedings where, under the illumination of camphor candles, the Maharaja held his court with grandly attired ministers or sat back to relish musical and dance performances by highly trained courtesans and instrumentalists.

Another substantial contributor to the splendor of the Durbar was the military processions that were often held. In these, uniformed soldiers marched in strict formation to showcase the discipline and preparedness of the army. Festivals, such as Holi and Basant Panchami, were celebrated with great pomp and ceremony. Guests were invited to witness the flamboyance of the festivities, with the Maharaja calling for all courtiers to dress for and participate in the occasion.

▶ **This gouache painting, c. 1864,** by artist Bishan Singh depicts Maharaja Ranjit Singh, seated on his famous golden throne, in his court at Lahore. The painting also features a self-portrait of the artist.

"The room the **entertainment** was given in was fitted up all round with **small mirrors**, **fixed** in the wall with **enamel**, which **shone like diamonds** in candlelight… **Nautching** [dancing], **drinking, and fireworks**, were … the order of the day: to me … it is **not disagreeable**."

HENRY FANE, *FIVE YEARS IN INDIA*, 1842

Treasures from the Sikh Empire

The 19th-century Sikh Empire boasted an array of artifacts that were a testament to the formidable might and glory of the courts of Maharaja Ranjit Singh and his successors. These works of art were of great value and had the ethos and the splendor of the Sikhs woven into the very fabric of their design.

Maharaja Ranjit Singh holding a white flower

▶ Insignia of merit

Maharaja Ranjit Singh initiated the *Kaukab-i-iqbal-i-Punjab* (The Order of the Propitious Star of the Punjab) in 1837, awarding it to those who had been of great service to the kingdom, for instance, his grandson Nau Nihal Singh. Supposedly inspired by the French Legion of Honour, this insignia given in the ceremony was designed as a radiating star in gold enamel, set with table-cut emeralds and diamonds, and held a painting of the ruler under glass.

Fashioned to resemble a sickle moon

▲ Crescent-shaped earrings

This stunning pair of golden loop earrings belonged to Maharani Jind Kaur, c. 1830–1840. Seed pearls and flat, leaf-pendants adorn the scalloped edges.

Diamond and pearl charm in the form of a lotus

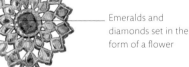

▼ Charm necklace

Maharani Jind Kaur's necklace, c. 1830–1840, features several pendants on a chain of pearls. Made of gold, emeralds, diamonds, and red spinel, it reflects the exquisite craftsmanship of the period. Similar necklaces in this style were part of the queen's treasury and provide an understanding of her aesthetic taste.

Emeralds and diamonds set in the form of a flower

◀ Maharani's earrings

These earrings, known as the *karanphool jhumkas* (flower-shaped earrings) were the property of Maharani Jind Kaur, c. 1830–1840. They are created with gold, diamonds, and emeralds. The domelike drops have more emeralds and diamonds, with three-tiered pearl fringes and glass beads.

◀ Gem-set bangle
This intricate bangle, c. mid-19th century, encrusted with precious stones, belonged to Maharani Bamba, the first wife of Maharaja Dalip Singh (see pp.218–219) who was the last ruler of the Sikh Empire. It features the heads of mythological sea creatures known as *makars* facing one another. The style of work suggests that it was made in Jaipur, in Rajasthan.

Floral designs in red and green enamel

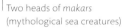

Two heads of *makars* (mythological sea creatures)

Central diamond set in an emerald

Octagonal emerald surrounded by diamonds set in gold

▲ Gold armlet
A gold *bazuband* or armlet, c. mid-19th century, worn by Maharani Bamba, the first wife of Maharaja Dalip Singh, on her wedding day. This beautiful *bazuband* is made up of three hinged pieces, and features emeralds and diamonds. The back showcases intricate enamel florals, a style of craftsmanship traditionally practiced by jewellers in Jaipur, Rajasthan.

Intricately carved geometric patterns

Locks imply that it probably held precious items

◀ Sandalwood casket
Reported to have belonged to Maharaja Ranjit Singh, this box is made with aromatic sandalwood and inlaid with tortoiseshell and ivory in geometric designs. Featuring small drawers in multiple tiers, it was probably used to store small valuables or letters.

The bloody diamond

One of the most famous diamonds in the world, in part due to its tumultuous history, is the Koh-i-Noor. The brilliant-cut, oval jewel was once the nonpareil treasure of Maharaja Ranjit Singh's collection. The British acquired it in 1849, and it is now set in the British Crown Jewels.

The Koh-i-Noor diamond, which translates to "Mountain of Light," was first referred to in the memoirs of the Mughal Emperor Babur in 1526. Its origins, though, can be traced to the famed mines of Golconda in the Godavari delta, in the south of India. The diamond's history, one of bloodshed and frequent changes in ownership, has given it the moniker "the cursed diamond." In India, the last keeper of the diamond was Maharaja Ranjit Singh, the founder of the Sikh Empire.

One stone, many owners

Over the course of several centuries, the Koh-i-Noor was owned and forcibly taken by many different rulers, which may go some way toward explaining its reputation for being cursed. After all, whoever owned the huge diamond was a target for attack.

Before the Mughals acquired it, the Koh-i-Noor had already had several owners. It had been in the possession of the Deccan kings and the erstwhile Delhi Sultan Alauddin Khalji. In 1739, the Persian king Nadir Shah, who invaded India, looted it from the Mughal treasury. Twelve years later, the Afghan ruler Ahmed Shah Durrani acquired it when the Persian Empire collapsed. The Koh-i-Noor then passed on to his grandson, Shah Shujah Durrani, under whom it returned to India. The Afghan had fled to Lahore in 1813 and Ranjit Singh allowed him to stay there. The Sikh ruler exerted his influence upon Durrani to hand the diamond over to him.

A symbol of power

The Koh-i-Noor held more value for Ranjit Singh than for any of his predecessors, especially since he had acquired it from the very people he had defeated to claim his throne (see pp.166–167). The Maharaja kept the diamond in his crown jewels. It was seen on his person on every public occasion and presented for viewing to all eminent visitors to his court. At other times, the diamond was guarded in the treasury at the Gobindgarh fortress. For Ranjit Singh, the jewel symbolized not just a prize, but the very essence of Sikh victory.

By 1839, a series of strokes had left Ranjit Singh unwell and he had to decide to whom to bequeath his possessions. This provoked a conflict over the possession of the Koh-i-Noor. While the Hindu priests of the Jagannath temple in Puri in south-central India claimed that Ranjit Singh had promised to gift the jewel to the temple, the royal treasurer Misr Beli Ram was convinced that the jewel belonged to the Sikh state. Ultimately, royal decrees and attempts at

> "He who owns this **diamond** will **own the world**, but will also know all **its misfortunes**. Only **God or woman** can wear it with impunity."
>
> UNKNOWN, A CURSE IN INDIAN FOLKLORE

concealment kept the diamond in Punjab. The next four rulers of the Sikh Empire were all assassinated while in possession of the stone, adding to the diamond's history of intrigue and violence.

In British hands

The Sikhs finally lost the Koh-i-Noor after the Sikh kingdom passed on to British hands following the Treaty of Lahore. In April 1850, the diamond was finally shipped to London where it would be presented to Queen Victoria. Though the royals were in awe of its beauty and proud of their possession, the public response to the diamond at its first appearance outside was indifferent. Displayed in a gilded cage at the Great Exhibition in London in 1851, the diamond failed to attract a crowd. Its Indian cut and lack of "shine" disappointed viewers and it was not the hit that British officials had expected.

Unhappy with this response, Prince Albert had the diamond re-cut in 1852 to match a more British style, which significantly diminished its size. The Koh-i-Noor, once 191 carats, was reduced to 105 carats. Since then, the stone has been set in the crowns of British queens, the last of which was the crown of Queen Elizabeth, the Queen Mother.

▼ **The Koh-i-Noor diamond,** which is part of the Crown Jewels of the United Kingdom, can be seen in this photograph in its original setting at the time of its acquisition by the British.

Illustration showing the young Maharaja **Dalip Singh** with Sir Henry Hardinge, British Governor-General of India. The British claimed the diamond as part of the Treaty of Lahore.

Lahore Fort

A UNESCO World Heritage Site since 1981, the modern structure of the Lahore Fort or Shahi Qila, as it is known, was constructed in 1566. Over the centuries, the sprawling fort has seen many invaders and rulers, each trying to leave their mark on this symbol of might and power.

A brief history

The city of Lahore had always been of immense strategic importance, militarily and economically. The earliest record of a fortified building in the northwest corner of the city, one made of mud bricks, can be dated to the 11th century and the reign of Turkish ruler Mahmud of Ghazni. Mongol invaders in 1241 left it in ruins, but it was reconstructed in 1267 under Ghiyasuddin Balban of the Delhi Sultanate and then destroyed by Timur's raids. The present fort was built by Mughal Emperor Akbar. Subsequent rulers added to its grandeur, including Ranjit Singh who occupied the fort in 1799. It here that he became the Maharaja of the Sikh Empire and held court at the Lahore Durbar. The fort changed hands once again with the fall of the Empire and the British annexation of Punjab, and remained in British control until independence in 1947.

▲ **A vintage, aerial photograph of the sprawling Lahore Fort,** including the Alamgiri Gate, the fortified wall, and the inner grounds.

The majestic Alamgiri Gate at the Lahore Fort was built by Emperor Aurangzeb in 1673. It is flanked by ramparts with lotus-petal detailing on their base. The gate's arch was tall enough to let the Emperor's elephant with a mounted seat to pass through.

Architecture and interior

This fort is an ideal example of Mughal architecture and has twenty-one key monuments from different time periods. The red sandstone buildings date back to Akbar's rule, the Persian styles can be attributed to Jahangir, and the marble to Shah Jahan's reign. Aurangzeb added buildings here and the Sikh ruler Ranjit Singh had modifications made and several structures added too, including a fortification wall and several pavilions, such as a haveli for Kharak Singh added to Jahangir's Quadrangle.

As Maharaja, Ranjit Singh used an elevated pavilion, which was known as the Atha Dara (building with eight openings), to hold court. Here, the frescos of the Hindu god Krishna along the northern wall represent the Kangra School of art. A floor was added to the Sheesh Mahal as well. It is believed that the Mahal is where Ranjit Singh died in 1839.

1. A Mughal garden as seen through a fort walkway;
2. Interior of the Sheesh Mahal; 3. Maharaja Ranjit Singh's statue in the exterior; 4. A Kangra School of Art mural;
5. Intricate ceiling work at the Lahore Fort; 6. Exterior of the Diwan-i-Khas; 7. Sheesh Mahal; 8. Badshahi Mosque;
9. Jehangir's Quadrangle; 10. Picture wall on the outside;
11. Mural at the Fort; 12. Beautiful Diwan-i-Khas pavilion;
13. Interior of Moti Masjid at the Fort.

Cultural heritage

From gilded artifacts, illustrated manuscripts, and educational opportunities to lush gardens and expansive *havelis*, the Sikh Empire crafted a landscape that simultaneously sustained lavish lifestyles, monumental piety, and secular sovereignty.

Maharaja Ranjit Singh's move to shift the capital to Lahore in present-day Pakistan, was a significant one. Once a representation of Mughal might, it was now a symbol of a flourishing Sikh Empire. Remnants of its rich cultural history, marked by magnificent productions of art, architecture, and literature are still found in the city.

Art and literature

Ranjit Singh was a patron of the arts. He invited local and foreign artists to paint portraits of Sikh leaders and illustrate manuscripts and religious texts. Exquisite artifacts made in Amritsar, Lahore, Multan, and Srinagar, including objects of gold and silver, coins, intricate weapons, pashmina wool shawls, and beautiful fabrics were often on display or given as gifts. The ruler commissioned literary works such as manuscripts of the Guru Granth Sahib, written

▲ **Painting of Maharaja Ranjit Singh** with his family.

and decorated in gold. Santokh Singh's *Gur Nanak Prakash*, its sequel, *Suraj Prakash*, and Rattan Singh Bhangu's *Sri Gur Panth Prakash* were also produced during this time. Ranjit Singh asked Sohan Lal Suri, a chronicler, to write about the court in *Umdat-Ut-Tawarikh*.

In *Royals and Rebels*, historian Priya Atwal notes that this indicated the ruler's intellect beyond his military might. It reflected that "the ideas he absorbed from such literature had an influence on the shaping of his ruling style."

Architectural splendor

The glamor of the Empire was best exemplified by its capital Lahore. The seat of the ruler was located here, within the Mughal fort which was refashioned to boast the riches of the kingdom. Occasionally, the court was held at Atha Dara, which

▲ **A 19th-century photograph of Hazuri Bagh.** Ranjit Singh had the garden complex constructed in Lahore, Pakistan, in 1813.

◀ **Maharaja Ranjit Singh rides an elephant** on a visit to a busy bazaar in Lahore in this painting by Sikh artist Kapur Singh, c 1860.

"In the center of ... [**Hazuri Bagh**] ... is an elegant little building ... where he [**Ranjit Singh**] transacts **business** in the hot season."

LIEUT. WILLIAM BARR, *JOURNAL OF A MARCH FROM DELHI TO CABUL*, 1844

translates to "eight openings." Ranjit Singh had this beautiful pavilion built, with white marble trellises and red sandstone pillars, as he refused to use the Diwan-i-Am, the hall the Mughals used.

The ruler also had a fascination for gardens, ordering repairs on Shalimar Bagh, which he often visited for leisure. Various gardens and pavilions around the perimeter of the city and outside were also repaired on Ranjit Singh's orders. After Hazuri Bagh in Lahore in 1813, he had Rambagh built in Amritsar in 1819. It was divided into four parts, with the Maharaja's summer palace in the center.

Life and education

Scholars suggest that the residents of the Sikh Empire were ahead of the rest of the country in terms of education. Most women were literate. People funded the setting up of educational institutions, including some only for women. The ruler himself patronized and granted funds from his treasury to existing institutions including madrasas set up by the Mughals earlier. Overall, many residents benefited from the rule of Ranjit Singh. Court officials and wealthy members of different religious communities supported his many social reforms, which impacted life in the Sikh Empire.

In brief

1809
Rattan Singh Bhangu begins work on the *Sri Gur Panth Prakash*

1813
Construction of Hazuri Bagh, Lahore

1819
Construction of Rambagh, Amritsar

1823
Santok Singh completes *Sri Gur Nanak Prakash*

Queens of the Sikh Empire

There was no dearth of prominent women in the Sikh Empire. Some of them were queens who rode into battle, influenced administrative decisions, exerted a presence through their patronage, and ultimately left an impact on the Sikh Empire in significant ways.

The queens of the Sikh Empire were not mere figureheads, but played a prominent role in matters of the state. They opposed the enemies of the Empire as warriors, brought forth new policies as regents, and even became *jagirdars*, or administrators of feudal lands. They are, however, not as well-celebrated as the male leaders of the time.

Queens as jagirdars

While queens as *jagirdars* were unconventional, they seemed to be the norm within the Sikh empire. Owning *jagirs* (landed estates) allowed them to maintain their autonomy, and also claim honor in some instances. Mehtab Kaur, the young wife of Maharaja Ranjit Singh was one such example. She was the daughter of Sada Kaur (see pp.168–169), one of the Maharaja's trusted advisors, and her marriage was a result of diplomacy between the Kanhaiya and Sukerchakia *misls*. One of her children, Sher Singh, even served briefly as the ruler. As the first wife of the Maharaja, Mehtab Kaur was the Maharani of the Sikh Empire, but chose to live away from the Lahore Fort, administering the *jagir* of Batala, in the Majha region of Punjab. Though she commanded much respect as the elder Maharani, she eventually distanced herself from political affairs.

After Mehtab Kaur's death in 1813, the title of Maharani passed on to Ranjit Singh's second wife, Datar Kaur. Though the marriage began as a diplomatic alliance with the Nakkai *misl*, unlike Mehtab Kaur, she enjoyed her husband's favor. Datar Kaur, also known as Mai Nakain, was the mother of the heir, Kharak Singh, but it was as *jagirdar* of Sheikhupura, near Lahore, that she contributed toward the shaping of the Sikh Empire. As a landholder, she paid tribute to the royal treasury and provided troops to fight in various conquests such as that of Multan in 1818. She is noted to have had the crumbling Sheikhupura Fort repaired, and bedecked with Pahari paintings.

Another wife of the Maharaja, Gul Begum, had been a courtesan prior to her marriage. She built her courtly status by directly managing the affairs of her *jagir* and dismissing officers from appropriating the position on her behalf.

The queen regent

Jind Kaur was the youngest wife of Maharaja Ranjit Singh and the mother of Dalip Singh (see pp.218–219), the last ruler of the Sikh Empire. Her father had been a keeper of the kennels in the

> "The Maharaja's **reign** was **built** with the **help** of his **family**—his **queens** and his princes."
>
> PRIYA ATWAL, *ROYALS AND REBELS: THE RISE AND FALL OF THE SIKH EMPIRE*, 2020

ruler's palace, and he suggested the marriage with his daughter as a means of social progression for his family. When her son inherited the throne as a nine-year-old, she served as regent on his behalf between 1843 and 1846. In order to do so, however, she had to wrench power from other contenders.

As regent, Jind Kaur was handed the challenge of reigning over an empire that had begun disintegrating after the Maharaja's demise. While she appointed ministers to handle administrative duties, she personally met with the Khalsa soldiers to unify the splintering allegiances among the troops. Her attempts failed after her brother killed Peshaura Singh, one of Ranjit Singh's sons, earning the wrath of the Khalsa, who put him to death.

Contemporary poet Shah Mohamad's *Jangnama* (Book of War) claims that Jind Kaur started the first Anglo-Sikh war to take revenge on the Khalsa. Other Sikh sources suggest that the relationship between the queen regent and the army had not yet fractured to such an extent. Rival forces and growing unrest made the Sikh Empire vulnerable to attack from English forces. The British won and restored control of a much smaller empire to Jind Kaur, who continued to exert influence and garner support despite her defeat. This prompted the British to impose labels of debauchery and misrule on her. Eventually, a British official was appointed as Dalip Singh's guardian.

Jind Kaur's continued influence over the court led the British to banish her to the Sheikhupura Fort, separating her from her young son. This made her a symbolic figure of resistance for the Sikhs, who had rallied under her during the 1848 Sikh rebellions (see p.207). She was finally arrested, but managed to escape to Nepal, where she stayed until she was reunited with Dalip Singh a decade later, when she was no longer considered a threat. She lived with him in England until her death in 1863.

Immortalized on canvas by Victorian painter George Richmond, in this 1863 oil portrait from London, Maharani Jind Kaur can be seen draped in exquisite jewelry. This is one of the most iconic portraits of the legendary queen.

► **This portrait of Maharani Chand Kaur**, by an unidentified artist, depicts her in bright royal attire, writing on a piece of parchment.

Chand Kaur

Chand Kaur's ambition was great, but her rule was short. The widow of the second Sikh Maharaja, Kharak Singh, she declared herself regent to her unborn grandchild in an attempt to thwart other claims to the throne.

The deaths of Kharak Singh and Nau Nihal Singh, the second and third Maharajas of the Sikh Empire in 1840, left the seat of the ruler vacant with no legitimate heir to claim the throne. Chand Kaur, who was the Maharani of the Sikh Empire through her marriage to Kharak Singh, and carried the title of Rajmata during her son's brief reign, seized power. This was to stall claims to the throne from her husband's half-brother, Sher Singh. In this period of intrigue, Chand Kaur managed to rule, albeit for a short while.

Role as regent

Chand Kaur came from the lower echelons of the Kanhaiya *misl*. Her marriage to the Kharak Singh was a result of the efforts of Sada Kaur, the leader of her *misl* and the first mother-in-law of Ranjit Singh. Sada Kaur was not directly related to the heir to the throne, and she wanted to retain some of her own authority in the Empire by arranging the match.

Chand Kaur, after the deaths of her husband and son, made a claim to the throne in 1840. This was not surprising since many women before her, such as Sada Kaur, had held positions of power in the Sikh Empire. Her own position, first as queen and then as Rajmata, bestowed her with the required legitimacy. It also worked in her favor that she appealed for support by insisting that she was ruling as the regent, and therefore not for herself, but on behalf of her unborn grandson.

Factional contestations

Despite the backing of influential men in the court, including Ranjit Singh's trusted ministers Fakir Azizuddin and Gulab Singh (see p.181), Chand Kaur did not accede to the position unrivaled. Ranjit Singh's second son, Sher Singh, challenged her rule.

The formation of two factions, each supporting a different leader, explains the contrasting views about Chand Kaur in the accounts of Sohan Lal Suri, her supporter, and Shah Muhammad, her critic. The latter's *Jangnama*

> "… Seikh law recognizes the claims of **females to inheritance**… Chund Kour … shewed how many ladies had **succeeded to the estates of their husbands**…"

H.M. LAWRENCE, *RECENT HISTORY OF PUNJAB*, 1844

contains misogynistic undertones that lay blame on the women, including Chand Kaur and Jind Kaur, in the Empire's eventual downfall. It also upheld Sher Singh as the legitimate heir to the throne. Suri's *Umdat-Ut-tawarikh,* on the contrary, points to the unjust attitude and actions of Sher Singh. These opposing views about Chand Kaur's claim to the throne can also be attributed to the past allegiances of the families of the writers.

Factionalism within the court intensified, with Chand Kaur coming to power, and splitting the courtiers and soldiers into two parties. Sher Singh launched an attack on Chand Kaur's forces in early January 1841, a mere month after she took over as regent. Within a few days of the siege, Chand Kaur was forced to surrender and sign a treaty giving up her claim as regent. Despite her eventual defeat, Chand Kaur fought passionately to hold on to the throne for as long as she could.

However, the stillbirth of her grandchild ended the last vestiges of legitimacy on her claim, and she retired to her son's home in Lahore. Despite this, Chand Kaur's position and presence in the city remained a threat to Sher Singh. A few months later, he conspired with Dhian Singh and had her murdered in her chambers.

Today, the only female ruler of the Sikh Empire is memorialized in a *samadhi* (shrine) in Lahore.

▶ **A lithograph of Maharaja Sher Singh**, who succeeded Chand Kaur to the throne, created in 1844 by Emily Eden, a correspondent of Queen Victoria of England.

Fall of the Sikh Empire

Maharaja Ranjit Singh's death in June 1839 set in motion a long period of turmoil within the Sikh Empire. Assassinations, coups, political maneuvering, and frequent changes in leadership left his Empire vulnerable to external influences.

The changes in succession that followed Maharaja Ranjit Singh's death led to the splintering of the Sikh Empire's administration and army into different factions. This weakened the foundation of the consolidated kingdom and ultimately led to a series of civil battles.

In 1839, the throne passed on to Ranjit Singh's first son, Kharak Singh. Though he was the legitimate heir, his administration was ineffectual and his reign lasted a little over a year. His only prominent achievements were the conquest of the states of Mandi, Saket, and Kulu in the hills, in the northern part of India. It is also during this period that his son,

Nau Nihal Singh, began trying to wrest power. As Kharak Singh's health started to decline, Nau Nihal Singh conspired to kill the court advisor and take over the kingdom.

Kharak Singh's death on November 5, 1840, made Nau Nihal Singh the next ruler, but this succession was short-lived. As Nau Nihal Singh returned from his father's funeral the next day, a gate fell on him, killing him. There was no legitimate ruler left to take over the Sikh Empire.

The vacant throne caused friction between Chand Kaur, the mother of Nau Nihal Singh, who took over as regent (see pp.198–199), and Sher Singh, the half-brother of Kharak Singh,

who was also vying for the seat. Within mere weeks of Chand Kaur taking over as regent, she was ousted in a coup by Sher Singh. This not only replaced the ruler but also caused animosity between the new administration and the factions that opposed Sher Singh. These political differences split the army into diverging allegiances and paved the way for rebellions in places such as Multan, Peshawar, Mandi, and Kashmir. The growing animosity ultimately resulted in Sher Singh's death, passing the throne onto Dalip Singh, who was five years old.

Contending with conspiracies

Besides Ranjit Singh's family, there were others who had eyes on the throne too. Gulab and Dhian Singh, the Dogra brothers who had been trusted administrators under Ranjit Singh, were now tempted to take advantage of the political chaos for personal gain. Siding with one or the other successor, they continued to conspire behind the scenes. Some accounts suggest that Nau Nihal Singh was killed by Dhian Singh, who had been his prime minister.

GULAB SINGH'S ROLE IN CHAND KAUR'S COURT

Gulab Singh repeatedly stole massive amounts of wealth from the state treasury and *jagirs* (revenue estates), transferring the riches to his stronghold in Jammu. Moreover, while claiming loyalty to Chand Kaur, he discreetly forged relations with Sher Singh, offering him the Koh-i-Noor, taken from the Lahore treasury, to profess his loyalty.

Dhian Singh, eager for his son Hira Singh to sit on the throne of the Sikh Empire, plotted to remove Chand Kaur and Sher Singh. He sent his brother to spy on Chand Kaur's court, while siding with Sher Singh, ultimately supporting the coup, and later aiding in her assassination.

Under Sher Singh's rule, Dhian Singh went on to enjoy a high seat. He secured good positions in court for his brother and son, and eventually got enough support to challenge Sher Singh's authority. However, Dhian Singh's past activities had not gone unnoticed. The Sandhanwalia clan, relatives of Chand Kaur, eager to avenge her death, assassinated both, vacating the throne for the last ruler of the Sikh Empire.

▼ **Ranjit Singh's tomb,** a mausoleum which features a large, ribbed dome, located in the Hazuri Bagh complex in Lahore, Pakistan, is depicted in this photograph dating c. 1863.

Weapons of the Sikh Empire

A potent force that faced several battles and invaders, Maharaja Ranjit Singh's army wielded many superior weapons. These form an intrinsic part of the martial history and military heritage of the Sikh Empire.

▶ **Dhal (shield)**
A steel *dhal* from the mid-19th century, adorned with depictions of a possible hunting scene with leaping animals and Maharaja Ranjit Singh riding an elephant.

◀ **Gold and ivory sword**
Maharaja Ranjit Singh gifted this sword to General Van Cortland, a commander of the Sikh forces in the Punjab.

Blessings for the Maharaja inscribed in gold, in the Gurmukhi script

The central stern is modeled after a double-edged dagger

▲ **Flintlock pistol**
Maharaja Ranjit Singh's flintlock pistol c. 1830–1839, with the barrel inlaid with gold at the front and the top.

◀ **Gajgah**
These "elephant Grapplers" are a set of totems that adorn the *dastar banga* of the Akalis. Tied with wire over the towering turbans, the *gajgah* has a central stern, a nasal guard, and curving crescents.

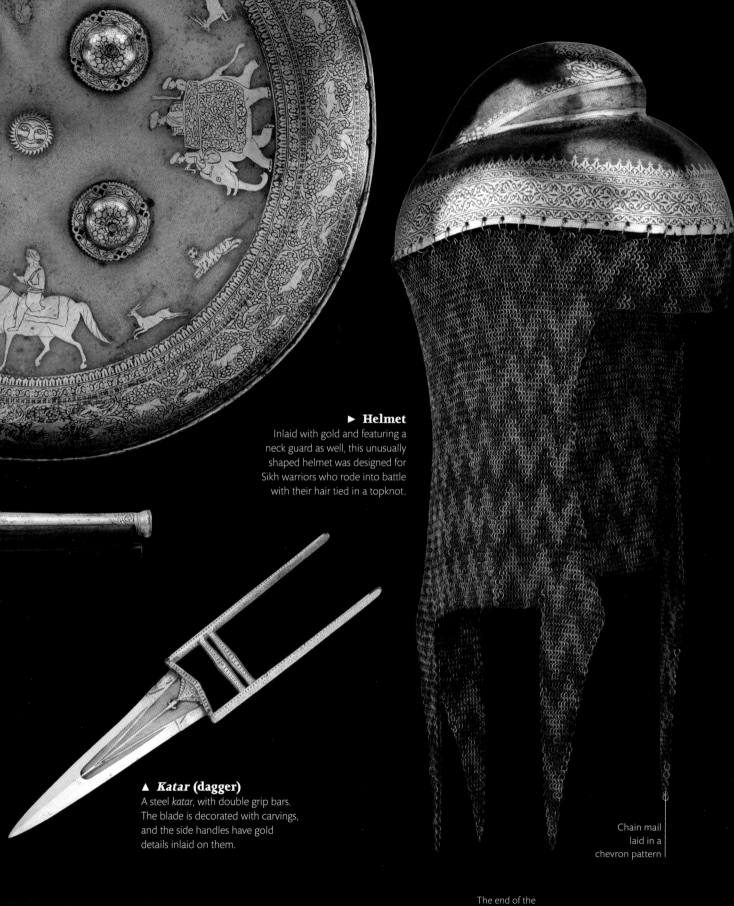

▶ **Helmet**
Inlaid with gold and featuring a
neck guard as well, this unusually
shaped helmet was designed for
Sikh warriors who rode into battle
with their hair tied in a topknot.

▲ *Katar* (dagger)
A steel *katar*, with double grip bars.
The blade is decorated with carvings,
and the side handles have gold
details inlaid on them.

Chain mail
laid in a
chevron pattern

The end of the
scabbard is embellished
with gold and
semiprecious stones.

The Anglo-Sikh Wars

The six years of the Sikh Empire were characterized by infighting as Sikh leaders sought to wrest power amid the rise of the British as a source of opposition. This culminated in two Anglo-Sikh Wars in the latter half of the 1850s, which ultimately allowed the British to take complete control of Punjab.

On September 15, 1843, the young Dalip Singh was placed upon the throne, with his mother Jind Kaur as regent and Hira Singh Dogra as prime minister. Being the son of Ranjit Singh did not guarantee a peace, however, and rivals soon cropped up both internally and externally. From within the Empire, Hira Singh's uncle and founder of the Dogra Dynasty, Gulab Singh; Dalip Singh's brothers Kashmira Singh and Peshora Singh; and the Sandhanwalia clan all challenged the arrangement. Then there was the larger threat in the form of the East India Company (EIC), which had consolidated its rule in almost all other parts of India and was now looking toward Punjab.

The internal rebellion was quelled after Hira Singh's forces attacked and killed Kashmira Singh and the Sandhanwalia chief, but fractures

emerged within the Sikh army as it considered Hira Singh an outsider who had eliminated a son of Ranjit Singh. Eventually, Hira Singh was put to death, and Dalip Singh's mother Jind Kaur became more proactive as the intermediary between the ruler and his Empire (See pp.218–219). Later, Jind Kaur's brother Jawahar Singh managed to contain Peshora Singh's rebellion and ordered for him to be killed. This incited the Sikh army even further and Jawahar Singh was murdered to avenge the prince's death in 1845.

The British watched these developments with great interest, at times meeting different Sikh players or passively meddling in court politics. However, the increasing supremacy of the army coupled with the growing instability within Punjab was a cause of alarm for the EIC. So, the British began preparing to annex the region under the new governor general Lord Charles Hardinge. They mobilized an army near the Sutlej River, and assembled fleets on the river under the excuse of an increase in commercial traffic. By December of 1845, their military units had assembled at Ferozepur.

The First Anglo–Sikh War

The Sikh army was acutely aware of their administrators' collusions with the East India Company. They also knew of the British advances and readied themselves to fight back. On December 11, 1845, the Sikh army stormed into British territory beyond Sutlej, launching the first Anglo-Sikh war. The war lasted for three months, generating heavy casualties on either side. Despite the loss of Ladwa, a key town, the army managed a few victories initially. However, they soon faced a major setback at Ferozeshah, where they met with the betrayal of their General Tej Singh, who

▼ This sketch by Major G.F. White of the British 31st Regiment depicts his men fighting the Sikh army during the second day of battle, at Ferozeshah, in 1845.

had struck a deal with the British to supply information. Soon, others, such as Gulab Singh Dogra, who later founded the Dogra Dynasty, also forged secret alliances with the British, undermining the power of the Sikh Empire.

When the British paused to reinforce its weaponry in January of 1846, the Sikhs swooped in to capture various strongholds, including Ludhiana, under Ranjodh Singh Majithia and Ajit Singh Ladwa. However, the British, along with their reinforcements, managed to win back these territories, handing a major defeat to the Sikhs at Aliwal.

The final battle took place at Sabraon where the British surrounded the Sikhs and unleashed a devastating defeat, thereby winning the war.

Treaty of Lahore

The loss effectively turned Punjab into British territory. The subsequent Treaty of Lahore only further weakened the political force of the Sikh Empire. It recognized Dalip Singh as the sovereign and Jind Kaur as the regent, but actual authority rested with the British Resident Henry Lawrence, who oversaw all decisions (see pp. 218–219). The regions between the Rivers Beas and Indus were seized as war indemnity, and handed to Gulab Singh Dogra, who had aided their victory. Nine months later, a new treaty was created that put the British in charge of Dalip Singh until he came of age, dismissing their rival Jind Kaur from power and imprisoning her. This sudden shift in

▲ A lithograph by **Dr. John Dunlop, assistant** surgeon to the 32nd Regiment of the British Army, portrays the army fighting in the trenches of Multan during the second Anglo-Sikh War.

In brief

September 15, 1843
Dalip Singh is crowned

December 1843
Jind Kaur takes over the reigns

December 3, 1845
British cut diplomatic ties with the Sikh Empire

December 11, 1845
The first Anglo-Sikh war begins

December 30, 1845
Tej Singh betrays the Sikh army

March 9, 1846
Treaty of Lahore is signed between the Sikhs and the British

December 16, 1846
The Treaty of Bhairowal is signed and Jind Kaur is deposed

April 1848
Rebellion in Multan

August 1848
Rebellion in Hazara

November 22, 1848
Battle of Ramnagar

January 1849
Battle of Chillianwala and the siege of Multan

January 21, 1849
Battle of Gujrat (fought in modern-day Punjab Province of Pakistan)

power dynamics sparked new rebellions and allegiances, especially rallying around Jind Kaur, who became the central figure of Sikh revolt.

The Second Anglo–Sikh War

British interference in the politics of Multan prompted a full-fledged rebellion from the Sikhs in that city under their governor Diwan Mulraj, and resulted in the deaths of two Englishmen in April 1848. The British accused Jind Kaur as the instigator and banished her to Benaras, in present-day Uttar Pradesh. This led to great unrest and protests even among those Sikh administrators who had, in the past, sided with the British.

In August, military commander Chattar Singh Attariwala launched his own revolt against the British, bringing more Sikhs into the cause, as did his son Sher Singh Attariwala. These widespread rebellions gave Lord Dalhousie, the new governor general, an excuse to declare war against the Sikh Empire. Mulraj and Attariwala became the two primary agencies of resistance during the second Anglo-Sikh war. The army under Sher Singh Attariwala bested the British troops at Ramnagar in November 1848 and then again at Chillianwala in January the next year, despite being weaker in numbers. A few days later, however, British troops succeeded in their

DECEIT IN THE FIRST ANGLO-SIKH WAR

The British won the Battle of Sabraon during the First Anglo-Sikh War, owing to their clandestine deals and deceptive pacts with various Sikh players. In addition to receiving reports from General Tej Singh about movements of the Sikh army, the British also forged a relationship with Gulab Singh Dogra, who was ready to win favors while watching the Sikh Empire fall. Such arrangements were condemned by those on both sides, including British historian J.D. Cunningham. After winning the battle and the war, the British appointed Gulab Singh Dogra as the ruler of Jammu and Kashmir.

siege of Multan, forcing Diwan Mulraj to give up his fort. The Sikhs fought a final battle against the British but were vastly outnumbered. They were defeated, and Sher Singh Attariwala was forced to surrender on March 11, one day before the same fate met the Sikh army.

The Lahore Durbar assembled for the last time on March 29, 1849, with Dalip Singh on the throne before the Sikh Empire and all of its wealth passed into British hands. The monarch was exiled and later sent to England. With the king deposed, the Koh-i-Noor diamond (see pp.188–189) ceded to Queen Victoria, and a new administration in Punjab, the Sikh Empire came to an end in its fortieth year.

This 19th-century painting in the Pahari style depicts the December 1846 Treaty of Bhairowal between the East India Company and Maharaja Dalip Singh. The king is accompanied by thirteen members of his court. An interesting aspect of the painting is that it provides an interior and exterior view of the tent, and the soldiers that stand guard outside.

5

Sikhism During the British Rule

1850–1947

In 1849, the British annexed the Sikh Empire. Exploitation, recession, and evolution marked this period of colonial rule. Managers of gurdwaras and religious leaders were co-opted by the administration, which triggered reformist efforts within the faith, such as the Singh Sabha movement. It also ignited the fire for independence.

Punjab under British rule

The British annexation of Punjab in 1849 transformed the nature of administration in the province. Not only did the new government change the economic structure of Punjab, it also implemented concrete measures that had an impact on the entire population.

▲ Illustration of Maharaja **Dalip Singh** visiting the British camp after the annexation of Punjab.

In 1849, Maharaja Dalip Singh and the British signed the Treaty of Lahore in the Lahore Durbar following which the Sikh Empire officially came under the latter's jurisdiction. As a territory of the British, the contours of the kingdom were administered under the province of Punjab, which encompassed various villages, towns, and even some princely states. A Board of Administration comprising of officials of the East India Company (EIC), which had been formed in 1600 to enable British trade in the Indian Ocean, would manage affairs in the Punjab. Following the Battle of Plassey in 1757, the Company had begun laying claim to the political sovereignty of the subcontinent. The onset of colonial rule integrated the province of Punjab into the expanding political geography of British rule over the entire subcontinent, bringing about several administrative shifts.

Administrative changes

Much like the rest of India, Punjab acquired new forms of transportation and communication such as the railways, telegraphs, and postal

BOARD OF ADMINISTRATION IN PUNJAB

Following the annexation of Punjab in 1849, the East India Company formed a Board of Administration that had both military and civilian administrators. The Board of fifty-six officials was helmed by Henry Lawrence, who served as president and also supervised defense matters; John Lawrence, who overlooked fiscal matters; and C.G. Mansel, who managed law and order. The Board was dissolved in 1853, after internal tensions heightened. Thereafter, the province was governed by a chief commissioner.

19th-century portrait of British administrator Henry Lawrence.

system by the mid-19th century. The province became even more accessible with the Grand Trunk Road, the construction of canals, and the regularization of taxes. The colonial government emphasized the implementation of revised revenue settlement systems, agricultural production, and irrigation projects.

While the Sikh Empire disintegrated, the British government had to contend with a large number of Sikh estate holders who wished to preserve their authority. The new administration chose to appease them by either monetarily compensating them or allowing them to retain some of their land, which in turn fostered an allegiance to the British. This sop, however, was denied to those Sikh leaders who had actively opposed the British, including Jawahar Singh Nalwa, Sardar Chattar Singh Attariwala, and Raja Sher Singh.

Changing social landscape

The administrative changes conformed with the Company's practice of exploitation in the name of increasing trade and economic process across India and even beyond, with the gains largely oriented toward Britain. On the sociocultural front, the government tried to imprint its mark by introducing English and western sciences into the education system, but it was eventually forced to restrict most institutions to the vernacular. The pedagogical incursions were allied with Christian missionaries, who tried to reform the linguistic and religious cultures of the province.

The administrative setup transformed the nature and lifestyles of the demography in Punjab, which had to adjust to a very different

system of rule that provided negligible representation. The land reforms increased revenues to some extent, but their exploitative nature continued. This left several peasants, especially small farmers, impoverished. At the same time, the system enabled the growth of middlemen, traders, and moneylenders who flourished through the commercialization of agricultural produce. In urban spaces, a middle class emerged, one that had received education in English, which sequentially opened up new avenues of employment under the British.

◄ **Coat of Arms of the East India Company,** a symbol of Queen Elizabeth I's royal patronage, featuring roses, sea lions, and ships.

In brief

June 23, 1757
The East India Company becomes the ruler of Bengal with victory in the Battle of Plassey

March 29, 1849
Establishment of the Board of Administration in the British Province of Punjab

1853
Abolition of the Board of Administration

"The **introduction** of the British administration … brought profound changes to Punjabi society … **colonial** rulers … established a **new** kind of **relationship** between the **individual** and the **state**."

PASHAURA SINGH, *THE OXFORD HANDBOOK OF SIKH STUDIES*, 2014

Weapons from the Anglo-Sikh Wars

Maharaja Ranjit Singh's efforts to create and acquire modern weapons, and train his soldiers in war tactics and traditional fighting, proved effective in establishing a strong Sikh army. These superior-quality weapons were employed during the Anglo-Sikh Wars in the late 1850s.

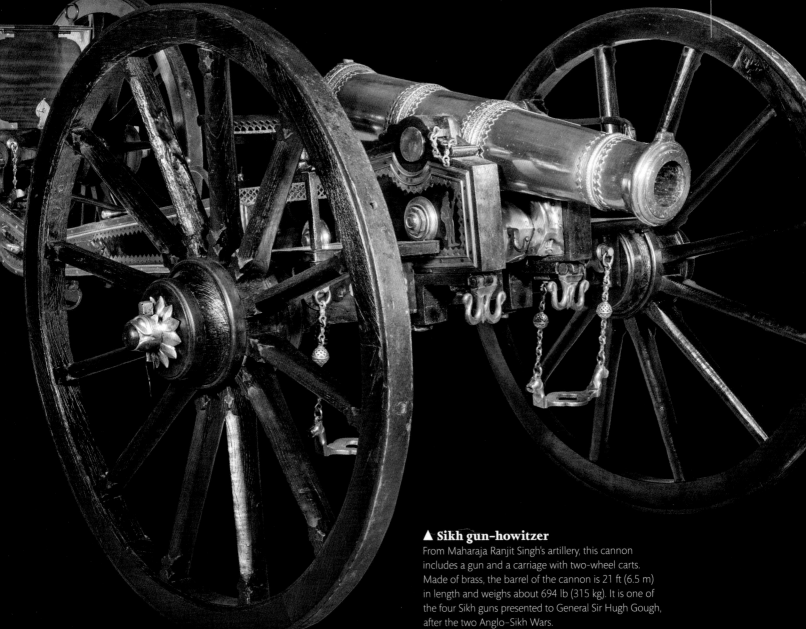

The wheels are 4.9 ft (1.5 m) in diameter

▲ Sikh gun–howitzer
From Maharaja Ranjit Singh's artillery, this cannon includes a gun and a carriage with two-wheel carts. Made of brass, the barrel of the cannon is 21 ft (6.5 m) in length and weighs about 694 lb (315 kg). It is one of the four Sikh guns presented to General Sir Hugh Gough, after the two Anglo–Sikh Wars.

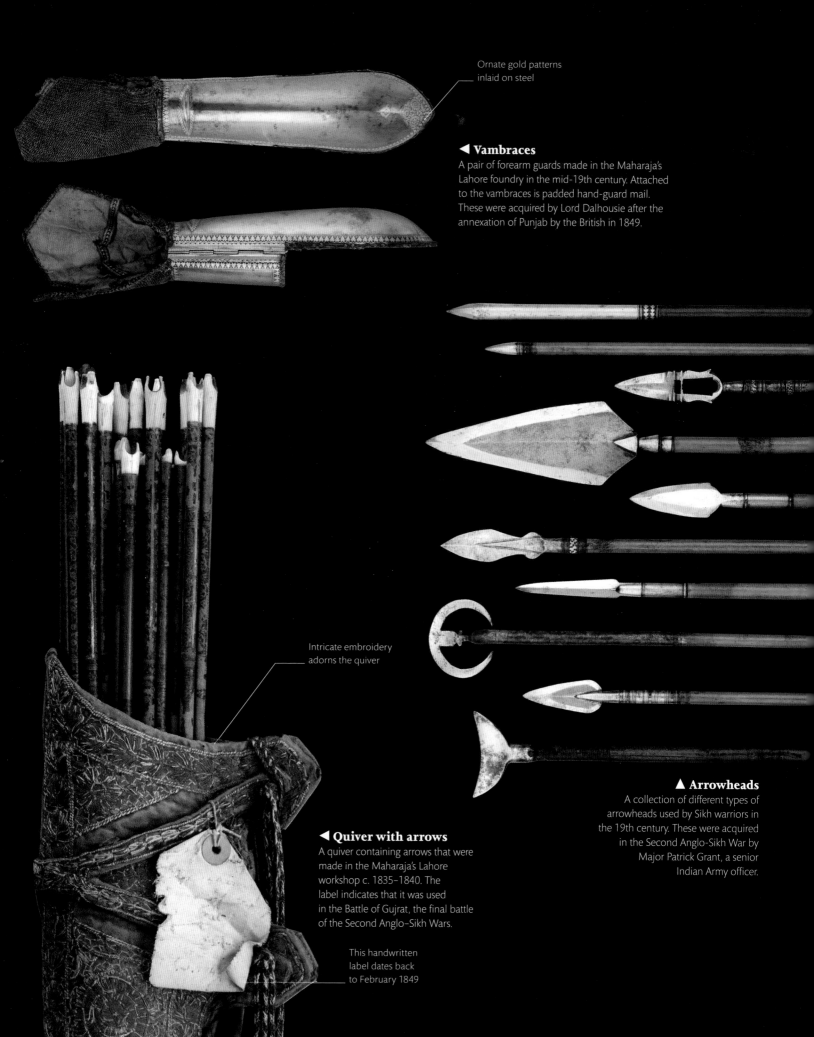

Ornate gold patterns
inlaid on steel

◀ Vambraces

A pair of forearm guards made in the Maharaja's
Lahore foundry in the mid-19th century. Attached
to the vambraces is padded hand-guard mail.
These were acquired by Lord Dalhousie after the
annexation of Punjab by the British in 1849.

Intricate embroidery
adorns the quiver

◀ Quiver with arrows

A quiver containing arrows that were
made in the Maharaja's Lahore
workshop c. 1835–1840. The
label indicates that it was used
in the Battle of Gujrat, the final battle
of the Second Anglo–Sikh Wars.

This handwritten
label dates back
to February 1849

▲ Arrowheads

A collection of different types of
arrowheads used by Sikh warriors in
the 19th century. These were acquired
in the Second Anglo-Sikh War by
Major Patrick Grant, a senior
Indian Army officer.

British policy toward Sikhs

After the annexation of Punjab in 1849, the British government tried to align the community with British objectives in the region. Strict measures were taken to assert its authority over Sikh leaders and Khalsa soldiers who were prone to rebellion.

The British government took steady measures to reduce the influence of Sikh leaders by discarding the *jagirs* (estates) of those who had fought the British. The government confiscated all the property and valuables it could lay its hands on, some of which was shipped back to England, including the Koh-i-Noor diamond from the Lahore treasury. The Board of Administration (see p.213) established a strong military and police force in the province. It had a large number of Muslims, but offered restricted employment for the Sikhs.

Restrictions and exiles

A measure to suppress resistance and maintain complete control was the imposition of exiles on rebels or leaders. The foremost example of this was the royal family; in 1854, Maharaja Dalip Singh was dethroned and sent to England to live under close supervision, while the queen regent was deposed and later imprisoned. A similar fate met other rebel leaders in Punjab, such as Bhai Maharaj Singh. A devout Sikh, he rallied his followers against the British, even calling for the assassination of the Resident, Henry Lawrence, an act which led to his exile to Singapore in 1850.

In brief

1849
The British start ruling Punjab

1850
Bhai Maharaj Singh is exiled to Singapore

1854
Maharaja Dalip Singh is sent to Britain

Bhai Maharaj Singh standing in a prison cell.

THE EXILE OF BHAI MAHARAJ SINGH

Bhai Maharaj Singh, the head of the Naurangabad Dera, actively opposed the British and was arrested for his insurgency in December 1849. He was exiled to Singapore the next year where he was held in solitary confinement at the Outram Prison. He died of an illness six years later. During his incarceration, Maharaj Singh requested the Governor General of the Straits Settlement for a copy of the Guru Granth Sahib. This was the first copy of the holy book to be sent to Singapore from India.

Social and religious control

The modernizing and westernizing aim of the British government had a deep impact on the Sikh community. The British set up new administrative structures, imposed western education in English, and encouraged Christian missionaries. They rejected traditional Indian education, philosophy, and religions, placing them at a lower level of intellectual hierarchy. Sikhs were impacted by this; some embraced the new system, converting to Christianity. On the other hand, it also led to a revivalist movement by Hindus and Sikhs who tried to counter British education by creating their own institutions.

The British followed a policy of appeasement of landlords in Punjab—they were even inducted into the British administration. However, the region suffered due to of a lack of an English-speaking middle class.

The Board of Administration was also eager to take control over the gurdwaras, havens of Sikh congregation. It established favorable ties with

> "As pieces of a **complicated** game every station in the Punjab now required attention and defense. The deluge of **rebellion**, but just shut in at Mooltan, **threatened** daily to inundate the land."

SIR EDWIN ARNOLD, THE MARQUIS OF DALHOUSIE'S ADMINISTRATION OF BRITISH INDIA

the Bhais, Sardars, and Mahants who were vested with the management of the gurdwaras under appointed committees. The Harmandir Sahib in Amritsar was administered by Sikh commanders, Raja Tej Singh and Sardar Jodh Singh. The appointments of all functionaries were made with the aim of regulating the activities of the Sikhs.

Changes in the community

The British suppression had an adverse impact on members of the Khalsa Army as well. Many were dismissed from their roles after the wars and no longer allowed to continue their military fervor. For sustenance and in rebellion, the demobbed soldiers roamed the districts of Punjab as dacoits and robbers, as they were left without a livelihood. This engendered further retaliation from the British government, which appointed a superintendent to clamp down on them and supervise their movement.

The other outcome of the soldiers' expulsion was a growing disaffection of Hindus within the Sikh fold. A large number of Hindus had turned to Sikhism in previous years encouraged by the Khalsa army that was capable of giving protection to all under it. The structure of the army made it possible for those Hindus that chose so, to be able to follow their own cultural customs and practices.

When the Khalsa Army was disbanded, such followers returned to mainstream Hinduism, which cemented the distinction between the two religions in an even more rigid manner.

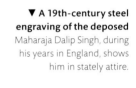

▼ A 19th-century steel engraving of the deposed Maharaja Dalip Singh, during his years in England, shows him in stately attire.

A maharaja without a kingdom

After the death of Sher Singh, Dalip Singh ascended the throne in 1843 at the age of five and went on to become an exiled dependant of the British state. His tragic life was marked by political intrigue and unrealized potential.

> "… there is something **too painful** in the idea of a **young deposed sovereign**, once so **powerful**, receiving a **pension**, and having no **security**…"

QUEEN VICTORIA'S LETTER TO LORD DALHOUSIE ABOUT
MAHARAJA DALIP SINGH, DATED OCTOBER 2, 1854

Ushered to the throne at the age of five, Dalip Singh found himself in the midst of political intrigue. His seat of authority never implied his actual rule; his mother, Jind Kaur, governed on his behalf.

Dependant of the British

Maharaja Dalip Singh was only nine when he was separated from his mother and regent, Jind Kaur, after the signing of the 1846 Treaty of Bhairowal. It made the British masters of the Sikh Empire. Dalip Singh handed over the Koh-i-noor diamond and stepped down from the illustrious throne. Henry Lawrence, Britain's Resident to Lahore, became Dalip Singh's guardian and the new regent, with the promise of merely holding the seat until the young king was of age at sixteen. In *Maharaja Duleep Singh Correspondence*, historian Ganda Singh asserts, "The worst hit and the most unjustly treated person in this affair was the innocent young Maharaja Duleep Singh who, for no fault of his, came to be reduced from a sovereign ruler to an exile, to be at the mercy of the British Government of India and England."

A king in exile

Tutors were organized for Dalip Singh to learn English and receive a western education. Under constant observation, Dalip Singh was limited to his quarters. Lawrence and his teachers were the only ones with access to the young king. He went hunting and riding but was kept away from administrative and military affairs.

After the Second Anglo-Sikh War in 1849, Lord Dalhousie, the Governor General of India, ordered Dalip Singh's exile from the Punjab, fearful of resentful Sikhs rallying around him. He was sent to the small village of Fatehgarh in the United Provinces in 1850, under the guardianship of Dr John Login, governor of Lahore. Surrounded by the children of serving officers,

Dalip Singh lived there without any contact with his countrymen. Here, he was introduced to Christianity and, in 1853, he quietly became a Christian.

In 1854, Dalip Singh sailed for England and that was the last he saw of Punjab. The British took this step to obliterate all that remained of the once powerful Sikh empire. He was received favorably by Queen Victoria, who took a liking to him, so much so that she commissioned paintings of Dalip Singh. She even sketched him herself. By now, Dalip Singh's Sikh identity had been all but erased. He was molded into an English aristocrat, who lived on a fixed stipend from the British and led an indulgent life.

An exile of no return

Despite his desire to return to India, Dalip Singh was only allowed to go back in 1861, where he met his mother after fifteen years, in Bengal, far away from Punjab. After her passing in 1864, he spent the next years of his life on his estate in England. Eventually, disaffected and embittered with the British, he sought to revive the Sikh Empire. The British discovered that he had rekindled ties with Sikh leaders, and was on his way to India when he was intercepted at Aden in Yemen. The British government in India believed that Maharaja Ranjit Singh still had many devoted followers who would rally around his son. This is why, perhaps, the government declared him an outlaw and forbade him from traveling to India. In 1886, Dalip Singh returned to the Sikh faith by undergoing an initiation ceremony (see pp.108–109) at Aden. He moved to Paris, where he conspired with Irish revolutionaries in a bid to regain his lost kingdom. He even traveled to Moscow in 1887 in an attempt to garner the support of Russians to invade Punjab, but to no avail. Dejected, he returned to Paris in 1888, where the heir to the once legendary Sikh Empire perished in 1893, in a shabby hotel room, partially paralyzed and in penury. *The Tribune*, a newspaper, reported, "… [at the time of his passing] there was no one with him to close his eyes."

◀ **A vintage print of a** young Dalip Singh with his mother, the regent Jind Kaur.

The 1857 Mutiny

When a band of soldiers mutinied against the British in 1857, there were a number of reasons why Sikh response was muted. Among these were the memories of the Anglo–Sikh Wars and the subsequent annexation of Punjab.

On May 10, 1857, a group of soldiers in Meerut rose in mutiny against their British employers, setting off a wave of rebellion that spread through parts of India. Within the Sikh community, some stood with the mutineers, but many aided the British, guided by a variety of complex motivations.

By the time the events of the 1857 revolt took place, Punjab had been annexed by the East India Company, and the events of the Anglo-Sikh Wars were still fresh in the community's memory. The powerful Sikh Empire that Maharaja Ranjit Singh had built had dissipated, and now a substantial number of Sikhs had been recruited into the British army.

The Purbia problem

The Sikh support of the British during the rebellion, for the most part, stemmed from the former's conflict with the Purbias. The Purbia garrison was part of the Bengal unit of the British army which aided the British during the Anglo-Sikh wars (see pp.204–207), and that saw the fall of the Sikh Empire. Later, the Purbias stationed in Punjab suppressed the Sikh army, leaving them without arms and any avenue to reconsolidate. So, when the garrison mutinied a mere ten years later, the civilian Sikhs were not particularly inclined to offer support, aligning themselves with the British by default.

The British turned to appeasement tactics to further garner Sikh support. The hostility toward the Mughals stood as another justification for the Sikhs to help suppress the revolt, as the mutineers had elected Emperor Bahadur Shah Zafar as their nominal head.

Supporters and dissenters

The Mutiny was restricted in Punjab by a large number of Phulkian and Jalandhar Doab states in the Cis-Sutlej region. In Patiala and Jind, Sikh soldiers restrained the movement of rebels into these districts, while the troops of the Nabha state provided protection to a siege train carrying reinforcements from the Chief Commissioner of Punjab, John Lawrence, to Delhi. Soldiers of the Kapurthala and Faridkot states went in large numbers to quell the uprising in Awadh. Moreover, the Phulkian states were strategically located to monitor communication from pro-Mutiny Sikhs in central Punjab to Bahadur Shah Zafar in Delhi. For this support, in 1861, Mahendra Singh, the Maharaja of Patiala, was nominated to the Governor General's Legislative Council.

When the British had established two battalions in Punjab in 1846, the total number of Sikhs in the British army was no more than a few thousand. Despite their small numbers, these regiments joined the Revolt in Benares and Delhi. Some Sikhs were arrested and executed in 1858, the first of whom was a man from Ropar. Raja Nahar Singh of the Ballabhgarh princely state was also an active opponent of the British during the Mutiny. He was charged with sedition by the British for raising an army and weapons to capture the road to Delhi, and was hanged.

> "The **motives** that brought the Punjab and the border to our **aid**, were no doubt **mixed** ones. Some content with our administration, some liking for English ways … all had, no doubt **their place**."
>
> MAJOR G.F. MACMUNN, *THE ARMIES OF INDIA*, 1911

A change in policy

Despite the divergent responses by the Sikhs during the Revolt of 1857, the British government acquired an admiration for their military prowess that had been showcased during the Anglo-Sikhs Wars and through the suppression of the rebels in 1857. From 1858, a large number of Sikhs were recruited into the British army as they were perceived as loyal fighters capable of countering even foreign attacks owing to their training. This allowed various Sikh farmers to find a more viable source of employment and also engendered the revival of the Khalsa culture, which was constricted in the years following the annexation of Punjab.

Sikh soldiers of the British 15th Punjab Regiment pose for a photograph with their weapons in 1858.

This late 19th-century photograph depicts Sikh troops in the North West Frontier Province (a region now in Pakistan). Earlier occupied by Maharaja Ranjit Singh until the early 19th century, it became part of British India in the aftermath of the Second Sikh War (1848–1849). Sikh infantries were deployed here by the British in the late 19th century to battle the Afghans.

At the crossroads

With the onset of British rule in Punjab, Sikhism encountered a diverse array of other religious movements that emerged from the late 19th century. Many of these directly impacted the Sikhs, in turn making their community reflect on its identity and future course of action.

The British government's suppression of local military activity in Punjab had a major religious consequence in terms of the decline of the largely Sikh army, which was considered hostile owing to its association with the erstwhile Sikh Empire. This also implied a restriction in the number of troops held by Sikh estate holders, who posed a threat to British authority. With the loss of power and prestige, a number of those who had converted to the faith reverted to mainstream practices.

At this time, the British government also started encouraging the inflow of Christian missionaries into Punjab. They not only interacted with the Sikhs in the sphere of education, but also endeavored to convert them to Christianity. Owing to the subsequent conversions that took place across religions, the Christian population surged in Punjab.

Perhaps one of the most distressing events for the community, however, took place in 1853, when the erstwhile Maharaja of Punjab, Dalip Singh, converted to Christianity. That year, a missionary school opened in Amritsar as well. Though initially, author and journalist Khushwant Singh notes, more Sikhs who had lower-caste Hindu associations converted to Christianity, their numbers dwindled, forcing the missionaries to look toward the Jats and Kshatriyas.

THE BRITISH RELIGIOUS POLICY

The latter half of the 19th century was a period of religious ferment in Punjab, marked by the presence of various sects, religious leaders, and saints. All British officials were Christian but the government chose to uphold a more liberal policy toward all Indian faiths in order to uphold law and order in the province. This implied official impartiality but did not condone excessive activity by any religious figure. One example of this policy was the expulsion of Hindu saint Sharda Ram from the city of Phillauri for strongly preaching the Sanskrit epic Mahabharata in a way that sounded like propaganda against the British.

Close up of Christ enthroned in mosaic.

▶ **Indian reformer Raja Ram Mohan Roy** founded the Brahmo Samaj and was responsible for key social reforms in India. This statue of the reformer stands outside Bristol Cathedral in the UK.

Reform movements

Simultaneously, the stress on western thought and rationality by the British engendered certain reforms within Hinduism. It witnessed the emergence of two distinct movements, which later entered Punjab. The first was the Brahmo Samaj, started by Indian reformer Ram Mohan Roy in Bengal. This was a radical movement inspired by the Christian ethic of the missionaries and espoused freedom, equality, and upliftment of the downtrodden.

The Arya Samaj, started by Indian philosopher Swami Dayanand Saraswati, was another reform movement. Widespread in Lahore in the late 19th century, it sought to reaffirm the authority of the Vedas and other ancient Hindu texts, and opposed ritual practices and discriminatory social customs. However, the Samaj had very stringent ideas about other religions, including Sikhism. In 1875, Swami Dayanand Saraswati published some of these ideas in his book *Satyarth Prakash*, which led to the beginning of hostilities that continued until the end of the 19th century.

Similar steps toward asserting identity were taken within Islam as well, through associations such as the Anjuman-i-Islamia. These promoted education, social reform, and even dabbled in politics to create a distinct consciousness about the Islamic community in Punjab. The associations established schools and orphanages that embraced western education as supported by the Christian missionaries. These and other factors significantly contributed to the religious melange and helped turn Punjab into a melting pot toward the end of the 19th century.

Changing Sikh consciousness

The continuously changing religious landscape in Punjab became a considerable source of concern for the Sikhs, who were eager to reestablish their identity as well as strengthen and fortify their community. Increasingly they became cognizant of the various steps taken by other religions in order to assert their identity and to appeal to new followers.

Moreover, the Sikhs recognized the need for the internal reform that was being carried out by other contemporary movements of the time. This, they believed, could further define Sikhism and make it more appealing to a wide variety of people. These self-reflections eventually gave rise to various developments within Sikhism, including the Nirankari, Namdhari, and Singh Sabha movements.

▲ A lithograph, c. 1860, depicts a German Protestant missionary speaking to Indians in what appears to be a bazaar.

In brief

1828
Formation of the Brahmo Samaj

1834
Arrival of the first Christian missionary in Punjab

1875
Formation of the Arya Samaj

1883
The Arya Samaj sets up a college in Lahore

1884
Creation of the Anjuman-i-Islamia

"This was the **land of the Sikhs**—a people of **fine physique**, and **unusually independent** character; [who] ... **discarded** the **idolatry** of Hindooism, and [**broke**], in some measure, the **bonds of caste**; and therefore might be **considered** to be in a **favorable** state to be influenced by Christian Missionaries."

HISTORICAL SKETCHES OF THE INDIA MISSIONS

Return to the roots

In the 19th century, the Sikh self-image came under severe threat with British annexation and consequent suppression. Alternate interpretations of what it meant to be a Sikh were presented to the community, and many embraced these ideas. This paved the way for the community's revival in the future.

During the span of the Sikh Empire, the Sikhs were a diverse community comprising fully converted Sikhs, semiconverted Hindus, and Hindus who continued with Brahmanical practices while donning the title of a Sikh. Through the 19th century, this diversity gave the religion a distinct character, and also prompted debates about its essence. It was this self-reflexive consciousness that engendered the birth of various movements within Sikhism.

The Nirankari sect

One of the first to found an offshoot movement was Dayal Das, a Khatri trader who had entered the Sikh fold in the early years of the Sikh Empire. His idea of divinity was opposed to all kinds of rituals and sacrifices, including any form of idol worship or pilgrimage. Instead, it centered on the "nirankari," or formless conception of the Divine. As his idea gained credence, he raised a group of followers around him who styled themselves as the Nirankaris, and stood in opposition to the beliefs of the Brahmins and the Sikh congregation at Rawalpindi, receiving hostility from both groups.

They established their center just outside Rawalpindi in present-day Pakistan. There, they built a temple named Dayalsar and continued their worship even after the founder's death, through veneration to his sandals and the Guru Granth Sahib. The sect continued to flourish many years after Dayal Das's death, when his eldest son Darbara Singh took over the spiritual reins. He established new centers and published spiritual orders for the followers. Darbara Singh's brother Sahib Rattaji succeeded him, followed by his descendants.

The sect shows the highest reverence to the Guru Granth Sahib, but diverges from mainstream Sikhism in the concept of the 10 living Gurus, extending the lineage to Dayal Das and his successors. It also digresses from traditional Hindu ritual practices that allowed it to don an identity of distinction from other mainstream belief systems of that time, marking its significance as a movement.

The Radha Soami Panth

The confluence of Sikh and Hindu traditions also gave rise to the Radha Soami, founded by a Hindu banker, Shiv Dayal Singh. For him, the Divine was a union of the soul, or *radha*, with the master, or *soami*. He built a large following of Hindus and Sikhs by drawing from the teachings in the Adi Granth and Hindu scriptures. His death fractured the sect into congregations, one at Agra and the other by the Beas River under the Sikh Jaimal Singh. His successors led the Beas Radha Soamis. Unlike the Sikhs, Radha Soamis have a living guru who initiates followers as his devotee-in-faith. Reverence is paid to this guru, and worship is devoid of any musical recitation. Teachings of the Sikh Gurus are quoted and used, as are also quotations from other faiths.

The Namdhari movement

A movement oriented toward establishing a distinct Sikh presence in religious and political spheres emerged in the colonial context of the 19th century. Started by Balak Singh, it gained a distinct form with Baba Ram Singh, who preached the importance of the reciting of *naam* or God's name in earning emancipation. He stressed following the Gurus' teachings and living an austere, disciplined life. Singh's *hukamnamas* gave ethical, social, and political directions to this largely underprivileged group of people, who now had self-worth and a distinct identity (see pp.228–229).

AKHAND KIRTANI JATHA

With Brahmanical customs taking root in Sikh traditions of worship, some Sikhs, such as Bhai Randhir Singh, found it unacceptable. He wanted devotees to strictly follow the *rahit maryada*. At the turn of the 20th century, he established a *jatha*, or group. The *jatha* expected its members to follow a strict code which included, among other things, baptism by *amrit*, vegetarianism, and a high moral code of conduct. Their devotion was showcased through *kirtan*, in which the devotees sat together to sing the *gurbani*, thereby earning the name of the Akhand Kirtani Jatha.

> "**Praise** be to the **Formless Creator; Worship of mortals** is of no avail."
>
> DAYAL DAS

In brief

1851
Dayal Das founds the Nirankari sect

1855
Death of Dayal Das

1861
Radha Soami Panth is founded

1878
Shiv Dayal Singh in Agra

1862
Ram Singh Namdhari takes over the Namdhari movement

1872
Sixty-six Namdharis executed by the British after attack in Malerkotla

◄ **A five-rupee coin released in 2015** with an engraving of religious leader and social reformer Ram Singh.

The Namdhari Movement

The name of this movement comes from the sect's emphasis on the practice of repeating God's name. Founded by Balak Singh, the movement advocated the revival of spiritual simplicity, free from materialism.

The Sikh Empire had fallen and the British had annexed Punjab. There were changes within the faith as well as a shift away from spiritual fulfilment. Eventually, reform movements began to make their presence felt, as they laid emphasis on both Sikh identity and a return to the Gurus' philosophy. The Namdharis, or the Kukas, were born during this time, seeking to revive the bonds of brotherhood as well as the restoration of Khalsa glory.

Back to the roots
Namdhari (literally, one whose heart is imbued with the Divine's name) drew its name from the importance the sect placed on chanting God's name, much like Guru Nanak's teachings. Its leader, Balak Singh, began preaching these ideas in Hazro, in the northwest frontier region near Attock in present-day Pakistan. He encouraged his followers to live simply and stressed the importance of *naam simran* (meditating on God's name) as the path to true existence. He also preached the strict adherence to the Khalsa codes (*rahit*).

Casting an identity
In 1857, Balak Singh's disciple Ram Singh took over the sect. Under him, the sect moved from Hazro to Bhaini in the Ludhiana region of present-day Punjab.

Ram Singh introduced several changes during his leadership that contributed to the Namdhari sect developing its own distinct identity. They dressed in modest, hand-spun clothing, wore white, woollen rosaries with 108 knots around their neck, and sported a turban that was tied horizontally across the forehead. They donned all five Khalsa symbols except the *kirpan*, which the state had banned. Instead, they carried a *lathi* (stick). *Havans* (fire ceremonies) and circumambulation of the holy fire during wedding rites were also introduced as a key custom. They also became protectors of the cow. It is during this period that the Namdharis came to be known as Kukas for their frenzied and passionate chanting of hymns in religious meetings.

A political connection
During this time, the Namdharis saw their numbers rapidly multiply, with Jats and Ramgharias from poorer classes making up their strength. This growing fervor attracted the British government's interest. Furthermore, Ram Singh's outspoken opposition to British authority, his condemnation

> "This **ideology** visualized, as is well known, a **nation of heroes**, who would give no quarter to **tyranny** in any form. **Freedom** from political tyranny was not excluded from this; but rather was very much part of the **goal** to be attained. The instructions as well as the personal **example** of **Guru Gobind Singh** left no doubt about it."

DR FAUJA SINGH BAJWA, KUKA MOVEMENT, 1965

of English education and imported mill goods, and his call to his followers to boycott government services led the imperial forces to impose restrictions in 1863. The British kept Ram Singh under strict surveillance and their suspicion of his rising power was expressed in various official exchanges at the time.

The collision between Ram Singh and the British authorities occurred when some Kukas attacked Muslim butchers of Amritsar and Raikot. Various activists were imprisoned and executed. The British also restricted Ram Singh's movement and forbade all assembly during Sikh festivals. However, resisting the orders, the Kukas flocked in their hundreds to Sri Bhaini Sahib, a sacred place of pilgrimage, on the occasion of the Maghi festival in January 1872. This was followed by an attack on the Muslim areas of Malaud Fort and Malerkotla. The district commissioner of Ludhiana then ordered the execution of forty-nine Kukas by cannons, without a trial. The commissioner of Ambala also ordered the execution of sixteen Kukas, after a brief trial. These incidents led to the exile of Ram Singh to Rangoon in Burma, where he remained for fourteen years until his death in 1885.

A photograph of a gathering of Namdhari Sikhs depicts them customarily dressed in white, with rosaries hanging around their neck, and turbans tied in a particular horizontal style across the forehead.

► **The Sikhs** wear a light-colored *keski* (small turban) under the larger *dastar* (turban). as in this image.

Keski and Dastar

The Sikh turbans

A long piece of cloth tied into a turban around the head is an integral part of Sikh practice and identity that goes back several centuries. When Guru Gobind Singh established the Khalsa in 1699, wearing a turban became intrinsically linked to the Sikhs' expression of loyalty to the new order. It also became affiliated to the practice of keeping unshorn hair (*kes*), one of the five Ks, as commanded by the Guru.

The Sikhs believe that covering their unshorn hair with a piece of cloth has spiritual and health benefits. The act of carefully combing one's long hair, tying it into a top knot and wearing a turban around it is considered a sign of Sikh discipline and obeisance to the Guru. The turban served to differentiate the Sikh community from other religious groups such as the Hindus and Muslims in Punjab.

Types of turbans

The *dastar*, *dumalla*, and the *keski* are all variants of the Sikh turban. The *dumalla* is a slightly rounded wrap, while the *dastar*, usually tied from a 19.4 ft (6 m) cloth, is more commonly worn by Sikhs everywhere. The *keski*, sometimes called the small *dastar*, is a shorter piece of cloth which is tied around the head, often under the main *dastar* by men to anchor it in place.

The Akhand Kirtani Jatha distinctly requires women to wear the *keski* as part of their belief in equality within the Sikh faith and the requirement that both men and women follow the code put forth by Guru Gobind Singh.

The practice of tying turbans is also emphasized by the American Sikh Dharma International, or 3HO, where both the women and men don tall white turbans. It is however more common for women to wear a *chunni* over their heads, instead of a turban, especially within sacred sites.

> "Sikhs cherish the **greatest respect** for it [the turban] … It may be observed how **lovingly**, **painstakingly**, **proudly** and **colorfully** they **adorn** their heads with neatly-tied **crown-like turbans**."

THE ENCYCLOPEDIA OF SIKHISM, EDITED BY HARBANS SINGH

Birth of Singh Sabha

By end of the 19th century, the socioreligious Singh Sabha movement emerged within Sikhism, giving rise to political yearnings, and bringing forth many significant changes to the fabric of the community.

The Singh Sabha Movement materialized from a meeting held between some prominent Sikhs at Amritsar in 1873. After the British annexation of Punjab in 1849, proselytization efforts of Christian missionaries (see pp.224–225) had set the stage. A growing awareness of decadence in the practice of Sikhism, the news of four Sikh mission school students' intention to be baptized as Christians, and a Hindu orator's inflammatory speech against the Gurus served to compel the Sikhs to consider this matter with urgency. They feared that these developments were weakening the Panth.

They decided to create an association that would adopt measures to defend the Sikh faith against the onslaught of religious conversions as well as the Arya Samaj, a Hindu reformist movement. Initially the Singh Sabha appraised the Arya Samaj (see pp.224–225) as a supportive force. But with the Samaj's insistence that Sikhs were Hindus, they were soon considered a significant threat.

Seeds of change

The Singh Sabha of Amritsar was established with the support of affluent, landowning, conservative Sikhs in 1873. Six years later, in 1879, another Singh Sabha was established in Lahore, by educated, middle-class men, with the patronage of the governor of Punjab. Evolving from a body to a movement, the Singh Sabha soon counted the peasantry and soldiers among its supporters. With this, it expanded to many locations. By the end of World War I, there

▶ **Photograph** of Singh Sabha leaders Tarlochan Singh, Bhai Vir Singh, and Bhai Sundar Singh Majithia.

were Singh Sabhas in almost all towns and villages of Punjab as well as several parts of India and abroad.

Reforms of the Singh Sabha

The clarion call of the movement was to rediscover and reinstate the purity of Sikh ideas and practices as propagated by the Gurus. It sought to eradicate illiteracy in the community with Western education and further the cause of female education among Sikhs. The movement also aimed at producing Punjabi literature and scholarship in Gurmukhi script, to champion the language of the Gurus. To achieve these objectives, a large number of reforms were enacted. These included reestablishing rites and customs that were consistent with Sikh doctrine and tradition. Several schools and colleges were set up in towns and villages, Sikh educational institutions were improved, and the Sikh identity was asserted with the help of Punjabi newspapers. In *Sikh Heritage: Ethos & Relics*, writers Bhayee Sikandar Singh and Roopinder Singh note that, "The Sikh mind was stirred by a process of liberation and it began to look upon its history and tradition with a clear, self-discerning eye." The Sabha also took up the reformation of Sikh shrines (see pp.260–261) with the help of legislative sanction.

Two factions

The Amritsar and Lahore Singh Sabhas were merged to form a coordinating body known as the General Singh Sabha. This was subsequently replaced by the Khalsa Diwan in 1883, which became an affiliating and controlling body for other Singh Sabhas. However, the fissures in

ARYA SAMAJ

The Arya Samaj, or "society of Aryans," was a Hindu revivalist mission founded by Dayanand Saraswati in 1875. It sought to restore the Vedas' infallible authority as the pristine Truth. The Arya Samaj was against idolatry and opposed the Hindu caste system. In the late 19th century, its progressive character gained traction in Punjab, and many reform-minded Sikhs joined the Samaj. The society, however, viewed Sikhism as an offshoot of Hinduism and initiated a *shuddhi* (proselytizing) campaign to reintegrate converted Hindus. This had a significant impact on Hindu-Sikh relations.

Members of the Arya Samaj pose for a photograph at a meeting in 1916.

the movement soon became palpable and a separate body, also called Khalsa Diwan, was formed in 1886 (see pp.238–239). The ostensible reason was that the Amritsar Singh Sabha did not endorse a pure Khalsa-style Sikh faith when compared to the Lahore Singh Sabha.

The Amritsar Sabha endorsed a wider definition of Sikhism whereby anyone following Guru Nanak's teachings was a Sikh, even if they worshipped local deities. This invited stiff opposition within the Panth as it furthered the claims of the Arya Samaj that Sikhs were a sect within Hinduism. Instead, the Lahore Sabha Sikhs promoted what they believed to be true (*tat*) Khalsa values, such as opposition to worshipping living gurus or observing caste structures, idolatry, and certain social practices.

The Tat Khalsa (the name used by the radical Lahore faction after the 18th-century Tat Khalsa) emerged as the more successful of the two because of its assertion of a distinct Sikh identity, which instilled pride in the Sikh people toward their institutions and beliefs.

In brief

1848–1849
Annexation of Punjab by the British

1873
First Singh Sabha founded in Amritsar

1875
The Arya Samaj is founded by Swami Dayananda Saraswati in Bombay

1879
The Singh Sabha of Lahore is established

1883
Khalsa Diwan Amritsar is established, bringing all the Singh Sabhas of Punjab together

"It **influenced** the entire **Sikh Community** and **reoriented** its outlook and spirit. Since the days of the Gurus nothing so **vital** had transpired to fertilize the **consciousness** of the Sikhs."

HARBANS SINGH, *THE HERITAGE OF SIKHS*, 1964

Bhai Vir Singh

Prodigious writer, scholar, poet, and philosopher, Bhai Vir Singh is considered the foremost figure in the revival of the Punjabi literary tradition. Over his lifetime of eighty-five years, he produced a voluminous corpus of literature.

He has been called the father of modern Punjabi literature, whose work was a marked departure from the conventional literature of the time. A key figure of the Sikh revival movement, his writing brought flair to Sikh literature, philosophy, and spiritualism, infused it with new inspiration, and set it on its modern path of development.

Beginnings

The 19th century was a challenging period for the Sikh faith. Besides the changing sociopolitical fabric and religious movements of indoctrination, there was a trend toward fusing Sikhism with Hindu elements. A direct impact of this was the emergence of reform movements, through the Nirankaris, Namdharis (see pp.226–227), and the Singh Sabha. Bhai Vir Singh, born in 1872 Amritsar, grew up during this period.

After completing his studies, he opened a lithograph press and became associated with the reformist Singh Sabha Movement (see pp.232–233). He launched the Khalsa Tract Society in 1894 to promote the movement's activities. The thought-provoking Punjabi weekly *Khalsa Samachar* followed in 1899, which published monographs with the objective of increasing awareness and pride in the Sikhs' sociocultural legacy. He wrote most of the 192 monographs produced within six years of the organization's existence, which were disseminated to almost 500,000 subscribers.

Sikh studies scholar Harbans Singh, in the seminal *Encyclopaedia of Sikhism*, notes that "the tracts produced by the Khalsa Tract Society introduced a down-to-earth literary Punjabi remarkable for lightness of touch as well as for freshness of expression. In this writing lay the beginnings of modern Punjabi prose."

Writing and compositions

Bhai Vir Singh chose to write in vernacular Punjabi, instead of Braj Bhasha, the western Hindi language prominent before the

19th century. In doing so, he placed Punjabi on the same pedestal as other modern Indian languages.

Vir Singh's earliest composition, in 1905, *Rana Surat Singh,* ran to 12,000 lines. Though a love story, there was no denying the philosophical underpinnings within the poem. Of his later compositions, the *rudais*, four-line poems employing the short meter, also became popular. He also wrote two biographies, *Kalgidhar Chamatka* on Guru Gobind Singh and *Chamatkar* on Guru Nanak. His literary genius is, however, best reflected in his novels, *Sundri* (1898), *Vijay Singh* (1899), *Satwant Kaur* (1900, 1927), and *Baba Naudh Singh* (1921).

His last collection of verses, *Mere Sayian Jio* (1957), published when he was eighty-one, allows the modern reader to appreciate the Guru Granth Sahib's spiritual, religious, and aesthetic grandeur using lyrical mien rather than commentary.

Spiritual inspiration

The most famous of his novels, *Sundri*, is based on a folk ballad, recounting the experiences of a young, newlywed Hindu girl, abducted by a Mughal soldier. Rescued by the Khalsa, she is finally initiated into the Panth and given the name Sundar Kaur, or Sundari. Woven intricately into the sociopolitical milieu of the time, the character reminds the followers of their true spiritual duty. Her profound realization of the *Akal Purakh* (the Timeless Being), her actions of *naam japna* (meditating on the Divine Word) and *sewa* (service), and her courage in the face of Mughal injustice casts her as the model of Sikh religious precepts.

Harbans Singh referred to Bhai Vir Singh as the person who "linked the past with the new," and whose works provide institutional and spiritual solutions by awakening the human soul. Bhai Vir Singh's contributions to Punjabi literature brought spiritual respite and hope for the revival of the true Sikh faith in the face of a volatile sociopolitical environment that had shaken Sikhism's core.

▼ The novel *Sundri* often referenced 18th-century historical battles: Sundar Kaur fought the Mughal Yahya Khan in 1746 as well as the Afghan Ahmad Shah Durrani.

The Khalsa College

Established in 1892 in Amritsar, Punjab, while the country was under British rule, the 330-acre (130-hectare) Khalsa College is testament to the efforts of countless Sikh scholars and leaders who raised funds, donated land, and collectively campaigned for this unique institute.

The second half of the 19th century saw the establishment of several mission posts and church-sponsored schools offering westernized education in Punjab. This began to be seen as a challenge to the predominance of traditional culture and faith in the region as these institutions often became associated with the proselytizing activities of the British. The period also saw an increase in conversions to Christianity, which caused worry among leaders of the different kingdoms in Punjab.

As a result, several societies sprung up in Punjab, reflecting the distinctive demands of their heritage, tradition, and evolving circumstances. The most notable among these was the Singh Sabha reform movement, launched in 1873, that aimed at asserting and reviving Sikh communal identity through educational and literacy programs (see pp.232–233).

Establishment of Khalsa College

In 1883, several prominent leaders organized a conference in Amritsar and adopted a resolution to set up a Sikh educational institution. Soon after, the group submitted a memorandum to the Lieutenant Governor of Punjab with the demand for a college. By 1890 a committee was set up with 121 members (including Sikhs and British) to oversee the project. They devised a plan and published a *hukamnama*, requesting residents to contribute a tenth of their income for the construction of the institution.

The request for funds saw the coming together of several intellectuals and rulers from across Punjab in a way that had not been seen in the century. Maharaja Rajendra Singh of Patiala was the first to donate to the cause, pledging about Rs 1,65,000. Following this, rulers of other princely states in Punjab, including Jind, Nabha, and Kapurthala offered generous aid. Along with the royals, the Sikh landed aristocracy also offered funds for the college. The Sikh public showed their support by organizing fundraising subcommittees, including well-wishers who lived in England. Then, in March 1892, almost a decade after the first conference, the foundation stone of Khalsa College was laid at Amritsar.

A new college council replaced the initially formed establishment committee and supervised the construction of the building, which was completed by 1912. The college

> "To promote **morality** and **sobriety** of life, to promulgate and to preach **teachings of Ten Gurus** as contained in **Sri Guru Granth Sahib** ..."

FROM THE MISSIONS OF KHALSA COLLEGE, AMRITSAR

council hired the teaching staff, and developed the college's various courses and their contents. In the 1920s, faculty members included Bawa Harkishan Singh, Professor Teja Singh, and Professor Nirarijan Singh, who, besides being well-known educationists, were active during the Gurdwara Reform Movement.

Intellectual and architectural splendor
Today, Khalsa College is an iconic institution in Punjab. Its sprawling complex was designed by the architect Bhai Ram Singh, and its splendor has not dimmed with time. The 130-year-old structure is a blend of Mughal, Rajput, and Victorian styles of architecture. There are four magnificent buildings, each dedicated to a different discipline: humanities and social sciences, commerce, agriculture, and computer sciences. The campus houses a gurdwara where prayers are held every morning and evening.

The college library and the museum on campus serve as repositories for Sikh history and culture. The library houses primary and secondary materials, over 6,000 books, and manuscripts such as the *Pothi Meharban* and the 1651 *Meharban Janamsakhis* of Guru Nanak. The museum is home to many unique and rare artifacts related to various incidents from Sikh history.

It also houses about 375 paintings, 601 manuscripts, a collection of old newspapers, weaponry from the 17th and 18th centuries, rare coins, and various exclusive photographs. These photographs include those of women who lost their lives during Partition and the Nankana Sahib tragedy, along with those that show the landscape of Punjab, among others. Exhibits also narrate the history of the founding members of Khalsa college.

Over the years, the college has produced many renowned alumni. Author Mulk Raj Anand; the third Speaker of Lok Sabha, Hukam Singh; two former chief ministers of Punjab, Partap Singh Kairon and Darbara Singh; the captain of the Indian hockey team in 1956, Olympian Balbir Singh Sr; cricketer Bishan Singh Bedi; litterateur Gurbaksh Singh Preetlari; playwright Atamjit Singh; and historian and professor Ganda Singh have all attended Khalsa College, adding to its legacy as a premier education institution in Punjab.

The expansive façade of the Khalsa College is an iconic landmark in the city of Amritsar. The building designed by Ram Singh, reflects different architectural elements, including Mughal, Victorian, and Rajput.

Consolidation for coordination

The establishment of the Chief Khalsa Diwan at the turn of the 20th century brought under its fold many Singh Sabhas and other similar societies. It worked to address the political rights of the Panth, promote literacy, and establish a distinct Sikh identity.

The Chief Khalsa Diwan was founded in 1902 and upheld the ideals of *tat*, or pure Khalsa, which fought for a distinct Sikh identity based on the norms of the orthodox Khalsa. The main council of the Sikhs, the Chief Khalsa Diwan was in control of religious and educational affairs of the Panth, and voiced their political rights.

Initially, it was formed as a central organization to replace the Khalsa Diwans of Amritsar and Lahore. Divided by conflict, they had begun obstructing the work of the Singh Sabhas affiliated to them. About twenty-nine Singh Sabhas joined this new unitary body, now presided over by Bhai Arjan Singh of Bagrian as president and Sundar Singh Majithia as secretary. With the rise in the reputation and legitimacy of the Khalsa Diwan, more Sabhas affiliated themselves to it, numbering at fifty-three in about a year's time.

The council aimed at promoting education, publishing texts for Sikhs, and setting up institutions of community welfare. It also had a constitution and a set of procedures and committees in place.

Religious and social reforms

This was the period of a growing print culture; the advent of printing presses helped to disseminate ideas more swiftly and widely than ever before. The Sikhs also employed existing Sikh publications to spread their message. They used the *Khalsa Samachar* in Gurmukhi and the *Khalsa Advocate* in English to distribute reports, pique public interest, and educate the masses on Sikh religious philosophy. Later, lithographed posters on social and religious themes were produced and distributed free of cost, particularly to influence rural Sikhs. The Diwan also advocated for the recognition of Punjabi in Gurumukhi script in government institutions. Literacy in the Panth was a major concern, so from 1908, the Diwan convened annually for educational conferences to assess the progress and to collect more funds to set up institutions.

The expanding Hindu influence, according to the Diwan, argued for the perversion of the faith. As a result, they declared a gurdwara reform, purging all non-Sikh elements and reclaiming sacred sites (see pp.260–261).

Rallying for political rights

The Diwan soon realized the significance of political recognition for a minority religious group, and swore allegiance to the British

ANAND KARAJ

The Sikh marriage ceremony or the *Anand Karaj* can be traced back to Guru Amar Das and Guru Ram Das, who composed hymns that were sung during the ceremony and recited to solemnize the marriage, respectively. During the reigns of Maharaja Ranjit Singh and his successors, the practice fell out of favor due to Brahmanical influences. The Nirankaris and the Singh Sabha sought to revive the ceremony, which was legally sanctioned by the Anand Marriage Act of 1909.

▶ Front pages of *Khalsa Samachar*, a weekly paper. It was established by Bhai Vir Singh in 1899 in Amritsar.

> "... the Singh Sabha **reformers** [Chief Khalsa Diwan] had **succeeded** in shaping a firmer **definition** of **Sikh identity** and in persuading a substantial proportion of educated **Sikhs to accept** that definition."

HARJOT OBEROI, *THE CONSTRUCTION OF RELIGIOUS BOUNDARIES*, 1994

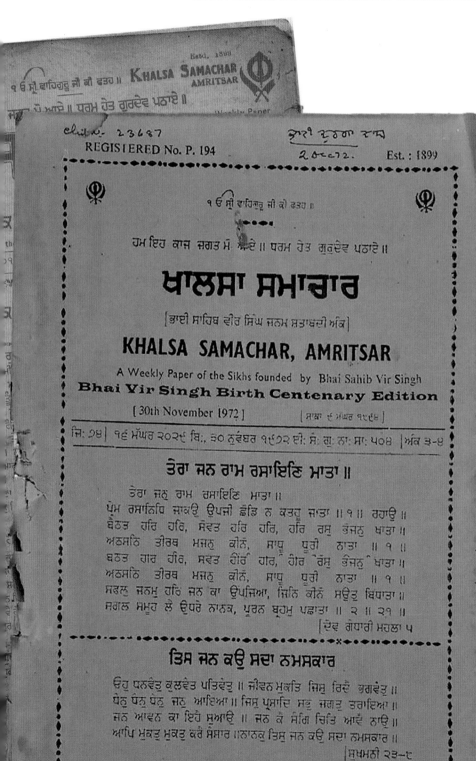

monarch in order to safeguard Sikh rights and campaign for representation in government posts. The Singh Sabhas used journals, resolutions, and tracts to mobilize support, while petitioning the British to navigate political issues. Sundar Singh Majithia was elected to the Imperial Legislative Council in 1909, where he advocated the Anand Marriage Bill, introduced in 1908 by Tikka Ripudaman Singh of Nabha. This was a major step toward institutionalizing Sikh rituals.

Sikh politics was not limited to constitutional lobbying: in 1907 they organized themselves ito protest against the British Colonization Bill of 1906, which transferred the land of a deceased man without an heir to the government. This exacerbated discontent with the Land Alienation Act of 1900, which limited the transfer of land ownership in Punjab Province. Demonstrations forced the British to amend the legislations.

During the Morley-Minto reforms of 1909, which limited the involvement of Indians in central and provincial administration, the Sabha pushed for separate electorates for Sikhs, a demand that remained largely unfulfilled.

Post-World War I, the Chief Khalsa Diwan's political strategies did not succeed as the British government's political priorities had shifted. The body then returned to its previous aim of amplifying the Sikh mission via educational and intellectual endeavors.

World War I and its aftermath

Sikhs in British India comprised less than two percent of the country's population, but were recruited in such great numbers for World War I that they made up over a fifth of the British Army's troops.

Sikh soldiers played a crucial role in World War I as part of the British Army and were important contributors to the victory of the Allies against the Axis powers. When they returned home from their battles, they found Punjab reeling under socioeconomic exigencies and a nationalist dissatisfaction against an apathetic and authoritative regime.

Sikh troops had been employed by the British after their action against the rebels during the mutiny of 1857, where sepoys rebelled against the army. The Sikhs had largely supported the British (see pp.220–221).

Sikhs in the War

The British government had raised a massive army in India for both internal protection and external defence. From the late 19th century, the army followed a recruitment policy based on a "martial race" theory whereby certain communities were considered naturally built to fight. From the 1870s, the government had tried to dismiss sepoys from races which were not "martial." As a result, there emerged a preference for specific groups such as the Jats, Purbias, Pathans, Gurkhas, and the Sikhs, which explains their enormous presence as soldiers in the war years. By 1915, there were around 35,000 Sikh soldiers in the British Army. By the end of the war, 60,000 more Sikhs had joined, making up one-fifth of the total number of soldiers. Most recruits hailed from the princely states, with some reinforcements being personally sent by rajas who had shown allegiance to the British after recognizing the latter's suzerainty.

The Sikhs were sent to fight in nations in Europe, Africa, as well as Turkey, and their bravery was noted with admiration by British officers. The Sikhs were awarded fourteen Military Crosses for their service, although this contribution has remained veiled in popular discourse. They were largely motivated by a loyalty toward the government which let them perceive their services as a sanctified duty.

Discrimination in North America

Among the migrants who worked in fields and factories across North America, many were Sikhs who moved as a result of British policies in India. They had been inspired by the labor movements in the US and Canada and came together to organize and exchange nationalist ideas. These resulted in the Ghadar movement (see pp.246–247), which gained popularity but also prompted biased treatment against Indians. The Ghadar movement actively sought to fan dissent against the British in India, and sent people as well as propaganda material to India itself.

Years after the war

The soldiers had expected an appropriate compensation after the war but they soon realized that their service did not lead to social elevation. They were still regarded with disdain by local law enforcement, which had also actively persecuted and coerced their families for war funds.

The socioeconomic situation following the war incited more dissatisfaction with the British, who imposed an indentured system on Indians, forcefully recruiting them to work overseas. These circumstances worsened after a drought swiftly raised the prices of crops. Meanwhile, as part of the Spanish flu pandemic, a flu outbreak in 1918 plagued the people of Punjab, while the British responded with a higher burden of taxes.

Crisis in Punjab

Things finally came to a head when the restrictive policies of the war era were renewed under the Rowlatt Act. According to it, certain political cases could be tried without a jury and suspects could be imprisoned without trial. This led to nationwide protests, brutal British retaliation, and subsequently the Jallianwala Bagh massacre (see pp.248–249) in 1919. However, the protests in Punjab further intensified. Demonstrators attacked all things and people associated with the British government, which led to the imposition of martial law in the province. The army and police under British command opened fire upon people, and arrested or executed others without trial.

A photograph from 1916 shows Sikh soldiers parading through Paris, France, during World War I.

Dispatches from war

Away from their homes, Sikh soldiers often took to writing their thoughts to survive their foreign stations. These missives reveal a melange of emotions and experiences around themes of circumstances, pain, gratitude, religion, and loyalty.

Sikh sepoys stationed at foreign locations in Europe, Africa, and the Middle East came face-to-face with new landscapes and lifestyles. Their amazement at this is prevalent in the letters they sent back to their families. Bakshish Singh, a Sikh soldier, considered France to be heaven, waxing at length about its bounty of apples and absence of crime. Yet, another sepoy Sant Singh, also stationed in France, described the extent of violence and death, painting a different picture of the same landscape.

Such duality of perceptions is quite common in the letters that relay the personal experiences of soldiers. Those writing from military hospitals generally relayed their pain and suffering, dissuading others from joining the war, while others wrote about the rumored preferential treatment of the British soldiers on the battlefield. There are other letters, however, that share the joy of charitable donations from the British, of items such as the *gutka*s or the five Ks (see pp.110–111) that allowed Sikhs to enjoy a semblance of normalcy.

A matter of duty and identity

Some letters portray an uneasiness over the lack of a distinct religious identity, which would allow the Sikhs to be seen as a brotherhood distant from the other faiths fighting alongside them. This loosely reflects the 19th- and early 20th-century discourse about the complicated relationship between Sikh and Hindu traditions that had prompted reform movements within both faiths. One conspicuous manifestation of this was through the self-identification of the Sikh community as a martial group that had fought for years and was fighting again, this time for the British.

Some Sikh sepoys showcased a loyalty to the British in their letters and perceived their sacrifice in the war as a spiritual and political duty. The imperial authority was conceptualized almost as a deity toward whom they had to show devotion, although much of this goodwill might have stemmed from the knowledge

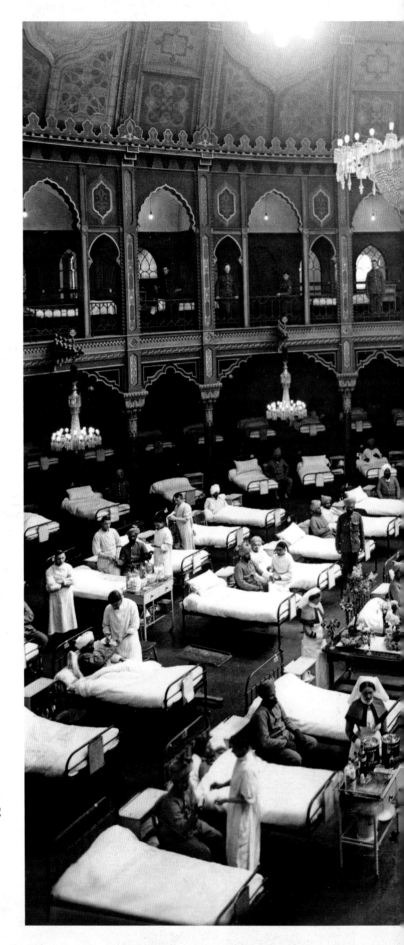

> "Do your **King's work well** and be **faithful**. It is the order of the **Guru** that one should be faithful to the person **whose salt one eats**, and this is the **time** for us to do all that is **possible** for the **King**"

EXCERPT FROM A LETTER BY A SIKH SEPOY

that the letters were screened before being dispatched. This attitude needs to be situated within the tradition of Sikh martyrdom that was meant to enable emancipation.

Upholding loyalty

"It is the finest thing in the world to die for [our] King. I believe that God will keep those men happy whose aim in life is to be brave and loyal. I must also remark that it is up to you to help us for this is the time of our lives. Such an opportunity will not occur again for a hundred years and succeeding generations will reap the benefits of your exertions," wrote a sepoy in one letter, encouraging fellow Sikhs to show courage and loyalty to the British, through the singular opportunity of fighting in the war as that would gift them with divine grace. A similar sentiment is expressed in another letter where the soldier stresses that he is wilfully fighting because that is what God wants him to do. The phrase "eating the salt" of the King is often repeated to celebrate their participation in the war as a way of repaying the generosity bestowed upon them. Being martyred on the battlefield hence was the highest accomplishment, as it fulfilled the twin duty toward the government and the Divine.

Loyalty, however, did not quite negate the dissatisfaction apparent in a few letters to and from Punjab, especially in the context of the Ghadar attitudes which were defining Sikh identity in new ways (see pp.246–247). Some soldiers spoke of mistreatment, while others chose to uphold the value of martial duty as an identity of the Sikhs, who were fighting the war not out of submission, but to forge favor with the British.

◀ **Wounded soldiers including** those from the Sikh community at the Royal Pavilion, a former royal residence in Brighton, UK, converted into a military hospital during WWI.

Sikhs comprised one-fifth of the Indian contingent of the British Indian Army at the onset of World War I in 1914. This 1918 photograph shows soldiers of the 45th Sikhs (52nd Infantry Brigade, 17th Division) marching with the Guru Granth Sahib held aloft, during the campaign in Mesopotamia. A soldier fans the holy book with a whisk, as is customary.

Ghadar movement

The early 20th-century Ghadar movement was meant to help foment a rebellion against British rule in India. It was supported by the Indian diaspora, with more than 90 percent of its members being Sikhs.

In 1913, a group of Indians in the US raised a call to overthrow British rule in India by armed rebellion. These men were members of the Pacific Coast Hindustan Association, also known as the Ghadar Party. Sohan Singh Bhakna was its founder president. The party took its name from its main organ, a weekly paper, published in Urdu and Punjabi, titled *Ghadar*. The name comes from the Urdu word for rebellion or mutiny. The party's intentions were stated clearly in its inaugural issue in November 1913: "To bring about a rising ... because the people can no longer bear the oppression and tyranny practiced under English rule."

Roots taking shape
In less than a year of the paper's circulation, the party's membership grew to thousands of members and dozens of branches spread across the world, to places such as Singapore, Hong Kong, and Tokyo, while the bulk of members lived on the Pacific Coast. Nearly 90 percent of its supporters were Punjabi Sikh males, nearly half of whom were veterans of the British Indian Army who had served in distant lands. Others were peasants and agriculturalists. The paper included statistics of India's poverty and the draining of India's wealth to England. The colonial establishment was characterized as an "ulcer" and a "plague" on the nation. Liberty, the Ghadar activists believed, was a natural right.

In a new world
What united the immigrants was the common belief that the source of their distress was located in India's subjugation by the British Crown. Lala Har Dayal, a revolutionary and the editor of the *Ghadar*, asserted that colonial policies had compelled many Indians to move overseas in search of livelihood. And in these foreign lands, he stressed, they were considered degraded subjects of the British, a people devoid of freedom and respect. Racial discrimination and violence in the host countries further fanned an anticolonial consciousness among Indians.

Stirring into action
With the outbreak of the First World War in mid-1914, the Ghadar Party sprang into action. On August 4, the newspaper ran an article entitled "The Trumpet of War," that gave a call to arms: "... the opportunity that you have been looking for has come... This is the right moment to start a war of independence. You can very soon expel the British from India." Between 1914 and 1918, the party would mobilize nearly 8,000 men from North and South America and East Asia to go to India to overthrow the British. Ship after ship carried hundreds of revolutionaries to Indian shores. However, alerted by an extensive intelligence network in Canada, the United States, and Hong Kong, British officials introduced a new measure called the Ingress into India Ordinance, on September 5, 1914. It imposed strict controls on those seeking entry into the country. Unsuspecting Ghadarites were arrested even before they could disembark from the vessel, dealing a severe blow to the party's plans. Reportedly, 1,700 were interned.

Those who were not detained established contact with Indian revolutionaries such as Rash Behari Bose, across the country, and fixed February 21, 1915, for the start of a synchronous revolt across India. The revolutionaries began convincing Indian soldiers in the provinces to strike against British commanders first, which they hoped would inspire the masses to rise up. Additionally, they collected arms and destroyed government property.

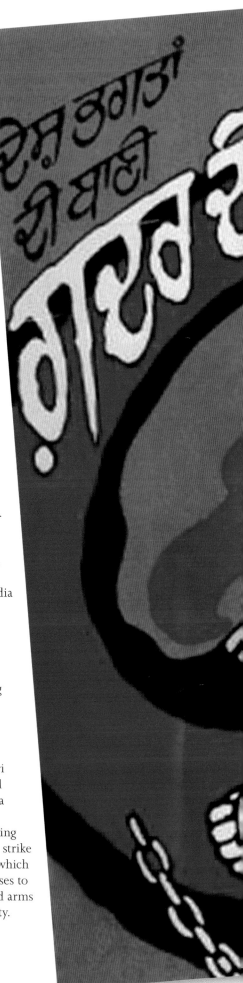

1915 DEFENSE OF INDIA ACT

The threat posed by the revolutionary activities of Indians during World War I prompted the British state to enact the 1915 Defense of India Act. The legislation empowered the state to detain anyone without trial, curtail movement and meetings, and censor writings and speech, among other provisions. Although it was implemented as a wartime measure, it was extended into the Rowlatt Acts of 1919, which led to mass agitations, culminating in the Jallianwala Bagh massacre the same year. It was also reenacted during World War II as Defense of India Act 1939.

By December 1914, these men had persuaded soldiers in Lahore, Ferozpur, Meerut, along with several other North Indian regiments. The Ghadarites did not succeed, however, as the British had planted spies in the party base at Lahore and uncovered their plans. Just before the fateful night of the planned revolt in February, the rebel army regiments were relocated or disarmed. Any help that the revolutionaries may have expected from outside army circles was minimal. Although Bose managed to evade the officials, almost all the leaders and hundreds of activists were arrested. The colonial state set up special courts to try them under the Defense of India Act of 1915. Many tried under the Lahore Conspiracy Case were executed and others incarcerated for life. Although the Ghadar movement was crushed in Punjab, many loyalists continued with their work.

In North America, the organization continued to publish *Ghadar*, undeterred by a drastically diminished membership. However, in 1917, after the entry of the US into World War I, all anti-British activities on American soil fell under sudden violation of its obligations toward neutrality laws. The American government arrested, charged, and jailed almost all active Ghadar members on conspiracy charges in 1918. This effectively put an end to the party's political work. After half a decade of its existence, the veritable threat posed by the Ghadar Party to the British government had been all but been neutralized by 1918.

◄ **Cover of *Ghadar di Gunj (Echoes of Mutiny)*,** an anthology of poems inspired by the movement that was published in 1913.

In brief

1907–1908
Indian-origin immigrants land in Canada and the US in significant numbers

1907
Anti-Asiatic riots take place in British Columbia, Canada, against immigrating Asians

1908
Exclusion riots occur in Oregon and California in the US

1912–1913
Pacific Coast Hindustan Association founded in the US. Newspaper *Ghadar* started

1914
First band of Ghadarites arrive in India

September 1914
Ingress into India Ordinance initiated by the British government

February 1915
Ghadarites collaborate with Rash Behari Bose for simultaneous uprisings across India

April–September 1915
Lahore Conspiracy trials take place in India and the US

April 1917
The US announces entry into World War I

Bloody Baisakhi

On April 13, 1919, the day of Baisakhi, hundreds of unarmed people were fired upon and killed by troops under Brigadier General R.E.H. Dyer at Jallianwala Bagh, a walled public garden in Amritsar, sparking widespread unrest against British rule.

Always apprehensive about any kind of revolt, the British government introduced the Rowlatt Bills, in March 1919. It made insidious incursions on people's civil liberties by authorizing tighter control over the press, arrests merely on suspicion, and detention without trial. These coercive measures were well-articulated in a contemporary slogan: *nā dalīl, nā vakīl, nā apīl* (no argument, no lawyer, no appeal). The Bills became law, popularly known as the Rowlatt Act.

This act instilled unprecedented upheaval in the country. Mahatma Gandhi called for people to "civilly defy" the act, which soon evolved into a nationwide defiance of British rule, and Gandhi's "messianic" appeal evoked massive support from the urban population. Agitations began across the province led by leaders Dr Saifuddin Kitchlew and Dr Satya Pal, which attracted thousands.

However, tensions soon mounted as Gandhi's access to Punjab was restricted and Kitchlew and Satyapal were unduly detained. In protests that erupted across the region, protesters destroyed government property, and were fired upon by the police. Several demonstrators as well as some Englishmen died in the violence that followed. Alarmed by these events, Brigadier General R.E.H. Dyer was dispatched to Amritsar from Jalandhar. While efforts were in place to declare martial law, Dyer issued a proclamation in Urdu and Punjabi prohibiting all assemblies and processions of more than four people in Amritsar.

The bloody massacre

On the evening of April 12, counter-proclamations were made by the beating of cans in the city—several local leaders had decided to convene a meeting at the Jallianwala Bagh on the following day of Baisakhi, the harvest festival. On April 13, thousands of people of all ages and religions gathered in the walled garden, near the Golden Temple. Some came to relax after offering their prayers, and others came to listen to messages from Kitchlew and Satya Pal. While the speakers were addressing the gathering, an incensed General Dyer reached the venue with fifty rifle-carrying troops. The

> ## "There was a **heap of the dead** and wounded **over, under and all around me.** I felt suffocated."

MOULVI GHOLAM JILANI IN A STATEMENT TO THE REPORT OF THE COMMISSIONERS APPOINTED BY THE PUNJAB SUB-COMMITTEE OF THE INDIAN NATIONAL CONGRESS VOL. II, 1920

soldiers occupied the entrance to the garden, sealing the exit. Without warning, they opened fire on the crowd. It is reported that 1,650 rounds were shot until the troops ran out of ammunition. Many fell dead or were crushed in the stampede as people tried to flee the hail of bullets. Some jumped into the nearby well in an attempt to escape and others lay wounded.

Official government records grossly underestimated the casualties. They claimed that 379 people were killed and over 1,200 wounded, however, the Indian National Congress estimated that nearly 1,000 died and 3,600 were wounded.

The days that followed

The massacre at the Jallianwala Bagh did not bring an end to Punjab's reign of terror. Amritsar was placed under martial law and Indians were forced to salute government officials and follow draconian orders such as a "crawling order" wherein people were forced to crawl on their bellies whenever they passed through the street where a British missionary had been beaten up. These rules were extended to other areas of Punjab as well. Bombings and air strikes were carried out on the towns of Gujranwala and Kasur.

Indian writer V.N. Datta asserts in his book, *Jallianwala Bagh*, that the incident "… changed the idiom of Indian nationalism." Gandhi assumed center stage and the Congress entered a different political phase of mass nationalism. The atrocities had added fuel to the fight for freedom.

Jallianwala Bagh

This watercolor painting by Indian artist Sumeet Aurora depicts the dead and wounded amid the chaos and massacre at Jallianwala Bagh.

Jallianwala Bagh

The walled garden, a stone's throw from the Golden Temple in Amritsar, is a poignant reminder of the lives lost in the Jallianwala Bagh massacre that took place on Baisakhi in 1919. A memorial, originally designed by American architect Benjamin Polk in 1961 and renovated in 2021, stands in the heart of the garden.

A brief history

On April 13, 1919, Brigadier General Dyer, the acting military commander for Amritsar, directed soldiers to block the only entrance to the compound. He then ordered them to fire upon a crowd that had gathered to celebrate Baisakhi and peacefully protest the unfair arrests of Indian activists. In the carnage that followed, hundreds of people were killed, and many jumped into a well to save themselves.

The complex itself is believed to have once been a flowering garden owned by a Sikh family from the village of Jalla in Punjab, which gave it its name (translating to "garden of the people from Jalla"). Today, the garden is a grassy expanse, featuring markers of the fateful event and memorials commemorating the martyrs.

▲ **Indian soldiers of the British army guard a street in Amritsar, Punjab.**
Riots broke out in the city in the days following the Jallianwala Bagh massacre.

The oblong memorial, the Flame of Liberty as it is known, is at the center of Jallianwala Bagh, Amritsar, built in memory of the lives lost in the massacre. The complex was preserved after India became independent, and was renovated in 2021.

Touring the site

A sculpture featuring the faces of known martyrs, with their names written in gold on a marble base, stands near the entrance to Jallianwala Bagh, as does a statue of Sikh revolutionary Udham Singh who assassinated Sir Michael O'Dwyer, the Lieutenant Governor of Punjab in 1919. The narrow path leading into the complex is lined with sculptures and is a new addition made in 2021. Inside is the martyr's memorial—the Flame of Liberty—a red-brick, oblong cenotaph visible from all sides. Inside, the Amar Jyoti, or eternal flame, burns all day and night.

Also preserved are twenty-eight bullet holes on the walls surrounding the garden and the now-covered well into which many fell or jumped to avoid the bullets. A gallery houses artifacts from the freedom struggle, including letters and photographs.

1. Marble carving of the martyrs; **2.** Hindi sign that reads: "Bullets were fired from this spot;" **3.** The eternal flame, Amar Jyoti, before renovation; **4.** Close-up of bullet holes in a wall, outlined in white; **5.** Entrance corridor with statues of martyrs; **6.** Inside view of the well before renovation; **7.** Udham Singh's statue at the garden's entrance; **8.** Udham Singh's ashes housed at the museum; **9.** Exterior view of the well; **10.** Brick archway with white outlines indicating bullet holes in the wall

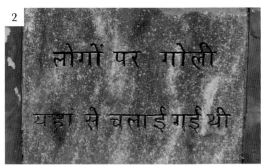

ਜਲਿਆਂਵਾਲਾ ਬਾਗ
जलिआंवाला बाग

JALLIANWALA BAGH

In search of freedom

Despite their allegiance to the British in the 19th century, many Sikhs eventually began fighting for political representation. By the 20th century, there were a large number of uprisings, nationalist in nature and focusing on several other issues, such as caste, class, and ethnicities.

While bitter about the fall of the Sikh Empire, most Sikhs still found it beneficial to side with the British after annexation, as seen during the 1857 Mutiny (see pp.220–221). Gradually, however, several collectives began to exert anticolonial sentiments through agitations, publications, and militancy. The 1880s saw the emergence of Muslim and Hindu associations to protect and represent their communities. Many Sikhs, too, began to see the need for separate electorates and weightage in governance. The first avenue for this emerged in the form of the Punjab Legislative Council, which had as its members several high-profile Sikhs.

Administrative disappointments

In 1909, when councils for Indian representation were established under the Morley-Minto Reforms, the Chief Khalsa Diwan demanded separate electorates for Sikhs, similar to those promised to Muslims. The demand went largely

▲ **Revolutionaries of the Indian freedom movement**, including Sikh leaders, at a meeting of the first Indian National Congress in 1885.

ignored and Sikhs were outnumbered by other communities in the subsequent elections. With the outbreak of the First World War (see pp.240–241), the focus shifted toward the safe return of Sikh soldiers, especially amidst reports of poor or no medical facilities for the wounded.

Nevertheless, the cause of representation stayed alive and the call for it became louder in 1916 and the signing of the Lucknow Pact. The Congress and Muslim League signed the pact and divided the Punjab electorates amongst them. As a reaction, the Chief Khalsa Diwan wrote to the Lieutenant Governor at the time rejecting the pact. He demanded a third of the seats for the Sikhs. Prominent Sikh leaders including Bhupinder Singh, the Maharaja of Patiala, responsible for pioneering social reform and education in Patiala, met the secretary of state, Edwin Montagu, and the viceroy, Lord Chelmsford, to voice the same demands. Consequently, the Montagu–Chelmsford Reform proposals added an amendment for Sikh representation, but this was later outvoted.

Nationalist uprisings

The Chief Khalsa Diwan persevered with support from the Punjab government that presented a case for the Sikhs before the Franchise Committee. They only conceded a separate electoral roll and some constituencies, which the Sikhs believed to be an underwhelming representation in the face of the community's service and loyalty. The first elections under this system happened in 1920, but by this time resentment had increased owing to the treatment of civilians and returned soldiers. The ignominy toward them and the Jallianwala Bagh incident resulted in many taking up the nationalistic cause and distancing themselves from the Chief Khalsa Diwan.

Many leaders, influenced by Swadeshi (nationalist) periodicals, called on Sikh peasants to fight the economic oppression. An early revolutionary who was vocal about the unjust Colonial rule was Sardar Ajit Singh. In 1907, peasants in Punjab launched an agitation over land legislations. Over time, people started speaking up about the racial prejudices of the government and the poor treatment of soldiers in publications such as *Sacha Dhandora*, started by former soldier and educationist Sunder Singh Lyallpuri, and the *Khalsa Youngman's Magazine*, inciting censorship and arrests.

Diverse manifestations

With the creation of the Central Sikh League in 1919, a new face of anti-imperialism emerged, especially among the middle class. Meanwhile, another group of Sikhs established the Shiromani Gurdwara Parbandhak Committee (SGPC) in 1920, launching the Akali movement (see pp.260–261). Debates over religious jurisdiction brought about anti-imperial sentiments, marked by episodes of police brutality. The fervor for nationalism persisted as Sikhs were repeatedly denied proper representation in the Round Table Conferences and the Government of India Act 1935.

Alongside these strands of nationalism, a more revolutionary action commenced with the Ghadar movement (see pp.246–247). Some Akalis joined the Ghadarites to avenge the deaths of Sikhs. The Babbar Akali Jatha became another militant force, which had a more international influence. Some Sikhs, such as Bhagat Singh (see pp.256–257) started the Naujawan Bharat Sabha to emancipate laborers and peasants. These revolutionary organizations were deemed illegal by the British, and as they were susceptible to arrest and execution, their members were forced to largely work underground.

In brief

1909
Morley-Minto Reforms

1916
Lucknow Pact

1920
Creation of Shiromani Gurdwara Parbandhak Committee

1921
Creation of Babbar Akali Jatha

255

Sikhism During the British Rule

" … experience has shown that they [Sikhs] go … **unrepresented**. To the Sikhs … we propose to **extend the system** already adopted in the case of Muhammadans…"

MONTAGU–CHELMSFORD REPORT, 1918

UDDHAM SINGH

A revolutionary associated with the Ghadar Party (see pp.246–247) and the HSRA (see p.257), Uddham Singh was involved in organizing Indians in the fight against the British. He was arrested in 1927 for shipping weapons into India. After his release, he escaped to London where he plotted to assassinate Michael O'Dwyer, who was Punjab's Lieutenant Governor during the Jallianwala Bagh massacre. He sometimes misspelled the name as Dyer, perhaps confusing his target with the perpetrator of the massacre. He assassinated O'Dwyer in 1940 in London, following which he was executed by hanging.

▶ An iconic 1929 photograph of Bhagat Singh. Taken when he changed his appearance to evade British officials, the image has since made its way into popular culture as well.

Bhagat Singh

A revolutionary and social visionary, Bhagat Singh played a key role in India's struggle for independence. His unyielding ideas and stirring writings resonated across the country even after his death and continue to do so today.

In a letter to his brother before his execution, Bhagat Singh wrote, "My ideas will remain forever, whether the self remains or not." Singh was barely twenty-four years old when he was executed in 1931 for the murder of an English policeman. Known as Shaheed-e-Azam (the Great Martyr), Bhagat Singh became enshrined in national memory, not just as a young revolutionary who challenged the British Empire, but also as a martyr who fearlessly sacrificed his life for the cause.

A rising star
Popular stories, apocryphal or not, have given shape to a certain view about Singh as a hero. One story states that at the age of four, he suggested sowing rifles in fields in order to reap a crop of freedom. Another story places him in Jallianwala Bagh at twelve, from where he brought back blood-soaked sand as a reminder of the brutality he had seen.

A shift in perception
In early 1922, Gandhi withdrew the Non-cooperation Movement of 1919 to prevent the escalation of violence after clashes broke out between the police and protesters at Chauri Chaura in modern-day Uttar Pradesh. This left many disillusioned, as they felt that the suspension was unwarranted. Singh was one of them, and had aligned himself with the Hindustan Socialist Revolutionary Association (HSRA). The group believed in taking up arms for freedom, if necessary. He took over the leadership after the arrest of HSRA members for looting a train carrying government treasure in 1925. The following year, he established the Naujawan Bharat Sabha, a socialist youth organization in Lahore. His ideas struck a chord with the youth, tapping into their anger and frustration with the British government.

Colonial repression
In 1928, the death of prominent freedom fighter, Lala Lajpat Rai, from severe injuries inflicted on

him by the police at a demonstration incensed moderates and radicals alike. An enraged Bhagat Singh and his comrades Shivaram Rajguru, Sukhdev Thapar, and Chandra Sekhar Azad decided to assassinate J.A. Scott, the police superintendent behind Rai's death. However, in an act of mistaken identity, they shot J.P. Saunders, the assistant superintendent of police.

In 1929, Bhagat Singh and B.K. Dutt, another HSRA member, planned a volatile bomb attack on the Central Legislative Assembly in Delhi to make the "deaf hear." Their two slogans, "*Inquilab Zindabad*" and "*Down with Imperialism*" caught the imagination of thousands of people. Singh and Dutt surrendered on site to implement their plan of using British courts as platforms to articulate and publicize their cause. The two accepted their crime and said, "By crushing two insignificant individuals, a nation cannot be crushed."

Later, Bhagat Singh, Rajguru, and Sukhdev faced a series of trials for Saunders' murder. Eventually, they were sentenced and hanged to death.

◀ A book and a small chest that belonged to Bhagat Singh.

Writings and beliefs
Singh had a voracious appetite for reading. It shaped his ideas on social equality and inclusive nationalism, considering religion secondary. A radical thinker and commenter, Bhagat Singh questioned the validity of the British government and socio-religious practices in his writings, which formed a large part of his legacy.

His first letter to his father informing him of his departure from home to fulfil his revolutionary mission was full of political rationalization. His 1924 article, "*Vishwa Prem*" (Universal Love), highlighted his commitment to a world that was built upon the ideals of brotherhood rather than "socioreligious othering."

He endorsed the philosophical tenets of religion, which, according to him, give it meaning, but dismissed its superstitious character. He also acknowledged that religion has pacified people in times of crisis, serving as their "last consolation." His disbelief in God was frequently misinterpreted as *ahankara*, or ego. However, it was a dual effort toward instilling a sense of scientific realism, which in turn would provide the vision for an equitable socialist world where power could not be used in the name of religion against those in distress. According to him, politics, strangled by religious superstition and intolerance, required intellectual liberation as it was this crisis in politics that hindered India's development for centuries.

"Bombs and pistols do not make **revolution**. The **sword** of revolution is sharpened on the whetting-stone of **ideas**."

BHAGAT SINGH IN A STATEMENT BEFORE THE LAHORE HIGH COURT BENCH, 1929

Audience see revolver dram

SIR M. O'DW
DEAD AT CAX

Lord Zetland and Lord Lamington wounded

HIT BY TWO SHOTS

Daily Express Staff Reporter

SIR MICHAEL O'DWYER, Governor of the Punjab a the time of the Amritsar "massacre" in 1919, was shot dead in full view of 180 people in London yesterday afternoon.

Just as a lecture in Caxton Hall, S.W., held by the East India Association and the Royal Central Asian Society, was about to end, six reports startled the audience. Sir Michael fell dead, with two bullets through his heart.

The Marquis of Zetland, Secretary of State for India, who was presiding, toppled from his chair, wounded in the ribs; Lord Lamington, seventy-nine-year-old ex-Governor of Bombay, had part of his right hand shattered; and Sir Louis Dane, eighty-four years old, whom Sir Michael succeeded in the Governorship of the Punjab, was shot in the arm.

The meeting had been called to hear an address on Afghanistan by Brig.-General Sir Percy Sykes. It was held in the oak-panelled Tudor room of Caxton Hall,

SIR MICHAEL O'DWYER
"I shall be back in time for tea" he said before leaving home.

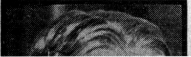

at London lecture

ER SHOT
ON HALL

...andcuffed man is taken from the Caxton Hall.

R.A.F. snap U-boat, then sink it

A British pilot sinks a U-boat . . . Two wonderful pictures, taken from his plane, are on the Back Page.

STOP PRESS

ITALY'S ANTI-RUSSIAN PLAN: TURKEY REPLIES

ISTANBUL, Thursday. — Turkey has replied to Italy's proposal of direct collaboration in event of Russian attack in the Balkans, according to authoritative source in Istanbul.

This is believed to state that Turkey is impressed by proposal as means of safeguarding Balkan peace, but will postpone decision until other countries concerned have been consulted.—British United Press.

FINNISH GOVERNMENT MAY RESIGN TODAY

COPENHAGEN, Thursday.—Finnish Government may resign today, according to Stockholm report. Provisional Government may be formed to ratify peace treaty and so relieve men who directed Finland's heroic defence of onus of having to sign humiliating peace. — British United Press.

MANNERHE...
THE BLA...

The front page of the Daily Express, a British newspaper, reports the assassination of Sir Michael O'Dwyer and the arrest of Udham Singh, a Sikh revolutionary, in London. Singh shot and killed O'Dwyer, the former Lieutenant Governor of Punjab on March 13, 1940, as revenge for orchestrating the Jallianwala Bagh massacre of 1919.

The Akali movement

The 20th century ushered in a stronger motivation among the Sikhs to control their own affairs, especially their sites of worship. Through the 1920s, a number of agitations were held by the Akali forces to assert Sikh authority over gurdwaras under the newly formed Shiromani Gurdwara Parbandhak Committee (SGPC), resulting in the Sikh Gurdwaras Act of 1925.

◀ **The present-day facade of Gurdwara Rakab Ganj Sahib** associated with the cremation of Guru Tegh Bahadur.

allowed the demolition was roundly condemned. The discord waned with the looming World War I but reignited in 1919 under the nationalist Central Sikh League, which set out to repossess the gurdwara land and halted only when the wall was rebuilt and the land restored to a Sikh management committee.

Organizational transformations

The fervor for self-management of shrines continued to fester, stirring major developments throughout 1920s. On October 12, a rally of Sikhs led by Khalsa College teachers marched into the Golden Temple with Dalits to give *karah prasad* (offering), which the priests had banned Dalits from offering. The priests were forced out and a new management instituted. The Akal Takht organized a meeting on November 15 to form a central committee for the management of gurdwaras. This was the Shiromani Gurdwara Parbandhak Committee (SGPC).

With many gurdwaras coming under their control, the Shiromani Akali Dal was also set up as the political arm of the SGPC. Its members promoted the ideas of the SGPC and worked with the committee on the collective mission of self-management. The gurdwara reform movement itself came to be known as the Akali movement and an eponymous Gurmukhi newspaper, the *Akali* was also started. The body adopted a largely nonviolent attitude toward takeovers. Even when the *mahants* attacked the Akalis at the Tarn Taran gurdwara, resulting in the death of two Akalis in January 1921, the Sikhs maintained a semblance of nonviolence.

Gurdwara reform agitations

Between 1921 and 1925, the Sikhs became more proactive in their demand for shrine control under the SGPC. In February 1921,

Spearheaded by the Singh Sabha, the gurdwara reform movement was instituted within the context of a growing dissatisfaction over the maladministration of gurdwaras by the *mahants* (hereditary priests). They had been managing these sites since the Mughal period and had introduced Hindu elements and practices into worship, misused funds, and excluded lower-caste Sikhs. The British government considered the *mahants* the legitimate caretakers, recording each gurdwara property against the name of a priest in its official documents. In 1859, a management body was established to reclaim Sikh places of worship, but it was unsuccessful in restraining the authority of the priests.

The Singh Sabha led protests for removal of Hindu images, icons, practices, and ideologies from its shrines. Due to this pressure, idols were removed from the Golden Temple premises in 1905. Matters came to a critical point in 1912, when the British government took over a plot of land outside the Rakab Ganj Gurdwara in Delhi and demolished a boundary wall in order to build the new capital. The demolition became a flash point and the management that had

Narain Das, the *mahant* at Nankana Sahib Gurdwara in Punjab, killed a *jatha* (band) of advancing Akalis, who had come to oust him. This led to a march of about 2,000 Sikhs to the shrine. The government intervened and handed the keys of the gurdwara to the SGPC and proposed the Sikh Gurdwara and Shrines Bill as conciliation, but it was rejected as an inadequate measure.

In November, upon becoming suspicious of Baba Kharak Singh, the new president of the SGPC, the deputy commissioner of Amritsar took the keys of the Golden Temple treasury. The SGPC held protests and issued a call to boycott the visit of the Prince of Wales. Sikh leaders were arrested, but under pressure of growing agitation, the government had to return the keys.

Another demonstration occurred in August 1922 after some Sikhs were arrested for meddling with the Guru ka Bagh shrine, near Amritsar, on a false complaint logged by *mahant* Sundar Das Udasi. The police brutally dispelled the agitating Sikhs, earning the censure of both Indians and the British. The latter eventually had to cease action and free the 5,605 arrested, of whom 1,500 were injured. Between August 8 and November 17, 1922, 12 people had died. Unrest broke out in 1923 after the police interrupted the reading of the Guru Granth Sahib in the village of Jaito, Faridkot district, because of SGPC's support for Maharaja Ripudaman Singh of Nabha, who the British had deposed. This led to SGPC being declared an unlawful organization.

Political consolidation

The Jaito agitation continued for several months until 1925, leaving many a large number of Sikhs imprisoned, injured, or martyred, which drew sympathy for the Akali movement. Finally, exhausted by the resilient passive resistance, the government opened negotiations with the SGPC, which resulted in the passing of the Sikh Gurdwaras Act in July 1925. This act made Sikhs custodians of their places of worship.

With this, the committee gained legitimate authority over both gurdwaras and Sikhs. The SGPC held itself responsible for the cultural and social uplifting of the faith and of Sikhs across the globe. In this pursuit, the SGPC published the official code of conduct, known as the *Sikh Rahit Maryada*, which defined the identity of a Sikh and underlined the conventions to be followed to foster religiosity and communality. The Akalis also remained dominant in Sikh affairs. In later decades, they were active in the Sikhs' campaign for a Punjabi-speaking state, which ultimately came to fruition in 1966.

▼ **A 1925 print depicting** a *shahidi jatha* (band of martyrs), involved in the Jaito agitation, marching through a village in Punjab.

The new leaders

In the 1930s and 1940s, key Sikh figures emerged who had a significant impact on the politics of the region, and went on to shape the future of Punjab in independent India.

By the mid-19th century, key Sikh political figures came together to battle the movement for the creation of Pakistan. Later, post-Independence, they represented the community and its interests on a national level and stood for its rights as well. Some of the stalwarts of the Akali Dal, a party established in 1920 which is considered the principal representative of Sikhs, included Master Tara Singh, Giani Kartar Singh, Uddham Singh Nagoke, and others.

Among them, "Master" Tara Singh (as he was popularly known due to his role as a headmaster), played an important role in the Sikh ideological framework. This was evident from his position at the helm of all the prominent Sikh organizations in the 1920s: Akali Dal, Shiromani Gurdwara Parbandhak Committee (SGPC), and the Sikh Central League.

> "The **Khalsa Panth** will either be a **ruler** or a **rebel**. It has no third role to play…"
>
> TARA SINGH IN BALDEV RAJ NAYAR, *MINORITY POLITICS IN THE PUNJAB*, 1966

A politico–religious leader

Tara Singh rose to prominence with the gurdwara reform movement of 1920 (see pp.260–261). In 1921, he became the secretary of the newly formed SGPC. His prominence was aided by the debate surrounding the Nehru Committee Report of 1928, to which he responded: "Regret, Sikh rights have been overlooked." Knowing that the Sikhs were in the minority, Tara Singh supported the Congress party but opposed the proposal and convinced the leadership to withdraw it. There were

▼ **Master Tara Singh** (standing) speaking at a conference with political leaders Kanaiyalal M. Munshi and Chakravarti Rajagopalachari.

detractors to Tara Singh's pro-Congress policy as well. Though he fought the 1937 elections with the Akali Dal, after striking a compromise with the Congress, he did not win.

A matter of identity

In 1940, under Tara Singh's leadership, the Akali Dal and SPGC pledged to oppose the Lahore session's proposal for a separate homeland for Muslims. He did not support the Muslim League and also refused various inducements that wanted him to cast the lot of the Sikhs with India and its leaders. He led the Sikhs during a very turbulent time, and many who worked with him would later, in independent India, rise to be political leaders in their own right.

After Partition, Tara Singh strongly campaigned for a re-demarcation of the boundaries of Punjab on a linguistic basis, as was being done for other states in India. He led the initial charge, but this change took a long time, a series of agitations, and the contribution of many leaders. Punjabi Suba (see p.276–77) came into being with the 1966 State Reorganization Act, with Haryana and Himachal Pradesh as separate territories. Tara Singh passed away in 1967 at the age of eighty-two.

Contemporaries of Tara Singh

Besides Master Tara Singh there were several Sikh leaders who played a key role in Punjab's political history, both in the years leading up to Partition and in independent India. Among them was Giani Kartar Singh (1902–1974), an active member of the SGPC and the Shiromani Akali Dal, who later served as an elected member of the Legislative Assembly. He proposed an Azad (independent) Punjab scheme for a Punjab that had no single dominant religious community, and he strongly opposed the formation of Pakistan. In the days leading up to Partition, he was instrumental in helping members of the Sikh community migrate from Lyallpur and Sheikhupura, located in present-day Pakistan. He was then revenue minister. In the 1957 Pratap Singh Kairon Cabinet, he was revenue and irrigation minister.

Another leader was Baldev Singh (1902–1961), the first defense minister of independent India who also represented the Sikh community in the pre-independence negotiations as well as the Partition.

Uddham Singh Nagoke (1894–1966), a freedom fighter, the *Jathedar* of the Akal Takht and a member of the Rajya Sabha, also took an

▲ **Photograph of British minister Stafford Cripps** standing next to Sikh leaders (seated from left to right) Baldev Singh, Master Tara Singh, Jogendra Singh, and Ujjal Singh, c. 1946.

active role in Sikh affairs. He was primarily motivated by the Nankana Sahib tragedy of 1921, where hundreds of Sikhs were killed (see p.261). He also took part in shrine reform and participated in Akali agitation for the recovery of the keys of the Golden Temple treasury (see p.260).

Hukam Singh (1895–1983) also rose to distinction through the Shiromani Akali Dal and was its president for three years. He stood for the protection of the rights of the minorities and refused to sign the new constitution of independent India after the protection for Sikhs as a religious minority could not be secured. Hukum Singh, along with Tara Singh and Gyani Kartar Singh, also put forward the demand for a Punjabi Suba. Later, he was elected to the Lok Sabha twice and became deputy speaker.

Ujjal Singh (1895–1983) was elected to the Punjab Legislative Council in 1926 and continued serving until 1956. Moreover, he became the Governor of Punjab from 1965–1966 and the Governor of Tamil Nadu from 1966–1967. Ujjal Singh participated in the First Round of Table Conference in 1930 and served as Minister of Industries and Civil Supplies, and again as Finance and Industries Minister between 1949 and 1956.

▼ **A 1946 photograph of Sikh political leader Baldev Singh.** He served as the first Defense Minister of India from 1947–1952.

Toward Independence

As the country edged toward freedom from British rule, the Sikh community, still fighting for adequate political representation, opposed the division of their land. However, it seemed that a partition of Punjab was inevitable.

The path toward Independence in the subcontinent was shrouded in uncertainty: an uncertainty that bred suspicion. The Sikhs felt a political alienation from the more dominant Congress and Muslim League, while increasingly losing their trust in the British administration.

Disenchantment with the political process only intensified when, in 1937, the Unionist Party came to power in Punjab. The Unionist leader signed a pact with Muhammad Ali Jinnah, forging a Muslim solidarity and appointing Muslim Unionist legislators in Punjab. Its strong Arya Samaj leadership, vocal in its support of a return to Vedic Hinduism and its refusal to give Sikhism a separate standing, made allegiance with the Congress difficult. The Sikhs had only the Khalsa Nationalist Party and the Akalis—the Shiromani Akali Dal had taken over the role as spokesperson for the Sikh community—for leadership.

The war years

The announcement of World War II presented a dilemma. While critical of the British government's actions since the annexation, the Sikhs were still eager to maintain their numerical strength within the armed force. The Khalsa stood by the British, the Akalis took a stand encouraging armed recruitment while censuring the British, while the Congress upheld the noninterference policy of the party.

In 1940, the Muslim League put forward its demand for the formation of Pakistan, a separate state comprising those areas of the subcontinent where Muslims were predominant; this included most of Punjab. In fear of the division of Punjab, an All India Akali Conference was organized, followed by a general Sikh conference in Lahore, where a resolution was created opposing Pakistan. It was at this time that the idea of a separate Sikh homeland was raised, as a region between Pakistan and India, in the case that the Muslim League's demands were accepted.

The Cripps Mission

In the face of the looming Japanese threat on the Indo-Burmese border, Sir Stafford Cripps came to India in March 1942 to negotiate political issues and garner full support for the British in India. Cripps proposed the creation of an elected body of Indians who would draft the new constitution of India at the end of World War II. The proposal stated that any province that did not want to join the Union was free not to do so. Congress and the Muslim League rejected the proposal. Sikh leaders, seeing the possibility of a concession to Pakistan (even though the League's rejection was because it did not), sided with the Congress, believing it stood against Partition. The Cripps Mission was a failure but, what it did do was establish the Sikh commitment to an undivided Punjab, and India.

▼ **The Sikh community** opposed the partition of Punjab. In this image from August 1947, a delegation leaves Downing Street in London, UK, after presenting a petition requesting that the entire Punjab region remain with India and not Pakistan.

alternative to Partition. Some believed that it was inevitable, despite the official stand. It was against this background that the Congress launched the Quit India movement in August 1942. Within a few days most of the leading Congressmen were imprisoned and the party declared illegal. The Muslim League, with M.A. Jinnah at its helm, took the opportunity to solidify its campaign for Pakistan.

Towards Partition

In July 1944, C. Rajagopalachari of the Congress, later the last Governor General of India, came up with a proposal to break the political deadlock between the Muslim and the Congress: both parties would work together toward immediate independence from the British; at the end of the War, a commission would be set up to demarcate areas with an absolute Muslim majority; and in these areas a plebiscite would determine whether the inhabitants desired to form a separate sovereign state or remain in India. The Sikh leadership did not take this proposal well and organized some protests against the division of Punjab. While these

separate Sikh state, most leaders felt it was an impossible demand.

In March 1946, the British Labour Government deputed a Cabinet Mission to understand the sentiments toward the formation of a separate Muslim state. The Sikh delegation of Tara Singh, Gyani Kartar Singh, Harnam Singh, and Baldev Singh opposed the idea of Pakistan, stating the impossibility of Sikhs living under Muslim majority. The Mission's proposal of a federation, though cautiously accepted by the Congress and the Muslim League, was also abjectly unacceptable.

The Sikhs, led by the Akalis, initially rejected this proposal but later accepted the interim government on promises from the Congress that the situation would be fixed through deliberations. As the League remained adamant about Pakistan, and the Congress remained unable to resolve the situation, it became clear even to the Sikhs that the division of Punjab was the only solution. By 1947, Partition had become inevitable and, while Britain worked to pass a bill that would make India independent on August 15, 1947, the Sikhs negotiated for the maximal inclusion of their population, land, and religious sites in East Punjab.

In brief

1939
The Second World War begins

1940
The Muslim League passes the Pakistan Resolution

1941
Khalsa Defense of India League is established

1942
Sir Stafford Cripps comes to India

1944
C. Rajagopalachari comes up with a plan for Partition

1945
End of World War II

1946
The Cabinet Mission is sent to India

1947
India attains independence

Rebellion in Malaya

Of the thousands of Sikhs who fought in Malaya for the British forces in World War II, many eventually turned against their employers, raising the cry of rebellion and self-rule after joining the banner of the Indian National Army. This was not the first occasion of such Sikh resistance. The region bore a strong precedent of revolt by Indian troops.

In the colonial period, British Malaya, often referred to as Malaya, was a term used to designate the British-ruled Straits Settlements, that is Melaka, Penang, and Singapore, and the British protectorate states located within the present-day territory of Malaysia. In the 1870s, many Sikhs sailed from Punjab to Malaya as recruits in the British police and paramilitary forces or employees in the government services, forming a major chunk of the population in the region. In late 1913, the Ghadar Party (see pp.246–247) began circulation of its Urdu and Punjabi newspaper *Hindustan Ghadar*, which was distributed internationally, including Malaya. Even earlier in the century, revolutionaries had arrived in Malaya from India. These included Bhai Bhagwan Singh, a Sikh *granthi* at a Penang gurdwara who wrote and distributed poems in Punjabi urging readers to fight the British; and Bholanath Chatterjee, who was associated with a revolutionary organization in Bengal and tried to establish contacts with other revolutionaries to build a network. All this sowed the seeds of rebellion among the Indian troops.

The beginnings

The main aim of the revolutionaries was to free India from British rule. To this effect, Ghadar leaders such as Jagat Singh organized collectives to incite Indian troops to mutiny, forged links with British enemy states, such as Germany, and collected funds for weapons. Gradually, a large number of Sikhs turned to the cause of liberation. By 1915, following a few years of tireless efforts, supporters of the cause tried to leave Malaya in large numbers for Punjab, where the Ghadar party and its supporters had planned a massive anti-British rebellion. The British clamped down on the instigators everywhere, including in Malaya. Many revolutionaries were arrested and others banished. As a result, this rebellion, and the one in Punjab, eventually failed. However, by this time many Sikh soldiers had left their posts to return to Punjab and the British were not able to catch the deserters.

Malaya in World War II

If the Sikh rebellion in World War I underpinned ties with Germany, it was the link with Japan that highlighted the nature of revolt in World War II. In 1941, Japan reached out to Indian revolutionaries across Asia who were opposed to British rule. Among them was Rash Bihari Bose, previously associated with the Ghadar movement, who forged links with Sikhs such as Sardar Budh Singh, an Indian nationalist living in Malaya. When Japan invaded the Thai–Malayan border, it captured several Sikh soldiers of the British army fighting there as prisoners. Most of them turned to the Japanese side, becoming members of the Indian National Army. One such soldier was Captain Mohan Singh.

Sikhs under Mohan Singh

In February of the following year, troops of the Indian National Army, under the command of Captain Mohan Singh, attacked Singapore on behalf of Japan. They used this opportunity to recruit more Sikh soldiers from the defeated British army, who made up over one-third of the entire force. Civilian Sikhs also supported the cause of the Indian National Army by providing food and clothing to the soldiers.

Within the next few months, however, certain Indians, including Mohan Singh, became suspicious about the actual intentions of the Japanese, who had tried to restrict the activities of the Indian National Army and had even interfered in its formerly discussed jurisdiction. Following disagreements, Mohan Singh was removed from his post as the commander of the Indian National Army in December 1942, returning to India after Japan was defeated in the war.

▶ A vintage photograph, c. 1941, depicts Sikh soldiers training with an artillery gun prior to the Japanese invasion of Malaya and the fall of Singapore.

"The attack on the loyalty of the Sikhs has come … from outside the Punjab and … outside India itself. **Malcontents** in America, China, and Malaya made **great efforts** to bring about a **rebellion** in India in 1915 but fortunately their **efforts were frustrated**."

C. HANNIGAN, FMS COMMISSIONER OF POLICE IN MALAYA, 1929

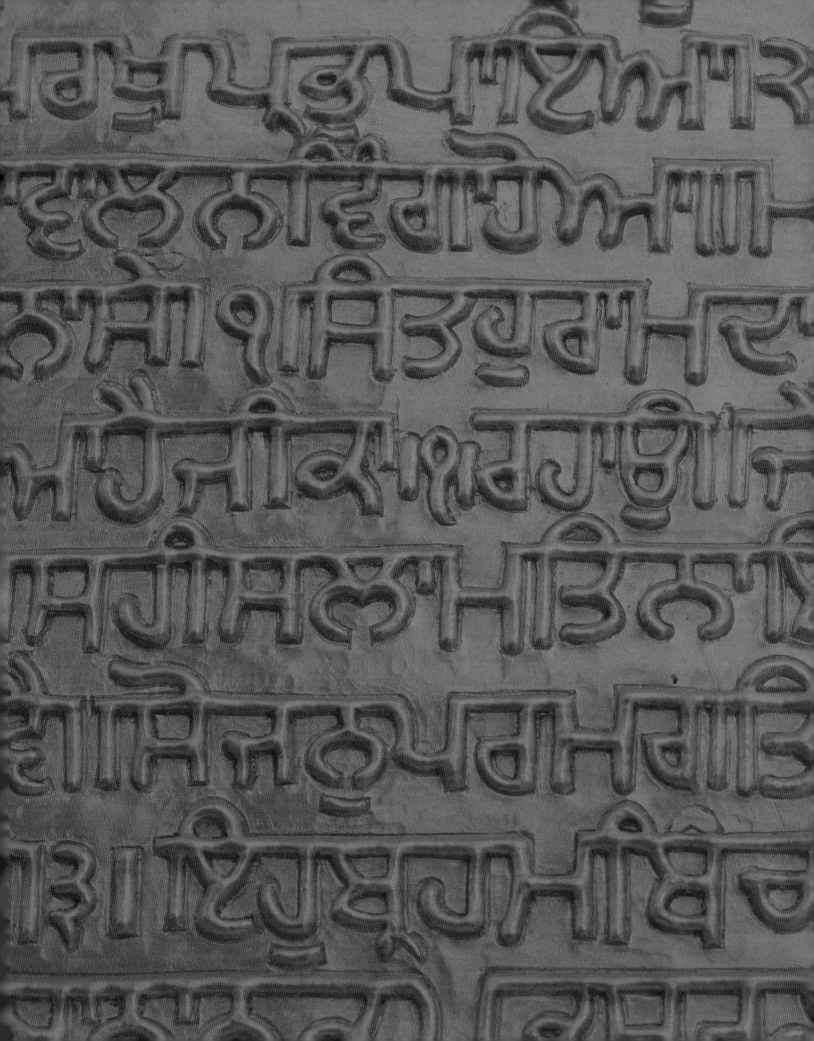

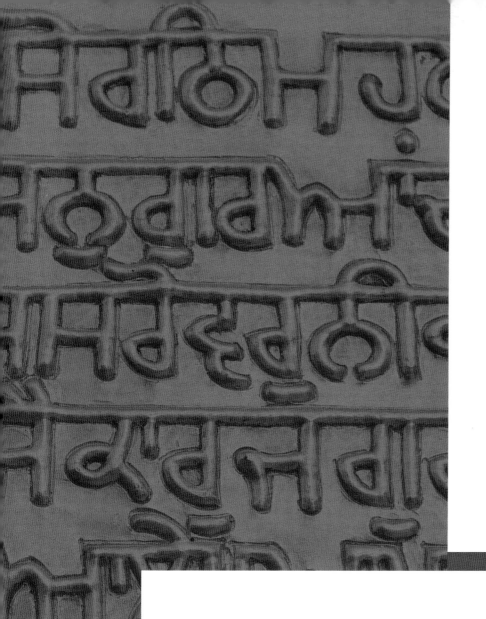

6

The Contemporary Sikh

1947 to present

Emerging from the horrors of Partition, the Sikhs established a distinct sense of identity. Not only did they make great strides in furthering the faith, but the community also contributed to the fields of sports, literature, and art. Most notably, their faith and belief in its tenets saw the Sikhs come together to serve humanity in its times of need.

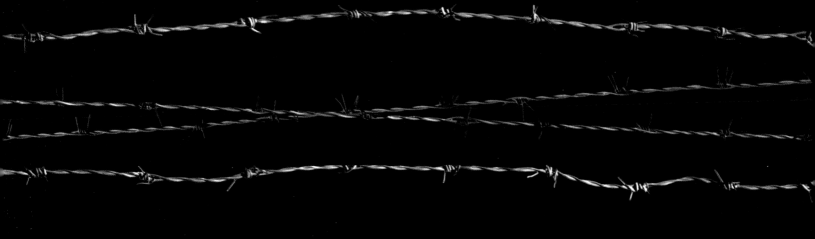

The two Punjabs

The jubilation of hard-fought independence from British rule in August 1947 was soon eclipsed by the trauma of Partition. As political lines split the Punjab region, forcing people to leave their homes, brutal violence broke out and massacres followed.

The buildup of tension and violence that had attended every decision on Partition erupted with ruthless barbarism at its implementation. Roughly 15 million people, Sikhs, Muslims, and Hindus, were displaced—leaving where they had lived for generations in search of a future amidst "their own communities." Even before the inevitability of Partition had sunk into the minds of the people of Punjab, the simmering violence became a palpable force in the province.

Sparks of hate

Tensions between communities—Muslims on one side and Sikhs and Hindus on the other— escalated in tandem with demands and debate at the political front. Although Sikhs were not the majority—they were about 13 percent of the population—they were politically active, and as landowners and prosperous agriculturists, had a significant presence. It was undeniable that if the new Muslim state was to provide itself a solid economic base, it needed control over rich, productive wheat lands that the Sikhs owned.

While the Sikhs had not initially declared any allegiance, they were identified as Hindu sympathizers and, as rioting became more aggressive, anti-Muslim. Their distinctive headdress made them easily identifiable on the streets and they were targeted more frequently than Hindus. The Muslim League made no attempt to reassure the community, and its rhetoric emphasized a purely Muslim state.

Misgivings and distrust intensified, fear and suspicion drew lines across towns and villages, dividing people who had been friends and neighbors for generations; violence festered. The series of riots that tore Calcutta in August 1946, in response to the call for "direct action" from the Muslim League, caught up with Punjab that December, when a number of Sikh villages in the North West Frontier Province were destroyed. In March 1947, Hindu and Sikhs students clashed with Muslims in Lahore, the turbulence swept other parts of the province; not just cities, but even far-flung villages. By the time normalcy was restored over 2,000 lives,

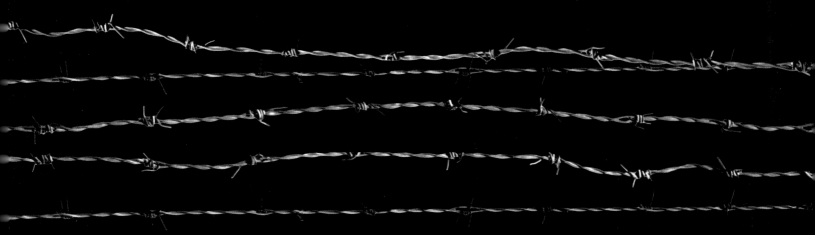

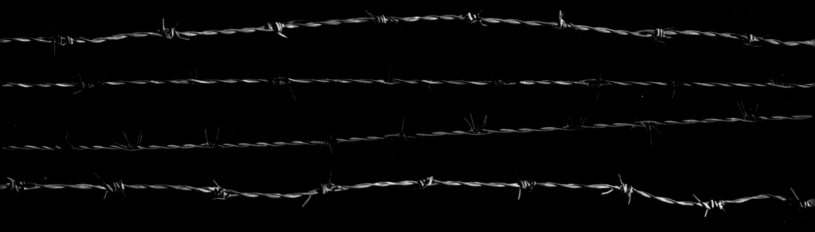

perhaps more, had been lost. As stories of rape, murder, and arson circulated, Hindus, Muslims, Sikhs, all armed themselves. Sikh *jathas* or bands were reorganized—the buildup to what would amount to civil strife was clear.

Division of lands

Partition became a certainty with the constitution of the Punjab Boundary Commission on June 30, 1947, with Sir Cyril Radcliffe as chairman. The commission was charged with demarcating a boundary based on contiguous areas with a Muslim majority, while taking into consideration "other factors." While these were not explicitly defined, they were understood to refer to Sikh claims based on issues including revenue paid, military services, development of virgin lands, and religious places. However, when all was done, over 150 shrines, half their population, and the richest of their agricultural holdings remained in the 52 percent of the province that now comprised West Punjab.

Perhaps, if the Punjab boundary had been announced sooner, the tragedy could have been contained. But Viceroy Louis Mountbatten delayed the announcement of the Radcliffe Line (the border between India Pakistan) until August 17, two days after Independence. This absolved the British government of any responsibility and left the fledgling governments in charge of populations terrified of being caught on the wrong side of the border.

MEMORIES OF THE SCHISM

It may have been decades since the Partition of the subcontinent, but the memory and trauma of the migration still haunts those who lived through it. Exhibitions of memoirs captured as conversations, reminiscences, and stories narrate these experiences. Works of artists such as Satish Gujral and Pritika Chowdhry; the writings of Saadat Hasan Manto, Bapsi Sidhwa, Khushwant Singh, and Urvashi Butalia; and filmmakers M.S. Sathyu, Deepa Mehta, and Chandraprakash Dwivedi all convey the reality of the tragedy to the generations that followed.

Partition

Millions of people were uprooted, while anarchy and terror prevailed. Violence was meted out on the streets, in homes, and in the trains carrying refugees from one side of Punjab to the other. Railway stations filled with migrants who had left their homes in haste in hopes of catching a train, but services had been disrupted, making the stations locales of crowds and pestilence. Those who managed to board risked being dragged out and massacred by mobs of the other community, and these incidents only multiplied as the spirit of revenge intensified.

Arson, looting, raiding, murder, sexual violence, and abductions became the tragic mainstay in Punjab during this period. No community was safe or blameless. The number of deaths has been estimated at between 180,000 to nearly 500,000, while there was a loss of property worth about 600 crores of rupees amidst the displacement. The subcontinent had been torn apart in a maelstrom of trauma and suffering that cannot be reported or imagined.

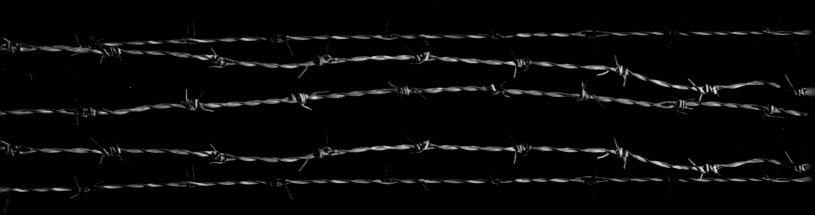

Beaming Sikh pilgrims wave from the window of a special train run for devotees to visit their sites of pilgrimage. The route, also known as the Gurdwara Circuit, covered five Sikh Takhts situated in three different states: Sri Damdama Sahib in Bathinda, Sri Keshgarh Sahib in Anandpur Sahib, Sri Akal Takht Sahib in Amritsar, Punjab; Sri Hazur Sahib in Nanded, Maharashtra; and Sri Patna Sahib in Patna, Bihar.

Ashes of Partition

The borders that were hastily drawn in 1947 birthed two nations and led to unparalleled violence. Its tragic legacy is inextricably woven into the lives of not just the survivors, but the countries of India and Pakistan as well.

On March 6, 1947, a few months before the partition of Punjab, sixteen-year-old Bir Bahadur Singh witnessed the death of his sister and twenty-six other women from his family at the hands of his father, Sant Raja Singh of Thosa Khalsa, a village in the Rawalpindi district, now in Pakistan. A Partition survivor who had managed to move to Delhi in 1947, Bir Bahadur told the Indian magazine *Open* that his father had learned of the inevitability of Partition and killed the women to protect their honor from attackers.

A darkness descends

The largest forced migration in human history began a few months before the Partition took place. Rumors and misinformation had started making the rounds and no one wanted to be caught on the wrong side of the border. Across the Indian subcontinent, communities that had lived side by side for many centuries attacked each other in an unprecedented and horrifying outbreak of communal violence across the country.

The partition of Punjab had a disastrous effect on India and Pakistan, leaving a bloody legacy that endures to this day. Families, friends, and neighbors were divided and millions were displaced or lost in the bloodshed that followed.

Tides of people spilled in and out of newly drawn borders, traveling in a variety of ways, from trains and cars to bullock carts and on foot. The journey was long and fraught with danger. Women, routinely targeted as symbols of family honor, were kidnapped and raped. Mob violence was common, and transit camps were often under armed guard, as were the trains, which in the first three weeks following Independence transported 7,00,000 passengers across the subcontinent. Author Nisid Hajari writes in *Midnight's Furies*, "Special refugee trains, filled to bursting when they set out, suffered repeated ambushes along the way. All too often they crossed the border in funereal silence, blood seeping from under their carriage doors."

Baljit Kaur Dhillon, a Partition survivor settled in the US, was still a child when her family fled from their village near Lahore to Amritsar. Her mother tried to shield her from the horrific scenes on the way, but she caught a glimpse of mutilated bodies scattered on the streets—a vivid memory that would haunt her for the rest of her life.

Partition caused terrible, gaping wounds that no amount of time could heal. Author Urvashi Butalia collected oral histories from survivors for her book, *The Other Side of*

> "… It was **then** that my **grandparents realized** that they were **never** to **return** to their ancestral **home**…"

TARUNJIT SINGH BUTALIA, DESCENDANT
OF PARTITION SURVIVORS

Silence, where she recounts the story of Kulwant Singh, a child at the time of Partition, who was afflicted by recurring nightmares as an adult. Butalia writes, "… his wife told us that he still had nightmares, that he woke in the middle of the night feeling an intense heat rising up around him, the flames which surrounded him as he lay by his father's body in 1947."

People's stories

Historical research gives evidence that fault lines existed before Partition but they were isolated events. Rami Ranger, a businessman from the UK, said in an interview to *The Guardian* that his father, who was assassinated before Ranger's birth in 1947, used to say that the country was not a shop that could be divided like property between brothers. Another interviewee from the newspaper, Surinder Shani, a retired architect, remembers that his father, a reluctant occupant, apologized to the Muslim man whose house they had to occupy in Jalandhar after escaping from Rawalpindi.

Sarjit Singh Chowdhary was a soldier who returned from duty in Iraq to find bloodshed at home. Put in charge of maintaining law and order, he accompanied a few hundred Muslims refugees safely across the border.

Alongside the tales of violence and loss were also stories of heartwarming reunion. In 2022, a pair of separated siblings, a Sikh brother and a Muslim sister, reunited after seventy-five years at Kartarpur Corridor (see pp.306–307).

It is the force of these accounts that drive home the sorrows and experiences of human beings, rather than disembodied maps, reports, or statistics.

A 1947 photograph shows a group of people crossing the Wagah border in a truck along with their belongings, which was a common sight in August 1947.

A Sikh majority state

The devastation of Partition, memories of violence, and forced migration, all fueled a deep desire in the Sikh community to protect its identity and demand a state that the Sikhs could call their own.

In the chaos that followed the Partition, Sikhs struggled to come to terms with the social, economic, and political changes they faced. The secular framework that independent India adopted was a profound shift from the system they were used to. As reservations of religious minorities were removed, many felt that the concessions they had were being stripped. Also, the Indian government nationalized the process of recruitment into all government posts, including the military.

As the fledgling Indian government dealt with overwhelming waves of refugees and fell short of expectations in terms of providing compensation, rehabilitation, or employment, many Sikhs wondered where their community was placed in a new political landscape where the Muslims had Pakistan and the Hindus had India. For many, the desire for a Sikh state remained alive and was further strengthened by the fact that while the migration had taken Sikhs to all corners of the country and the globe, it had created a concentration of Sikh settlements in some areas of east Punjab.

Princely states and a bilingual Punjab
In 1948, the princely states in Punjab acceded to the Union of India and formed a collective called the Patiala and East Punjab States Union (PEPSU), which comprised the states of Patiala, Nabha, Jind, Faridkot, Kapurthala, Kalsia, Malerkot, and Nalagarh. The Maharaja of Patiala, Yadavendra Singh, presided over this collective, which had several Sikh principalities. The creation of this body rekindled aspirations for a Sikh state, which was now seen as a mere merging of PEPSU with the other Sikh-dominant districts in east Punjab.

The pre-Partition Congress program of creating states along linguistic lines made these aspirations more imaginable. The Shiromani

Akali Dal, speaking on behalf of the Sikh community, maintained that this creation of provinces on a linguistic and cultural basis was vital for the Sikh community, in helping them experience the intellectual and spiritual freedom that an independent India stood for.

The Congress, however, seemed wary of creating a Sikh majority state. In 1956, the PEPSU merged with Punjab, expanding the state into one where the Sikhs comprised only a third of the population. The same year, Punjab was declared a bilingual state with both Hindi and Punjabi as official languages.

Toward state formation
The Akalis intensified their agitation for a separate Punjabi-speaking state. The demand was for the division of the state into Hindi-speaking

▲ **Riots broke out between** the Hindus and Sikhs over the future of the Punjab state. In this image from 1966, a mob pelts stones at a shopping center.

Haryana and Punjabi-speaking Punjab. This would make Punjabi-speaking Sikhs the majority in the new Punjab. With the basis of most of the literature of the Punjab being Sikh sacred texts and the writing in Gurmukhi (see pp.54–55), it would create, in effect, a Sikh majority state.

Despite the efforts of the Akalis, it was only in 1966 that the Congress Working Committee agreed to create a separate state of Punjab on the basis of language. A Boundary Commission was set up in April to delineate the existing linguistic homogeneity in the state. Soon, the East Punjab state was divided into Haryana and its hill territories transferred to the then centrally administered Himachal Pradesh. Chandigarh, built as the administrative headquarters of Punjab, was declared a Union Territory that would serve as the joint capital to Punjab and Haryana.

SHIROMANI AKALI DAL

The Shiromani Akali Dal is a political party closely associated with apex Sikh religious institutions, such as the Shiromani Gurdwara Prabandhak Committee (SGPC). It is generally accepted as being the voice of the Sikh community in India. It played an active role in the freedom struggle and lays claim to being the oldest regional political party in India. It traces its lineage to the 1920s as a movement that challenged the British to win control over the management of gurdwaras through the Sikh Gurdwara Act of 1925.

In brief

1948
The PEPSU is created

1955
State Reorganization Committee publishes its report

1956
PEPSU is merged with Punjab

1961
Tara Singh holds a hunger strike in the Golden Temple to demand a Punjab Suba

1966
The State of Punjab is created

Panj Takhts

The word *takht* or *takhata*, which means "seat of authority," is the highest emblem of temporal sovereignty and a cornerstone of the Sikh faith. The Takhts represent the dispensation of the community's worldly affairs, embodying authority and sovereignty.

In 1609, Guru Hargobind established the first and most important Takht, the Akal Takht (throne of the Timeless God) at Amritsar in Punjab. From here the Guru presided over secular judgments for the community and deliberated on political matters, and where the assembly heard ballads extolling heroic feats of Sikhs. In 1708, when Guru Gobind Singh vested the authority of the Guru in the Adi Granth, the Akal Takht became the seat where decisions on both religious and secular matters were debated and decided. All resolutions passed by the Akal Takht were regarded as *hukamnamas* (orders from the Guru) and were binding on all Sikhs.

There is no doubt regarding the predominance of the spiritual authority over the secular. The architecture of the Takht in relation to the gurdwara shows it. While both occupy a seat, the Guru Granth Sahib is always placed at a higher level in the sacred shrine within the gurdwara complex.

The Akal Takht, located across the entrance to the Harmandir Sahib (the Golden Temple) is the first and oldest of the five Takhts. Attacks and desecrations throughout history have only served to enhance its symbolic embodiment of the Sikh spirit. This paramount Takht has its own unique traditions. The *Jathedar* of the Akal Takht is the highest spokesman and the spiritual leader of the Sikh Panth. The cleric here recites the evening prayer and *Ardas* while donning an unsheathed sword.

Remembering Guru Gobind Singh

There are four other Takhts that the Panth has established over the last few centuries. Takht Sri Patna Sahib, also known as Takht Sri Harmandir, is in Patna, Bihar, at the birthplace of Guru Gobind Singh. The gurdwara is also linked to Guru Nanak, who visited Patna on his first *udasi* (holy tour), initiating the ritual of *langar* (communal eating). The ninth

The Contemporary Sikh

> "**Sri Akal Takht**, the Throne Of Immortal is ... **non-violent**, yet so self-respecting, most **secular** but deeply **religious**, dedicated to **self-sacrifice**, yet pledged to self-preservation."

H.S. DILGEER (SIKH POET AND SCHOLAR)

Guru, Tegh Bahadur also visited it, and considered it *Guru ka ghar* (adobe of the Guru). The original gurdwara, built in 1666, suffered damage after a fire, and was reconstructed by Maharaja Ranjit Singh in 1839. An earthquake damaged it again in 1935. The edifice as it stands today was completed in 1954 and was extensively renovated some years ago.

The Takht Keshgarh at the Gurdwara Sri Keshgarh Sahib in Anandpur is where the tenth Guru, Guru Gobind Singh, spent most of his life, expanding the existing city and renaming it Anandpur. This is where the Guru established the Khalsa and performed its first initiation in 1699.

Takht Sachkhand Sri Hazur Sahib, along the banks of the Godavari at Nanded, Maharashtra, is where, in 1708, Guru Gobind Singh passed away and was cremated. His followers installed the Guru Granth Sahib on the Takht where the Guru would sit, and built a room over it. They named it Takht Sahib. Raja Chandu Lal of Hyderabad supported the shrine and its caretakers. In time, Maharaja Ranjit Singh sent resources and men to build a grand edifice.

Takht Sri Damdama Sahib (Guru Ki Kashi) at Talwandi Sabo in Bhatinda, Punjab, is also linked to Guru Gobind Singh. It marks the site where he held his daily assemblies when he was staying at Damdama while preparing the Guru Granth Sahib. It was in this version of the holy book that he designated the eternal Guru and spiritual leader after him in 1705. The legendary Baba Deep Singh (see p.102), who was appointed as Damdama Sahib's first *Jathedar* (appointed head), prepared copies of the Guru Granth Sahib and distributed them to other gurdwaras so that Sikh doctrine might spread further. However, it was only in 1966 that the Takht was given official recognition as the fifth Takht.

The Takhts are, therefore, at the heart of the Sikh faith. Acknowledging the desire of every Sikh to visit all five Takhts at least once in their lifetime, a train service was started in 2014, linking the Panj Takhts (five Takhts) across different states in India, providing pilgrims the opportunity to visit them all in one trip.

Harmandir Sahib

Harmandir Sahib, which translates to "Abode of God," is the primary place of worship for members of the Sikh faith. Also known as the Golden Temple, it has survived the ravages of time, including attacks by foreign invaders. Today, it attracts many pilgrims and is home to the world's largest *langar*, which serves more than 100,000 people every day.

A resplendant site

The beautiful main sanctum with its golden dome can be seen through the Darshani Deori, the arch that stands at the entrance of the complex. The main hall or sanctum is situated on a small platform in the center of the Amrit Sarovar, which means "pool of nectar." While the bottom half of the structure is covered with white marble, the upper level is adorned with about 880 lbs (400 kg) of gold leaf, which was added during the restoration of the site in 1830 during the reign of Maharaja Ranjit Singh (see pp.182–183). Since then, the Harmandir Sahib complex has undergone many refurbishments. Its premises are also home to a clock tower and a Sikh history museum.

▲ **An archival photograph, c. 1880, of the causeway** linking the entrance arch to the Darbar Sahib or the sanctum.

Contemporary photograph of the Harmandir Sahib Gurdwara. The gold-leaf encrusted upper-half and dome, which can be seen reflected in the Amrit Sarovar, gives the site its popular name, Golden Temple.

Architecture and interior

The complex has four entrances to welcome people from all directions. This reflects the Sikh faith's egalitarian nature, embracing people of all faiths and social backgrounds. The walls around the Amrit Sarovar are etched with stories of those who have been healed of their ailments. The sanctum's ground level is home to the Guru Granth Sahib in the day, where it is placed beneath a gem-encrusted canopy for visitors to offer prayers. At night, the holy book is taken to the five-storeyed Akal Takht, which stands in white and gold opposite the causeway.

The sanctum interior is decorated with gold plates, precious stones, and mirror work, which reflects the influence of both Rajput and Islamic artistic styles. A flight of stairs leads to the Sheesh Mahal, or the Hall of Mirrors, and golden domes rise above this pavilion.

1. Causeway to the main sanctum; **2.** Carp in the Amrit Sarovar; **3.** Arched entrance; **4.** Guru Granth Sahib inside the sanctum; **5.** Rich inlay work on marble and frescos on the roof, along with embossed doors of the window in the interior; **6.** Exterior view; **7.** A window in the sanctum; **8.** Pilgrims on the causeway; **9.** *Langar* being served; **10.** Gilded Gurbani text; **11.** Volunteer making food for the *langar*; **12.** Vessels in the kitchen; **13.** Ceiling pattern from the Sheesh Mahal; **14.** Musicians performing; **15.** A machine making chapatis.

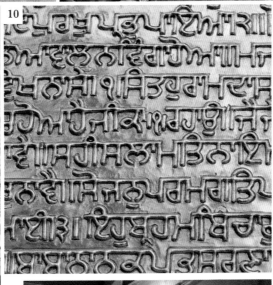

A tradition of divine music

The holy recitations, the ragas that complement them, and the classical and folk music singing styles are all elements that form the essence of the Sikh music tradition, and help the devotee on their journey toward the Ultimate Truth.

The origins of *Gurmat Sangeet*, also known as the *Gurbani Kirtan* or *Shabad Kirtan*, can be traced to Guru Nanak, who composed *banis* or hymns in diverse traditional Indian musical meters and singing styles. He incorporated some complementary string and percussion instruments and went on to formalize the *Shabad Kirtan*. This musical rendition of Guru Granth Sahib's poetic *bani* is used to disseminate the sacred word of the Gurus.

The Gurus' words in ragas

Endowed with a specific identity, *Shabad Kirtan* has become an intrinsic element of the Sikh ethos. The classical traditions of *Gurmat Sangeet* were enriched and preserved during the lives of the ten gurus. The Gurus composed several hymns in various musical modes and ragas, which were then passed down until Guru Arjan (see pp.76–77). The fifth Guru compiled these compositions in the Adi Granth in 1604, which he then installed in the Harmandir Sahib.

> **GURBANI**
>
> *Gurbani* stems from two words, *gur* (Sanskrit, "guru") meaning "enlightener or spiritual teacher" and *bani* (Sanskrit, "van") meaning sound, word, or speech. It refers to the sacred compositions and utterances of the Gurus and other holy saints as compiled in the holy Scripture, the Guru Granth Sahib. For Sikhs, *gurbani* is the revealed word – the way God discloses and communicates Itself to humanity.

The successive gurus expanded the anthology, adding more verses with a comprehensive indication of the various *ragas* mandated for each of the poems. The collection of the whole *bani* or *gurbani* (Divine Word) in various *ragas*, *raga* forms, music signs, and a variety of musical directions, is a one-of-a-kind example in the world-music landscape.

The Sikh scripture is, thus, a collection of around 6,000 *shabad* (scriptural verses). The Sikhs contemplate the *Akal Purakh* (the timeless being, God) through this recitation, in pursuit of divine enlightenment and eternal bliss. Performed in all congregations and during religious activities and rituals, the recitation of *kirtan* elevates the soul from the material to the transcendental realm of spiritual ecstasy. In most instances, *kirtan* is performed by volunteers. In smaller groups, this tradition is visible in villages, towns, and in the diaspora. However, some of those that perform *kirtans* are professionals.

The expression of an ethos

Historically, there have been three types of Sikh musicians: Rababis, Ragis, and Dhadhis. Guru Nanak established the Rababi tradition with Bhai Mardana; Guru Arjan promoted the Ragis lineage. Dhadhis have sung *Vaars*

▼ **A 1915 photograph of Sikh men** singing *banis* in a barn in France.

(ballads) to inspire the community to deeds of heroism and valor, and they are a distinctive feature of Sikh music.

Over the years, Sikhs have used music to invoke their heritage and affirm their identity. In the face of oppression and injustice, the Dhadhis came to the forefront, composing songs of resistance that evoked Sikh history, religion and gallantry—referencing Punjabis in the armed forces, the spirit of the Punjabi diaspora overseas, or the camaraderie of Sikh farmer communities.

Today, there are different styles of Sikh devotional music. Sikh music is also emerging as a unique heritage in modern music. Many schools, colleges, and institutions in Punjab and around the world teach *Gurmat Sangeet*. Sikh musicians, *kirtaniyas*, and instructors of the *Gurmat* tradition are in high demand, to illustrate Sikh musicology's predominance in the larger cultural narrative, its spiritual capacity to bring the community together, and its aesthetic sensibilities that rouse bravery in the face of injustice—the Khalsa's central message.

"If we **sing** of God and **listen** to his praises and let **divine love** arise within, all our suffering will disappear, and we will experience **enduring peace** within our **heart**, **mind,** and **soul**."

GURU NANAK, *GURU GRANTH SAHIB*

Ragis, **or artists, performing *Gurmat Sangeet*** at the Parliament of the World's Religions, an international event which was hosted by Australia in 2009.

The princely states

The many rajas and maharajahs had always had an important role in Punjab's political, cultural, and military landscape, before and during Ranjit Singh's time, under the British, and even later in independent India.

Insignia of the rulers of Patiala

Before its consolidation under Ranjit Singh, a number of chieftains controlled Punjab. Local titles varied but, regardless of their territory size, all were rulers. It is also why Ranjit Singh was hesitant in taking on the title of Maharaja: it would have been a clear declaration of his rule over all other rulers in Punjab. However, he was successful in forming the most illustrious kingdom of Punjab. His death in 1838 threw the kingdom into chaos. The East India Company took advantage and, by 1849, Punjab was under the British. Under the Raj, the states were formalized, titles awarded, a protocol established, and hierarchy expressed in terms of gun salutes.

The princes remained autonomous, in principle, but the British held the reins of power and authority. The valor of the princely lords was now in service of the Empire, and they served Imperial forces in the two World Wars. They also encouraged widespread recruitment to the British Indian army, leading from the front as they joined the war effort themselves.

The magnificence of the princes

Their power may have been diluted, but the opulence and grandeur of the Sikh rulers did not wane. Maharaja Bhupinder Singh of Patiala (1891–1938) is symbolic of the time. His treasury included priceless jewellery—the Cartier necklace with around 3,000 diamonds being the most famous. Known for his appetite for sports cars, he owned a fleet of more than twenty-seven Rolls-Royces and the rarer Maybach, which Adolf Hitler gifted him in 1935. However, he was more than the epitome of luxury: He played a significant role in Sikh affairs, was present at festivals, where he financed *langars* and gave liberally to gurdwaras. He functioned as an intermediary between the British and the Akali Sikhs of the Shiromani Gurdwara Prabhandhak Committee (SGPC), even as he funded other religious institutions, such as the Kali temple in Patiala. He was a patron of religious Sikh music and significant to the development of modern Sikh *kirtan*. When the greatest khayal

A black-and-white photograph from the Diamond Jubilee celebrations of the Maharaja of Kapurthala depicts the Maharaja seated in the back, watching an Indian dancer perform at the palace in Kapurthala, Punjab.

singer of his time, Tanras Khan fled the Delhi court, he sought refuge in Patiala, establishing the Patiala khyal gharana or school of music, and making it the musical capital of Punjab.

The maharaja also played a prominent role in sports, being the founder of BCCI (Board of Control for Cricket in India). He is attributed to have started the prestigious Ranji Trophy in honor of his cricketer friend—Ranjitsinhji, Maharaja Jam Saheb of Nawanagar in Kathiawar (now Gujarat).

Many princely rulers were known for their syncretic sensibilities, promoting not just the Sikh religion through the propagation of art and architecture, but other faiths as well. Maharaja Jagatjit Singh, the Ahluwalia ruler of Kapurthala State, built the Moorish Mosque for his Muslim subjects. His royal residence was inspired by the European-style Château de Fontainebleau and the Palace of Versailles in France.

With music at the heart of the Sikh tradition, Kapurthala, like many princely states, nurtured numerous gharanas or schools of music such as Patiala, Talwandi, Kapurthala, and Shamchaurasi. Sikh princes, such as Hira Singh of Nabha and Rajinder Singh of Patiala were instrumental in establishing the Sikh Press. The scions from the royal families donated to Amritsar's Khalsa College (see pp.236–237), and educational institutions in their own states, such as Mohindra College in Patiala, which was founded in 1875. They patronized works on Sikh history and tradition as well. For instance, the *Guru Shabad Ratnakar Mahan Kosh*, a four-volume, Punjabi encyclopedia, which Bhai Kahn Singh Nabha compiled, had three patrons before it was published in 1930—Maharaja Brijindar Singh of Faridkot, Maharaja Ripudaman Singh of Nabha, and Maharaja Bhupinder Singh of Patiala.

Legacy in independent India

After independence in 1947, the princely states of the now-partitioned Punjab signed the instrument of accession and formally joined the Union of India. The Patiala and East Punjab States Union (PEPSU) gave eight princely states— Patiala, Jind, Kapurthala, Nabha, Faridkot, Malerkotla, Kalsia, and Nalagarh—a distinct identity before it was merged into Punjab in 1956. The royal scions retained their honors and titles until 1971 when the 26th Amendment of the Indian Constitution dissolved the royal titles and abolished the royal privy purse.

Despite this, the descendants of the kings of Punjab continue to have significant influence and impact, be it in politics, sport, art, or culture. The descendants of the royal house of Patiala have been active players in the political and sports scene. Nabha's Pratap Singh Malvendra Bahadur, who served in World War II, ended his military career as colonel of the Sikh Regiment of the Indian army in 1951. The royal scion of Kapurthala State, Sukhjit Singh, was awarded the Maha Vir Chakra, India's second highest award for gallantry, for his courage during the 1971 India–Pakistan war.

Royal jewels

Rulers have always surrounded themselves with grand accoutrements of office to affirm their exalted status, and the princely states of Punjab were no exception. Royal states, such as Patiala and Kapurthala, patronized artists and commissioned jewelers from India and abroad to create stunning pieces that reflected and added to their prestige.

▼ Regal dinner set
Maharaja Bhupinder Singh of Patiala commissioned an opulent 1,400-piece, gold-plated silver dinner set from London, in honor of a visit from Prince Edward, Prince of Wales, in 1922. The royal tour reportedly culminated in a lavish banquet serving 200 guests. Seen here is part of the set.

Coffee or hot water pots, engraved with the Patiala coat of arms

Vessel handles featuring a lion's face

Tongs fashioned with a crown and flowers

► The Patiala Choker
French jeweler Cartier crafted this stunning multi-layer necklace with rubies, natural pearls, and diamonds for one of Maharaja Bhupinder Singh's queens in 1931.

Oval ruby cabochon beads

18-carat tobacco-colored diamond

◀ The Patiala Necklace

The Maharaja of Patiala commissioned this iconic, five-tiered, Art Deco diamond necklace from the French jeweler Cartier in 1928. It disappeared for a time, but was later found and reassembled using some replica stones.

Ornament fanning out like a tuft of feathers

Large ruby in the center

▶ Maharaja's sarpech

This turban ornament (*sarpech*) was crafted around 1910 for Maharaja Bhupinder Singh. The gold trinket is encrusted with 15 rubies, 133 diamonds, and a natural pearl drop.

The centerpiece, the "De Beers" diamond, was reputed to be the world's seventh-largest diamond

Blue-feathered neck in enamel

▲ Peacock accessory

This charming ornament in the shape of a peacock was made by French jewelry house Mellerio dits Meller, in 1905. Fabricated in vibrant enamel and set with rose-cut diamonds, it was worn by Maharaja Jagatjit Singh of Kapurthala as a *sarpech* and by his wife Anita Delgado as a hair pin.

Sporting glory

Sikh athletes have had an influential impact in Indian sports in the last seven decades, be it as members of the hockey team that won gold in the 1948 Olympics, or as practitioners of the nationally recognized martial-art sport, Gatka.

"I am **inspired** by **honest** people who don't cheat others. To me the famous are those who are **kind** to fellow human beings and **dedicate** their life to **charity**."

FAUJA SINGH

Fauja Singh, the 102-year-old celebrated marathon runner on a run in Jalandhar, Punjab, in India.

The iconic Kikkar Singh and Dara Singh were the epitome of Sikh sportsmen, defined by their height, complemented by wide shoulders and a deep chest. Popularly known as Kikkar Singh Pahilvan for having uprooted an acacia (kikkar) tree with his bare hands, Prem Chand was a legendary Sikh wrestler (pahilvan). He enjoyed the patronage of many rulers of princely states in pre-Independence India and was famous for his unrivaled strength and world-class skill. Dara Singh's illustrious career as a 1956 Commonwealth champion wrestler brought him accolades not just in the ring and on the mat, but also in politics and on the silver screen. During the three decades of his wrestling career, he competed in over 500 bouts, defeating many stalwarts and earning the coveted title of *Rustom-e-Hind*, or the Champion of India. He was inducted into the WWE Hall of Fame in 2018, six years after his demise. Wrestling, however, was just one of the many sports where the Sikh community found glory. Their success is often associated with the uncompromising physical fortitude, mental strength, and indomitable spirit that fired their forefathers on the battlefield.

Making history

The Indian hockey team's gold medal at the 1948 London Olympics was a defining milestone in Indian sports history. Coming months after India got its independence, it also heralded the emergence of Balbir Singh Dosanj. The beloved sportsman won three Olympic gold medals, scoring two of the four goals in the London Olympics, and five of the six goals in the Helsinki Olympics in 1952. After him, five other Balbir Singhs would go on to represent India at the national level, though none matched his success.

In 2021, when the Indian hockey team made it to the semifinals of the Olympics after forty-nine years, the three winning goals were scored by players from the Sikh community. Sikh representation has, however, not been confined only to India. There have been 157 Sikh hockey players who have competed in the Olympics, representing nine different countries.

The racing stars

Olympics and Sikh athletes also bring up the image of another great Sikh sportsman—Milkha Singh or the "Flying Jat" (see pp.292–293). He won India gold in the 1958 and 1962 Asian Games as well as the 1958 Commonwealth Games. However, he is most recognized for finishing fourth in the 400m race in the 1960 Olympics in Rome.

Fauja Singh is another famous athlete. A Sikh who migrated from India to the UK in the 1960s, and who took up running in his eighties, Singh broke the world record for the fastest marathon in the ninety-plus age bracket. An athletic icon but also a celebrity, in 2004 Fauja Singh earned a spot in an Adidas advertising campaign alongside international sportsmen David Beckham and Jonny Wilkinson. At the

▲ **Bishan Singh Bedi holds up the trophy** as his team, Northamptonshire, celebrate their victory against Lancashire in this photograph from the 1976 Gillette Cup Final held at the Lord's Cricket Ground in London, UK.

age of one hundred, he attempted and accomplished eight world records in the age group in one day at the special 2011 Ontario Masters Association. In 2012 he carried the Olympic torch. When asked about the rigor of running a marathon, Fauja Singh said, "The first twenty miles are not difficult. As for the last six miles, I run while talking to God."

On the cricket field

One of the most magnificent spectacles in cricket history was when left-arm spinner Bishan Singh was called to bowl. He was a key member of India's renowned spin quartet in the 1960s and 1970s, securing 1,500 wickets in 237 matches. The third most successful test spinner, Bishan Singh, is known for his performance in the 1976 World Cup, when he bowled an incredible 12-8-6-1 session to lead India to their first One Day International cricket victory against East Africa.

Another celebrated cricketer is Harbhajan Singh, a specialist spin bowler who rose to fame during a Test series in 2001, where he became the first Indian bowler to take a hat trick in a test match. Named the Sikh Sports Person of the Year in 2011 for his contribution to the Indian cricket team's World Cup victory in 2011, Harbhajan Singh has had a dramatic yet illustrious career. In his twenty-four years as a cricketer, he has claimed 711 international wickets from only 367 matches.

▶ **Legendary sprinter Milkha Singh is** the first to cross the finish line during the AAA Championship in London in 1960.

Milkha Singh

From running to save his life during the violence of the Partition in 1947 to running for gold in the 1960 Rome Olympics, Milkha Singh's journey of grit and perseverance inspired an entire nation.

In 1958, Milkha Singh was at his peak. He had bagged the gold medal in the 200m and 400m events at the Asian Games in Tokyo and become the first Indian athlete to win gold at the British and Commonwealth Games in Wales. The win was so momentous that Jawaharlal Nehru, the prime minister of India at that time, announced a government holiday in the country.

Two years later, at the 1960 Rome Olympics, Milkha Singh was one of the best, moving into the men's 400m finals, with compelling timings in the preceding races. The hopes of a young India were pinned on him. Blazing off the blocks, Singh seemed certain of the top spot, however, an error in judgment made him slow down just before the final turn. This difference of a mere 0.1 seconds cost him the bronze medal. Although he set a national record that day, one that stood unbeaten for nearly forty years, the lingering pain of this loss shadowed Singh all his life.

Early life

Milkha Singh was born into a large family of farmers in the small village of Govindpura (now in Pakistan) in the early 1930s. Running was a regular feature of his life. As a child, he ran to school each day or raced moving trains for fun. At the age of fourteen, he ran to escape the mobs that massacred his family during the brutal partition of British-ruled India. In his autobiography, *The Race of My Life*, Singh recounted witnessing his father being murdered.

▲ Milkha Singh (right) meeting Prince Philip, the Duke of Edinburgh during the Commonwealth Games in Wales, 1958.

▶ **Milkha Singh passes the baton** at the Queen's Baton Relay for the launch of the Commonwealth Games in 2010, in London.

"As he fell, Father screamed 'Bhaag Milkha, bhaag' (run, Milkha, run). With my father's warning … running through my head, I fled for my life." Singh escaped and hid in a blood-smeared, India-bound train and found his way to safety at his sister Isher's house in Delhi, in independent India.

Experiments to fame

In 1951, Singh joined the Indian Army as a sepoy, a career that offered stability for young men with little education.

Although he had a penchant for running, Singh was introduced to the sport of track and sprinting while in the army. One Saturday morning in 1953, he heard an announcement for a six-mile race. The prize—an extra glass of milk every day—was attractive enough to motivate him into winning his first race. Over the next few years, Singh was selected for cross-country races and he trained relentlessly. However, a dismal performance at his first Olympics, held in Melbourne in 1956, ignited a fire in him. "In my determination to avoid failure, I set myself a goal … to transform myself into a running machine," he wrote in his autobiography. "Running had thus become my God, my religion and my beloved." Singh reportedly won seventy-seven out of the eighty races he ran in his career.

After his heartbreaking loss at the 1960 Olympics, Singh redeemed himself when he beat Pakistani athlete Abdul Khaliq at the Indo–Pak meet in Lahore the same year, and earned himself the moniker, the Flying Sikh, coined by General Ayub Khan of Pakistan.

An icon

Milkha Singh's sporting legacy is tied to a new republic rising out of its many troubled phases. His determination and grit to do better became an inspiration to many. After an illustrious sports career, Milkha Singh worked for the Punjab government as a deputy director of sports. He made impactful efforts toward nurturing young talent, setting up summer camps, making sports class compulsory in school curriculums, building sports wings for different disciplines, and improving the quality of sports education in India.

In 1958, Singh was awarded the Padma Shri, India's fourth-highest civilian honor, and a Bollywood movie about his life, *Bhaag Milkha Bhaag*, was released in 2013.

"Even today, if I look back on my **life**, there are only two **incidents** that still **haunt** me—the **massacre** of my family during Partition and my **defeat** at **Rome**."

MILKHA SINGH, *THE RACE OF MY LIFE*, 2013

Identity politics

The loss and displacement of Partition led to the quest for a distinct political identity by Sikh leaders. Post-Partition politics, divisions aggravated by the vernacular press, and socioeconomic discontent were all exploited by cynical politicians.

After Partition, the only area where the Sikhs were in the majority in East Punjab was Patiala and the East Punjab Union, created by merging princely states. The government did not recognize the demand for Punjabi as a medium of instruction in schools and there was strong opposition from the Arya Samaj movement. The Sachar Formula of 1949 sought a compromise by creating Hindi and Punjabi zones for schools. However, Arya Samaj and others asked Punjabi Hindus to declare Hindi as their mother tongue in the 1951 and 1961 census. Competing with this was the Akali Dal–led Punjabi Suba Movement, which, after a prolonged agitation, largely prevailed. The Punjabi University was created at Patiala in 1956 to serve the language.

Haryana was carved out of the Hindi-speaking areas of Punjab in 1966, with hill areas going to Himachal Pradesh. The now-truncated Punjab with 54 percent Sikhs, benefited tremendously from the agrarian Green Revolution that in time, tripled rice yields in the state. Sikh farmers led development in the agricultural sector, which outpaced industry, leading to an increase in unemployment, economic disparity, and social discontent.

The Indian National Congress that formed the government at the center and the Akali Dal emerged as two key players in the political sphere. Congress chief ministers ruled Punjab from 1947 to 1966, but came under President's Rule twice. Post-1966, Gurmukh Singh Musafir became chief minister for a short period, but as acknowledged representative of the Sikh ethos in a Sikh majority state, the Akalis were in a strong position. Their coalition won the election of 1967, but could not follow up their victory by addressing the challenges facing the state. Tara Singh's death (see pp.262–263) in November 1967 saw the Akalis becoming increasingly divided.

The politics of power
Quick to take advantage, the Congress, secure in its position as a national party, did everything to increase support from Sikh factions looking for personal gain to win over Punjab. Defections and regroupings of political alliance became the order of the day, and it was not long before linguistic and religious chauvinism reappeared.

The 1971 parliamentary elections were disastrous for the Akali Dal. Far from having the support of the Sikh masses, it won just one of the thirteen seats from the state; the Congress took ten. President's Rule was imposed when the chaos of dissension and defection followed. The 1972 general

◄ **The Indian Army entered the premises of the Golden Temple** as a part of Operation Bluestar after Jarnail Singh Bhindranwale militarized the Golden Temple complex. This first image of the damaged Akal Takht after Army action in 1984 depicts the damage done to the shrine as a result of the fighting between the Indian Army and Bhindranwale's men.

ANANDPUR SAHIB RESOLUTION
The Resolution, among other things, asked the central government to award greater autonomy to the Indian states, and give Chandigarh and other Punjabi-speaking areas to Punjab. However, there is some debate about the exact wording of the Resolution since different factions circulated different versions. Harchand Singh Longowal, the Akali Dal president, sent a version to both houses of Parliament, which is considered official. While most Akalis denied that the Anandpur Resolution implied separatism, the complex terminology leaves it open to interpretation. The references to the Sikhs as a separate *qaum* or community entitled to govern itself gave separatists scope to assert themselves.

election did not change the picture: the Congress won sixty-six and the Akalis twenty-four, of the total 104 seats. As chief minister, Zail Singh promoted Sikh identity through the formal celebration of historic figures and events, striving to make clear that his membership of the Congress did not affect his identity as a Sikh: there was no reason for the community not to rally around him. The Akalis adopted a more religious rhetoric. At times, both came together to mark religious events.

Jarnail Singh Bhindranwale entered the political sphere within this context. A fundamentalist, he encouraged Sikhs to eschew modernization, alcohol, and drugs. His popularity among the peasantry ensured he was courted by Congress and Akali politicians, including Zail Singh. The 1978 clash with Nirankaris in Amritsar brought him into the spotlight.

Anandpur Sahib Resolution and after
In October 1973, a list of demands on behalf of the Sikh community, known as the Anandpur Sahib Resolution, was presented at the eighteenth session of the All-India Akali Conference and passed. Akali Dal, the ruling party at the time, did not see the need to push for any action. It was in 1980, when Congress won the national election and dismissed the Akali chief minister of Punjab, Prakash Singh Badal, that the Resolution became the cause for agitation.

As these demands were ignored, the Akalis launched the Dharam Yudh Morcha (righteous demonstration) in 1982. Bhindranwale, now a force to be reckoned with in Punjab, allied with them.

In time, he became more powerful and a new spate of violence ensued. Anyone opposed to Bhindranwale was attacked. Gurbachan Singh, the third Nirankari guru, was assassinated in 1980, journalist and editor Lala Jagat Narain in 1981. Hijacking, looting, and killing became commonplace, paving the way for President's rule in the state. Anticipating arrest, Bhindranwale moved from the periphery of the Golden Temple complex to Akal Takht, which he fortified. He established himself at the shrine and conducted all activities from there. He would be killed in June 1984.

1984

Indira Gandhi's assassination led to a surge of violence against the Sikh community. For three days, mobs murdered women, men, and children and destroyed property in Delhi and elsewhere. The chilling pogrom left scars that have never really healed.

> "I **apologize** not only to the **Sikh community**, but to the **whole** Indian **nation** because what took place in **1984** is the **negation** of the concept of **nationhood** enshrined in our **Constitution**."

DR MANMOHAN SINGH, FORMER PRIME MINISTER, IN 2005

On October 31, 1984, then Prime Minister Indira Gandhi's bodyguards, Satwant Singh and Beant Singh, turned their guns on her in an act of vengeance. Nearly five months before this assassination sparked a brutal pogrom against the Sikh community in India, Gandhi ordered the Indian Army to enter the Golden Temple in Amritsar. The aim of Operation Bluestar was to flush out Jarnail Singh Bhindranwale and other militants from the Sikh shrine. The move created a chasm of animosity between the Sikh community and the Central government.

From the government's point of view, the militants incited and organized violent incidents and killings across the state. They had fortified themselves inside the holy shrine, taking advantage of the government's reluctance to breach the sanctity of the temple. For the Sikhs, none of this mattered in the face of the guns, artillery, and tanks that had violated the sanctity of Harmandir Sahib, killing devotees and priests, and extensively damaging the Akal Takht. This desecration had shattered the trust of the Sikh community and led to a deep sense of outrage. Gandhi's assassination, the bodyguards had confessed, was an act of retribution for Operation Bluestar. In the hysteria that followed Gandhi's death, the Sikh community indiscriminately faced hostility, even violence and killings—not just for the assassination of the prime minister, but for earlier extremist violence in Punjab.

Absence of law and order
Rioting mobs first arrived at the hospital where Indira Gandhi had been taken and died. The volatility of the situation became apparent when a mob stoned the then President of India Zail Singh's motorcade. The crowds soon fanned out and attacked gurdwaras, looting Sikh property, and setting their vehicles on fire. Rioting spread to the outer areas of Delhi, as flames were fanned through rumors and false news. The mobs attacked members of the Sikh community. Iron rods, clubs, knives, acid, kerosene, and petrol were used to maim, slaughter, and burn. Sikh men were dragged by their hair, beaten, and set on fire, Sikh women were tortured, raped, and killed. One block in Trilokpuri, Delhi, witnessed the massacre of, it is reported, 350 Sikhs. The police, it seemed, were complicit as no help arrived.

Between October 31 and November 3, when Gandhi was cremated, 2,800 Sikhs were killed in Delhi alone. While these are the government's figures, some suggest that the number was as high as 8,000. The killings were not limited to Delhi, but extended to Haryana, Madhya Pradesh, Uttar Pradesh, Jharkhand, and Bihar as well.

The years after
Investigations following the riots found some Indian National Congress members, local authorities, and the police complicit in the prolonged violence. Witnesses spoke of mobs being incited to brutality and given weapons, of organized attacks, and assailants with voter lists to help identify homes of the Sikhs. Gandhi's son Rajiv was in West Benghal when he received news of the assassination on October 31. He was sworn in as prime minister that evening. However, no curfew was imposed nor was the army called to contain the violence. The killing ended after the army was deployed on November 3.

In 2005, in parliament, the then Prime Minister Dr Manmohan Singh offered an apology to the Sikh community on behalf of the nation. In December 2018, former Congress leader Sajjan Kumar, who had been acquitted in 2013, was sentenced to life imprisonment for his role in the riots, one of only a handful to have been convicted.

A car set ablaze in Delhi after the assassination of Indira Gandhi in October 1984. Mobs raged in the city and other parts of northern India between October 31, and November 3, 1984. They killed members of the Sikh community, destroyed their property, and burned their vehicles.

Sikh art and literature

Though the themes in art and literature have evolved over the years, the legacy left by writers such as Amrita Pritam and Puran Singh, and artists like Sobha Singh, has lasted over centuries and remains pertinent to this day.

Sikh writings in the initial years focused on religious themes meant to spread the word of God and enshrine religious practices in text, much like art focused on depicting stories from the lives of divine figures. Gradual shifts had begun to take place as the Mughal Empire spread, with Islamic influences making a mark in both literature and art. However, art in the 18th and 19th centuries was largely historical and represented important Sikh figures.

As the Mughals ruled India between the 16th and the 19th centuries, Urdu and Persian were official languages. In Punjab, this meant that the vernaculars faded into the background. The situation remained so until the 1860s, which saw the beginnings of modern literature in the Punjabi language.

Literary accomplishments

After the 1860s, Punjabi literature was dominated by Sikh writers, who imbued it with egalitarian Sikh ideals. The writer at the forefront of this was Bhai Vir Singh (see.pp 234-235). This was followed by scientist, poet, and mystic Puran Singh, who was inspired by American poet Walt Whitman, and wrote free verse on nature, freedom, individualism, Punjab, and its people.

A noteworthy Sikh writer of the 20th century is Amrita Pritam. Her early work was inspired by Romanticism, a 19th-century European literary and artistic movement. She wrote extensively about the female experience, and the effects of Partition, by which she had been affected. In the novel *Pinjar*, she narrates the story of a woman caught in the crossfires of the event.

▼ **Photographs depicting eminent figures:** painter Amrita Sher-Gil (left), author and historian Khushwant Singh (center), and the author Amrita Pritam (right).

Another stalwart is Khushwant Singh, one of the most famous Sikh writers. He wrote in English, penning newspaper columns, translations of *gurbani*, a well-regarded multivolume *History of the Sikhs*, and works of other nonfiction and fiction. He is best-known for the novel *Train to Pakistan*. His political commentary, humor, and wit, and stark truths about people and politics, made him one of the most-read Indian writers.

A platform for both established and budding writers were Punjabi literary magazines such as Labh Singh's *Pritam* (1923), Gurbaksh Singh's *Preeetlari* (1933), Bhapa Pritam Singh's *Aarsi* (1956), and Amrita Pritam's *Nagmani* (1966).

On the canvas

The evolution of Sikhism can be observed through the themes present in art. Paintings reflected the ways in which Sikh society progressed—from a focus on its religious and political leaders to a more individualistic approach that chronicled the nature of being Sikh. Sikh women, who had not been visible as artists until the 20th century, became one of the community's strongest voices in the years that followed.

> "O, nowhere did I find an **air cool** as the **Punjab's** Nowhere the **water** as **sweet** and suited."

PURAN SINGH, "PUNJAB DI AHIRAN GOHE THUPDI"

Prominent among them was Amrita Sher-Gil. Influenced by miniature Mughal paintings, Sher-Gil used intense colors to portray ordinary women in their everyday lives. She effectively captured the melancholy and loneliness of her subjects on canvas. Though Amrita Sher-Gil's interest was not in faith-oriented themes, she is undoubtedly emblematic of modern Sikh artists by virtue of her immense contribution to the field. In contrast, contemporary artist Arpana Caur delves into Sikh themes through works such as her series on Guru Tegh Bahadur's execution, and "1984," which depicts anti-Sikh violence.

However, no conversation about Sikh art is complete without the mention of Sardar Sobha Singh, considered to be one of the greatest 20th-century Indian artists. His simple yet powerful paintings, especially the portraits of the Gurus, are perhaps some of the most widely recognised works of Sikh art. Moreover, author Nikky-Guninder Kaur Singh notes that Sobha Singh's experience of violence during British rule pushed him to reimagine "prototypes of peace and love on his canvas," from stories of Heer-Ranjha to Sohni-Mahival—the ultimate tragic romances of Punjab.

SIKH NEWSPAPERS

The first newspaper written in the Gurmukhi script was believed to be *Akhbar Sri Darbar Sahib Sri Amritsar Ji* that started circulation in 1867. It was a pro-British paper, and did not accurately reflect the sentiments of nationalism brewing in Punjab at the time. In the late 19th and early 20th centuries, Punjabi newspapers such as the *Khalsa Akhbar*, edited by Giani Ditt Singh, and the *Khalsa Samachar*, started by Bhai Vir Singh, became tools of resistance against the British, along with the Ghadar Party's *Ghadar*, which first printed its Punjabi edition in 1913. Other publications included *Akali Patrika*, *Ajit*, and *Parkash*. These newspapers became an intrinsic part of community life.

Baptized by steel

The Sikh Regiment of the Indian Army today comprises twenty battalions. It is one of the highest decorated regiments and has a 176-year history of bravery and fearlessness. Its origins are from July 30, 1846, when the East India Company raised the XIV Ferozepore Sikhs as among the "bravest of the martial races in India."

Having fought against the Sikh army, the British, with their admiration for "good fighting spirit," were not without appreciation for the bravery and valor displayed by the Sikhs in battle (see pp.204–207). The annexation of Punjab was followed by its demilitarization. The Sikh army was disbanded and had to surrender its swords. Only a small number of troops were retained under the British.

Then came the revolt of 1857, focused in the region around Delhi. Not sure of whom they could trust, the British turned to mercenaries and Sikh forces from the Punjab who were, more or less, isolated from the events in the plains. The British played on the anti-Mughal sentiments of the Sikhs and were rewarded with their loyalty at this critical time. Quick to see the benefits of such a force, the British made a shift in their policy on military recruitment. Not only were Sikhs actively sought after as recruits, but their separate identity was

to be encouraged. The traditions of the Khalsa would not be overruled by those of the military—to the extent that once recruited, a Sikh, even if he voluntarily decided to give up the symbols of the Khalsa, was to be discouraged, and even asked to reenlist.

An army for the Empire

This strategy proved so successful that the British diversified their campaign of recruiting soldiers from "martial races," and encouraged loyalties based on perceived identity. Regiments of Sikhs, Dogras, and Gorkhas were divided into homogeneous communal battalions, and their communal ethos was infused into their disciplined structure. The Battle of Saragarhi, in which the 21 Sikhs fought to the last man against Afghan tribesmen to defend their post on September 12, 1897, cemented the Sikh soldiers' reputation for valor.

Soldiers of the Sikh Regiment of the Indian Army participate in full dress rehearsals for the Republic Day Parade in New Delhi, 2022. The regiment was first raised in July 1846.

> "They all **died** or were **wounded** for the freedom of … world … with **no** other **protection** but the **turban**, the **symbol of their faith.**"

GENERAL SIR FRANK MESSERVY, KNIGHT COMMANDER (BRITISH ARMY OFFICER, WWI AND WWII)

The Anglo-Boer war (1889–1902) and later, World War I, saw the Sikhs as an integral part of the British military. In the Gallipoli campaign, the 14th Sikh regiment was almost wiped out, having lost 379 officers and men in a day's fighting on June 4, 1915. They also fought in Mesopotamia and Flanders, and were known as the "lions of the Great War." Their numbers in the army surged from 35,000 in 1915 to almost 100,000 by the end of the war in 1918. They distinguished themselves in China in 1939–1942 during the first Opium War. This contribution continued in World War II as they became the mainstay of the British Indian force. Despite accounting for barely one per cent of the British Indian population at the time, young Sikhs enlisted and increased the Indian army from 189,000 to 2.5 million. They resisted the Japanese invasion in the Burma campaign and led a siege in Malaya for months. They fought Nazi forces in France, Belgium, the Netherlands, and Luxembourg.

During this time, the Sikh cultural ethos obtained a new distinctiveness, such as Belgian children paying their respect to the soldiers by donning turbans and marching, and the establishing of two gurdwaras in Paris.

Defenders of the nation

Post-independence, the army continued to recruit Sikh personnel. The Sikh regiment served as a defensive wall against the first onslaught on independent India's territory; they were airlifted to Srinagar where they battled against infiltrating tribal forces and Pakistani soldiers in 1948. They also played a crucial role in other major wars, including the Indo-Sino war of 1962, the wars with Pakistan in 1965 and 1971, and Kargil in 1999.

Awarded the honorific title "Bravest of the Brave" by the Chief of the Army Staff in 1997, the modern Sikh Regiment is a direct descendant of the British Indian Army's 11th Sikh Regiment. It was established in 1922 as the first multibattalion regiment. The post-independence Sikh armed fraternity began with two battalions and has now grown to twenty. The XIV Ferozepore Sikhs, the first Sikh military unit under the British, the forefather of them all, is now the 4 Mech or 4 Mechanized Infantry.

The Sikh diaspora

The Sikh community's migration from India can be traced to their recruitment in the British army as well as becoming workers in railroad projects in various parts of the world. Today, the reasons for migration have changed and there are millions of Sikhs living around the globe.

The beginning of Sikh migration from the subcontinent can be traced to the British annexation of Punjab in 1849. Today, there are about 16 million Sikhs living outside India, with a significant majority residing in North America and the United Kingdom.

There were two key changes after the annexation that led to Sikhs venturing out in search of new opportunities. The first was agricultural changes, including the Land Alienation Act (1901), which banned the transfer of land from an owner who belonged to an "agricultural tribe" to a buyer or creditor who was not from this tribe. The destruction of the artisanal sector further adding to the burden on the agricultural sector. The second was the recruitment of Sikhs into British Indian regiments, the police, security services, and railways in the Far East and Africa. By the 1890s, there were three Singh Sabhas in

Singapore, Penang, and Taiping. The British had deployed Sikh regiments in East Africa, but it was the thousands of Sikhs recruited as labor for the Kenya–Ugandan railway line that solidified their presence in Africa. Between 1895 and 1901, around 3,000 Sikhs worked in Kenya's railways and security services. In 1898, these workers established a gurdwara—the first one overseas—in Kilindini. A gurdwara was also established in Hong Kong in 1906.

In 1897, Sikh regiments traveled with the British army to Canada to commemorate Queen Victoria's Diamond Jubilee, and again in 1902 to celebrate the coronation of King Edward VII. Intrigued by the agricultural potential of the land, and perhaps drawn by a nostalgia evoked by the landscape, Sikhs migrated to British Columbia in significant numbers. Between 1904 and 1908, about 5,000 men from the Punjab, mostly Sikhs, moved to Canada.

However, the initial lack of attention toward these migrants did not last long. In 1908, in a bid to control migration from South Asia, the Canadian government decreed that migrants from the region would only be allowed entry if they had made a "continuous journey" from their country of origin. Direct passage to Canada from South Asia was not easily available at the time. As such restrictions grew tighter, many made their way to the US to work on railroads and lumber mills in Washington, Oregon, and California. The first record of Sikh settlers in California is a report in the *San Francisco Chronicle* dated 6 April 1899, on four Sikh men who were permitted to enter San Francisco.

In 1907, motivated to organize themselves and mobilize demands for protection and fair treatment, the Sikh communities in the US founded the Khalsa Diwan Society—a network of gurdwaras and educational institutions. The first gurdwara in California, Gurdwara Sahib Stockton, established in 1912, sponsored students—Sikh and non-Sikh—to study at the University of California, Berkeley. The establishment of the Vancouver and Pacific Khalsa Diwan followed. In the mid-1920s, migrant Sikh revolutionaries of North America organised the Ghadar party to fight for Indian independence (see pp.246–247).

Post-colonial Sikh diaspora

The partition of the subcontinent in 1947, which split Punjab, set off the second major wave of Sikh migration. Immigration policies in Britain and North America had seen some liberalization and, in the 1950s, thousands of Sikhs departed for Britain and Canada. Many who had stayed on in Kenya, Uganda, East Asia, and Hong Kong also moved west in what seemed like a concerted migration.

In the 1960s, the slogan of independent Punjab and the articulation of the demand for a "Sikh homeland" was initiated among migrant Sikhs. Jagjit Singh Chohan and others gave it the shape of a Khalistan demand in the UK and the US. It got a boost after the 1984 Golden Temple attack and the anti-Sikh violence in India, and many organisations started demanding Khalistan. The anti-Sikh riots transformed the Sikhs into international refugees and they sought shelter in some European and East Asian countries.

In recent times, most instances of Sikh migration are based on educational, economic, and professional needs and desires. The power of globalization, print culture, and sociopolitical events that influenced the community's history, reinforced the community's ethnic identity, social values, religious traditions, and linguistic affiliations, establishing it as a distinct diaspora.

Now, Sikh studies is a growing academic field in many countries, especially the US. Many museums hold events to showcase Sikh art and have permanent exhibitions. Online platforms join hands with the Punjabi press, gurdwaras, and Sikh organizations in articulating the Sikh faith to a global audience. Projects in Punjab supported by migrated Sikhs in Canada, the UK, and the US involve a transnational flow of capital, ideas, people, and images. The networks and linkages that have developed between the Sikh diaspora and Sikhs in India have resulted in the emergence of a global Sikh community.

▲ A 2015 photograph of dancers performing the Bhangra, a traditional Punjabi dance, as part of Baisakhi festivities in London, UK.

THE FIRST "BOAT PEOPLE"

In 1914, to adhere to the continuous journey regulation, a Sikh businessman chartered the Japanese carrier *Komagata Maru* to transport 376 migrants, mostly Sikhs, to British Columbia. Upon arrival, however, the ship was not allowed to dock. The local South Asian community fought the decision for two months without success. During that time, the conditions on board the carrier got increasingly worse. The *Komagata Maru* was turned away—initially without even provisions for the return journey—and had to return to India. Approximately 102 years later in 2016, Canada's Prime Minister, Justin Trudeau, officially apologized for the *Komagata* tragedy.

The Guru Nanak Darbar Gurdwara, located in the town of Gravesend in Kent, is one of the largest Sikh places of worship in the UK. The gurdwara was established in 2010, and its expansive complex houses prayer rooms, langar halls, a library, and soccer grounds. The UK has one of the largest Sikh populations outside India, and Gravesend alone is home to about 15,000 Sikhs.

Passage of faith

The Kartarpur Corridor, also known as the Peace Corridor, is a pilgrim passageway connecting the Sikh shrine Kartarpur Sahib, in Pakistan, with India. It is considered a symbol of religious and political connectivity between two neighboring countries with traditionally hostile relations.

About 2.7 miles (4.5 km) from the Indian border, along the western banks of the Ravi River, within Pakistan's territory, lies Kartarpur Sahib, a 16th-century gurdwara that holds great significance and meaning for the Sikhs. This is where Guru Nanak, the first Guru of the Sikhs, established the first Sikh community and where he is believed to have died.

In 1947, with the partition of Punjab, Kartarpur became a part of Pakistan and inaccessible to Sikhs living on the Indian side of the border. Escalating hostilities between the two countries made it almost impossible for the Sikh community to travel to Pakistan on a pilgrimage to Kartarpur Sahib. Until recently, pilgrims had to rely on a *darshan sthal*, a viewing platform fitted with binoculars at the Indian border from where they could catch a glimpse of the holy site on a clear day.

Within reach

Then, in 2019, as a part of a long-standing request from the Indian government, Pakistan constructed a corridor that connected Kartarpur Sahib in Pakistan's Narowal District with the Dera Baba Nanak shrine in Gurdaspur, India. The talks for such a corridor started in 1999 but were abandoned in the face of hostilities between the two countries.

Talks resumed in 2008, although without any resolution. Finally, in 2018 the Indian and Pakistani governments took the historic decision to establish the 2.5-mile (4-km) visa-free crossing for Sikh pilgrims. The route, the governments

> "The **political division** of the Indian subcontinent in 1947 was ... a **spiritual division** as the new states established complex systems of regulation to control the **access** of **pilgrims** from the two countries."

GURHARPAL SINGH, "THE CONTROL OF SACRED SPACES," *SIKH FORMATIONS: RELIGION, CULTURE, THEORY, VOL 15*, 2019

DEWAN ASTHAN ਦੀਵਾਨ ਹਾਲ دیوان استھان

▼ **Kartarpur Sahib, also known as** Gurdwara Darbar Sahib Kartarpur, can be seen in the foreground of the vast white complex in this image.

declared, was open to an unlimited number of devotees. It was inaugurated on the occasion of the 550th birth anniversary of Guru Nanak.

Spread across 42 acres (17 hectares), the temple complex includes a courtyard, a museum, a library, an immigration center, and an embankment to protect the shrine from floods in the region.

Continued legacy

The symbolic importance of Kartarpur Sahib lies in its association with Sikh religious heritage. It was here, in 1504, that Guru Nanak settled after decades of ceaseless travels, and established Kartarpur along the western banks of Ravi River in Punjab. It is here too that he spent the last eighteen years of his life, continued spreading the word of God, and also wrote many hymns including the sacred Japji Sahib. Soon, a commune settled around him and people from different faiths started gathering, drawn to the place by his message (see pp.28–29).

▶ **A contemporary miniature** gouache painting by Saira Wasim titled, *On road to Gurdwara Kartarpur Sahib*, a tribute to the Sikh community.

The Kartarpur Sahib Gurdwara was built after Guru Nanak's death in 1539. Many essential Sikh traditions, such as *kirtan* (communal singing of hymns) and *langar* (communal meals) were practiced here. Over the years, floods destroyed the original structure. Maharaja Bhupinder Singh of Patiala gave a "princely" donation of Rs 1,35,600 from 1920–1929 to protect the gurdwara from flooding and to renovate it. Popular Sikh accounts state that Guru Nanak's devotees had built shrines in his memory, however, the ravages of time and nature have destroyed them. Today, the Kartarpur corridor is a symbol of political cooperation and tolerance. It is also an embodiment of the Sikh community's dream to have unhindered access to all their shrines.

Selfless service

Within the Sikh faith, serving humanity or *sewa* (service) is an integral part of worship. For the Sikhs, this means devoting themselves to a life in service through physical, intellectual, or material means.

Sikhs across the world employed the basic Sikh philosophical underpinnings of service and humanitarianism to help millions during the outbreak of COVID-19 in 2020. Volunteers and organizations came forward to provide food, shelter, medical assistance, and supplies to anyone in need.

In service of humanity

Gurdwaras extended the practice of *langar* (communal meals) beyond the walls of the Sikh temples to guarantee that no one went hungry during the pandemic. In India, the Delhi Sikh Gurdwara Management Committee delivered meals to the homes of COVID-afflicted people who were unable to arrange food themselves. Some Sikh volunteers set up a "*langar* on wheels" program using food trucks to serve thousands of citizens who lost their livelihood and earnings during the pandemic. Various Sikh diaspora communities, such as at the Slough Gurdwara in the UK, harnessed the tradition

of *langar* to serve the afflicted, regardless of their religious leanings. They established an emergency food bank, supplying meals to thousands of homeless people and medical staff. Khalsa Aid, a UK-based Sikh organization, provided food packages in the UK as well as India. Additionally, many gurdwaras and organizations also arranged medical help and provisions such as free ambulance services. Another unique initiative was "oxygen *langar*," which extended the custom of *langar* to go beyond food. Stories also emerged of individuals who even sold their assets in service to fellow citizens.

Such occurrences of selfless collective action are not an exception, but rather the norm in Sikh religious tradition. Guru Arjan served those afflicted with leprosy by opening an asylum at Tarn Taran in Punjab and Guru Harkrishan attended to the needs of those suffering from smallpox and cholera in Delhi. Sikh accounts tell of Bhai Kanhaiya, a soldier from Guru Gobind Singh's army, who gave water

During the service of *langar,* people sit side by side in rows, irrespective of religion or class, as volunteers serve them meals free of charge as seen here at the *langar* in Gurdwara Sri Guru Singh Sabha, New Delhi, India.

> "In **Sikhism**, it is **not** the **great**, the **gifted**, the **sage** who **serves ordinary** people, **but** it is **ordinary** people who serve **ordinary people**."

DIPANKAR GUPTA, SOCIOLOGIST, "SIKHS ARE DIFFERENT," *THE TIMES OF INDIA,* 2021

to injured enemy Mughal soldiers during a battle. When questioned, he said he had not seen friend or foe, but the Guru's face while serving water on the battlefield.

The philosophical tenant

In Sikhism, everyday acts of service such as the putting away of worshippers' shoes at gurdwara gates, preparing food in the community kitchens, or sweeping floors are forms of worship. It is believed that through serving others, one is serving God, because divinity permeates every aspect of the world.

In the Sikh way of life, *sewa* (service) is considered the prime duty and followers are exhorted to lead a purposeful life, directed by individual virtues as well as the overarching social prerogative of *sarbat da bhala* (well-being of everyone). True *sewa*, according to the Sikh scriptures, is done without desire, in humility, and with pure intentions. *Sewa* can be dedicated in the form of *tan* (services rendered), *man* (by preaching the Divine Word), or *dhan* (money). Thus, it may take on many forms within a gurdwara setting, including monetary and food donations, helping *langars*, reading the scripture, or attending to the holy book.

A legacy of equality

Every day at the end of worship, gurdwaras offer *langar,* consisting of simple vegetarian dishes, to the community with the help of volunteers. Guru Angad institutionalized *langar* as a groundbreaking act in favor of equality against the existing social hierarchies, whereby people of different castes did not eat together. Mata Khivi, Guru Angad's wife, prepared and served l*angar* to all, regardless of any distinctions such as religion, caste, or social class. Guru Amar Das also strengthened the institution of *langar* and made "*pahile pangat, pachhe sangat*" (first comes eating together, then meeting together) a rule.

Langars continue to form an integral part of Sikh worship and of gurdwaras across the world. *Sewa* is not contained to Sikh temple premises, but pervades all social spaces where humanity can be served.

Every fall and winter, many fields across Punjab in India are awash with flowering mustard crops. Even though the state's farmers grow a variety of crops, from millet and wheat to rice, it is these small, bright yellow flowers that have captured the imagination of writers, artists, and scriptwriters—so much so that these fields of gold have even been immortalized in movies from the Hindi film industry.

Sources for writing Sikh history

In addition to the reliance on communal memory, much of Sikh history is reconstructed using literary sources, which were created by a diversity of personages, from Sikh leaders and their followers to Persian courtiers, British officials, and modern Sikh organizations.

The earliest attempt at recording a history of the Sikh faith manifested as hagiographies of Guru Nanak. These texts or *Janamsakhis*, penned by Sikh followers, record the life history of the Guru and the key events that engendered the formation of the Sikh faith.

Allied to this tradition was the creation of *Gurbilas* for the succeeding Gurus. These follow the hagiographical pattern of the *Janamsakhis*, and extend the narrative on the history of the Sikh faith in the years after Guru Nanak's death. These texts often positioned themselves around debates within the Panth, which also help chart the trajectory of the community.

Besides writings by the devotees themselves, there is also a corpus of textual orders written by the Gurus. These fall within the literary banner of *hukamnamas*, where *hukam* translates to order, and *nama* means letter. These official edicts, issued for dissemination within the community, relay invaluable historical information such as names, dates, places, and objects.

Court records

Historians also rely on Persian sources mostly associated with the Mughal court and written under the patronage of the rulers. These texts, dating to the 16th century or earlier, often discuss the Sikh community and events. These include general histories of emperors, such as the *Akbarnama* and *Khulasatu't Tawarikh*; specific histories such as the *Nushka i Dilkusha*; semiofficial reports such as the *Akham-i Alamgiri*; and memoirs and documents, such as the *Dabistan-e Mazaheb* and *Jangnama*.

Historians also have access to the chronicles written by Sohan Lal Suri, an attorney at the Lahore Darbar. These document the history of the faith from the beginnings in the 15th century to the times of Maharaja Ranjit

Singh, and the 1849 British annexation of the Sikh Empire. Over five volumes, the *Umdat-Ut-Tawarikh* provides key insights into the trajectory of the religion and its community from a 19th-century perspective.

Colonial documentation

The British started taking an interest in the affairs of the Sikhs from the 18th century. While some accounts, such as those of Warren Hastings and Henri Polier, center around the threatening might of the Sikh army and tactics, others, such as that of Charles Wilkins, focus on their religious practices.

British administrators compiled reports on the community throughout the Colonial period. This was mostly to keep a check on their congregations, to subdue rebellion, and look into Sikh history to find justification for British rule to foster collaboration.

The first "histories" written under the East Indian Company and the British crown can be considered a colonial analysis of the community. The works of Orientalist and founder of the Asiatic Society, Charles Wilkins, and Swiss soldier-trader Antoine-Louis Henri Polier, come under this umbrella. John Malcom's *Sketch of the Sikhs* (1812) and Henri T. Princep's *Sikh Power in the Punjab and the Political Life of Muha-Raja Runjeet Singh* (1834) provide a study of the region from the Company's point of view. J.D. Cunnigham's *History of the Sikhs* (1849), which initially did not find favor because of its criticism of the British, is now considered an important documentation of the period.

Indian historians under the British

The late 19th and 20th centuries saw publications by Indian writers educated in the western tradition. Influenced by the socioreligious, political resurgence

> "They are by their **bodily frame** and **habits** of life eminently **suited** to the military profession... Every village has its **separate** ... **ruler** acknowledging no **control**..."

during the Colonial period, their scholarship reflects the prevailing environment. Much of the writing centered around the faith. Some key works of the period include Sewaram Singh Thapar's *A Critical Study of The Life* and *Teachings of Sri Guru Nanak Dev: The Founder of Sikhism* (1904); Bhagat Lakshman Singh's *A Short Sketch of the Life and Work of Guru Govind Singh: The 10th and Last Guru of the Sikhs* (1909) and *Sikh Martyrs* (1923); and Khazan Singh's *History and Philosophy of the Sikh Religion* (1914).

The common thread in these works was the emphasis on understanding the doctrines and institutions, the distinctiveness of the faith, and the establishment of the Sikh identity.

The works of two Bengali historians, Indubhushan Banerjee's *Evolution of the Khalsa* and Narendra Krishna Sinha's *Rise of Sikh Power and Ranjit Singh*, published in the 1930s, took on a more nationalist flavor. As did *Transformation of Sikhism* by Punjabi historian Gokul Chand Narang (1912), which went through several revisions until the 1960s.

Post–Independence writings

The seminal *A Short History of the Sikhs* by Dr. Ganda Singh and Teja Singh (1950), published five years after Independence, presented Sikhism as an original faith using mostly Sikh sources. This approach situated it within what is called the *Tat Khalsa* tradition that began in 1879 under the Singh Sabha movement (see pp.238–239).

New Zealand scholar W.H. McLeod is also considered one of the principal scholars of Sikhism, whose publications in the 1960s and 1970s prompted immense debate. His view of Sikhism as a breakaway from Hindu

practices gave rise to disagreement over whether Sikhism was an independent faith or an ideology evolved from within Hinduism. It was a viewpoint echoed by several scholars, such as Harjot Oberoi, Pashaura Singh, and Louis E. Fenech.

However, the most definitive Sikh studies scholar of the 21st century, with a notable body of work, is J.S. Grewal, former vice chancellor of Guru Nanak Dev University, in Amritsar, Punjab. Scholars of Sikhism in the US include Gurinder Singh Mann, Pashaura Singh, John S. Hawley, Mark Juergensmeyer, I.J. Singh, and Nikky-Guninder Kaur Singh.

Other eminent voices on Sikh history include Indu Banga, Roopinder Singh, and Simran Jeet Singh, who have published extensively in the field, including books and articles.

The preservation of Sikh history is also aided by prominent art collections including Dr Narinder Singh Kapany's Kapany Collection and Davinder S. Toor's Toor Collection of Sikh Art, which introduced Sikh culture, art, history, and ethos to the people across the globe.

READING BETWEEN THE LINES

It is not enough for historians to read sources to arrive at a true narrative of Sikh history. Much of the historical analysis also has to evaluate the biases inherent in these sources, as they are written by people within particular temporal and physical contexts, often with a specific agenda. The inclination of the writer often determines the tone and content of the text and can at times obscure more than what is revealed. Besides careful scrutiny, studying sources in conjunction is another way in which historians can test the biases and write a more nuanced history.

Glossary

26th Amendment Enforced since December 28, 1971, the 26th Amendment to the Constitution of India abolished the privy purse paid to former rulers of princely states that were incorporated into the Indian Republic. See Privy purse.

amrit Sweetened holy water used in religious ceremonies; specifically utilized in the Sikh ceremony of initiation.

Bhakti Movement The word Bhakti means intense devotion toward a deity leading to salvation. The Bhakti movement emerged in South India in the 7th–10th century and spread across the north as well. It emphasized the intense love of a devotee toward a personal god.

Brahmin The highest-ranking class according to the Hindu caste system, or *varnas*. A privileged and priestly group, its members hold the hegemonic position by virtue of their birth. They are said to be the repositories of knowledge and they are the only Hindus who can perform yagnas and rituals to propitiate the gods.

caste system The Hindu system of grouping people as "higher" or "lower" in the social order as per the nature of their work. This includes Brahmins (priests), Kshatriyas (warriors), Vaishyas (merchants), and Shudras (peasants).

Civil Disobedience MK Gandhi launched this movement on April 6, 1930, with a handful of salt after the historic Dandi March, thus violating the British government's salt law. This act become a symbol of the people's nonviolent defiance of the government.

Dalit Derived from the Hindi term "*dalan,*" meaning oppressed. Today, it refers to someone outside of the caste system. Legally the term is used for members of Scheduled Castes as defined by the Constitution.

Deccan Derived from the Sanskrit word "*daksina,*" which means south. Refers to the southern Indian peninsula, south of the Narmada River.

Delhi The present capital of India is associated with seven cities. Of them, the walled city of Shahjahanabad was built in the region in 1639 by Mughal emperor Shah Jahan. It remained the capital of the Mughal empire until its fall in 1857.

Deputy Speaker Lok Sabha's presiding officer is known as the Speaker, who conducts the business of the House. A Deputy Speaker performs the duties of the Speaker when the latter is absent or while the office of the Speaker is vacant. See Parliament.

Dharma Hindu scriptures describe dharma as a way of life that follows the path of righteousness. The main objective of dharma is the attainment of *moksha* or ultimate liberation.

doab Originating from the Persian for two and water, a doab is the land or region between two converging rivers.

general election When the members of Lok Sabha or the House of the People are elected by all adult Indian citizens through their constituencies. The elected members are known as Members of Parliament and hold their seat for four to five years until the next election.

granthi An official who takes care of the Guru Granth Sahib and the gurdwara. A *granthi* is also a skilled reader of the sacred book.

Jat Traditionally a rural, agricultural community.

Jathedar Literally a leader, of a group, political dispensation, or a seat of spirituo-temporal authority.

khanda A two-edged sword of the kind used by Guru Gobind Singh in a ritual that marked the founding of the Khalsa; now a symbol of Sikhism.

khatri A mercantile caste.

langar A free communal kitchen and dining hall, which is a part of all gurdwaras. Also a practice, where everyone sits in lines (*pangat*) and eats food without knowing who has prepared it. Langars served to eliminate caste distinctions and uphold the Sikh principle of equality between all.

Maratha A confederacy established by Shivaji Bhonsle, comprised of a peasant warrior group.

Mool Mantra A statement of Sikh belief in the oneness of God, composed by Guru Nanak. A *mantra* is a sacred sound, word, or verse. In Sanskrit, the word literally translates to instrument of thought. A *mantra* is used in multiple ways, such as to build concentration during meditation or invoke deities (see p.45).

Nanakshahi calendar Widely adopted calendar of the Sikhs.

Operation Bluestar Code name for the Indian Army's military operation from June 1–10, 1984, at the Golden Temple in Amritsar. It had two subcomponents: Operation Metal focused on dislodging Jarnail Singh Bhindranwale and his armed supporters, who had sought shelter in and fortified the complex. Operation Shop was to capture suspects in other areas. The operation involved the use of heavy artillery. On June 5, tanks and troops were deployed inside the temple. By June 7, the army had full control of the Harmandir Sahib complex: Bhindranwale and most of his leading supporters were killed but the temple complex had suffered tremendous damage and the Akal Takht had been destroyed. Many devotees visiting the shrine had also been killed. Operation Bluestar caused immense anguish to the Sikh community and still remains one of the most debated and controversial internal security measures undertaken in India.

Panth A Sanskrit word for "path," Panth is used to describe follower groups of particular doctrines. The Sikh Panth, or the Sikh community, was also known as the Nanak Panth (followers of Nanak). After the establishments of the Khalsa, the community came to be known as the Khalsa Panth.

Parliament The supreme law-making and governance body of India. It comprises the President and two Houses—Lok Sabha (the lower) and the Rajya Sabha (the higher). The Houses constitute representatives of the people of India.

Parliamentary system A system of democratic governance where the executive derives its democratic legitimacy from the confidence of the legislature, typically a parliament, and is also held accountable to that parliament.

Princely states Territories ruled by princes during the British rule in India.

Privy purse A specific amount of tax-free payments guaranteed to be paid annually by the Indian government to the rulers of princely states and their successors who had acceded to India under Article 291 of the Constitution of India. See 26th Amendment.

Quit India movement A nonviolent movement that MK Gandhi launched on August 8, 1942, seeking an immediate withdrawal of the British from India.

Rajput Meaning "son of a king," the Rajputs, who are mostly from Rajasthan and Punjab, belong to the Kshatriya class of warriors and rulers.

Sufi A member of one of a number of mystical Islamic orders, whose beliefs center on a personal relationship with God.

Union Territory Also known as centrally administered territories, these are governed directly by the Union Government of India, unlike an Indian state that has a separate governing body.

Varnashramdharma The Hindu society is defined by a caste system from the late Gupta period. People are divided into four varnas (classes) with designated social roles and order of hierarchy: Brahmins (priests), Kshatriyas (rulers and warriors), Vaisyas (farmers, artisans, and traders), and Sudras (serfs and laborers). Varnas were further subdivided into jatis (castes), each with a specific occupation. Jati means birth; birth determines a person's caste, and caste determines their class. Neither caste nor class could be changed. There were only four classes, but the number of castes varied as old castes died out and new ones emerged. Varnashramadharma refers to the duties performed according to the system of the four varnas and the four ashrams (stages in life: student life, household life, retirement, and renunciation).

Index

Selected Bibliography

Amini, Iradj. *The Koh-i-Noor Diamond*. Roli Books, 2013.

Asher, Catherine B. and Talbot, Cynthia. *India Before Europe*. Cambridge University Press, 2006.

Atwal, Priya. *Royals and Rebels: The Rise and Fall of the Sikh Empire*. Oxford University Press, 2020.

Bains, J.S. "Political ideas of Guru Gobind Singh," in *The Indian Journal of Political Science* 24, 3 (1963): 239–250.

Bains, J.S. "The Ghadr Movement: A Golden Chapter of Indian Nationalism," in *The Indian Journal of Political Science* 23, 1/4 (1962): 48–59.

Ballantyne, Tony. *Between Colonialism and Diaspora: Sikh Cultural Formations in an Imperial World*. Duke University Press, 2006.

Ballantyne, Tony. "Looking Back, Looking Forward: The Historiography of Sikhism," in *New Zealand Journal of Asian Studies* 4, 1 (2002): 5–29.

Banga, Indu and Grewal, J.S., eds. *History and Ideology: The Khalsa over 300 Years*. Tulika, 1999.

Boparai, Hari Singh. *Revolt of 1857 in Punjab and Role of the Sikhs*. Gyan Sagar Publications, 2000.

Brown, Kerry. *Sikh Art and Literature*. Routledge, 2002.

Butalia, Urvashi. *The Other Side of Silence: Voices from the Partition of India*. Penguin Random House India, 2017.

Dahiya, Amardeep S. *Founder of the Khalsa: The Life and Times of Guru Gobind Singh*. Hay House, Inc, 2014.

Dalmia, Yashodhara. *Amrita Sher-Gil: A Life*. Penguin Random House India, 2013.

Dalrymple, William and Anand, Anita. *Koh-i-Noor: The History of the World's Most Infamous Diamond*. Bloomsbury Publishing, 2017.

Datta, V.N. *Jallianwala Bagh: A Groundbreaking History of the 1919 Massacre*. Penguin Random House India, 2021.

Deol, Jeevan. "Eighteenth-century Khalsa Identity: Discourse, Praxis and Narrative," in *Sikh Religion, Culture and Ethnicity*, eds. Christopher Shackle et al. Curzon, 2001.

Dey, Susnigdha. "Guru Nanak as a Poet" in *Indian Literature* 15, 1 (1972): 21–26.

Dhavan, Purnima. *When Sparrows Became Hawks: The Making of the Sikh Warrior Tradition, 1699–1799*. Oxford University Press, 2011.

Fenech, Louis E. and McLeod, William Hewat. *Historical Dictionary of Sikhism*. Rowman & Littlefield, 2014.

Fenech, Louis E. *The Sikh Zafar-namah of Guru Gobind Singh: A Discursive Blade in the Heart of the Mughal Empire*. Oxford University Press, 2013.

Gajrani, Shiv. "The Sikhs: The revolt of 1857 in Punjab," in *Proceedings of the Indian History Congress*, 61 (2000): 679–85.

Gandhi, Rajmohan. *Punjab: A History from Aurangzeb to Mountbatten*. Rupa Publications, 2015.

Gill, Harjeet Singh. "The Gurmukhi Script," in *The World's Writing Systems*, eds. Peter T. Daniels and William Bright. Oxford University Press, 1996.

Gohain, Hiren. "The Labyrinth of Bhakti: On Some Questions of Medieval Indian History," in *Economic and Political Weekly* 22, 46 (1987): 1970–72.

Grewal, J.S. and Habib, Irfan. *Sikh History from Persian Sources*. Tulika, 2001.

Grewal, J.S. *Guru Gobind Singh (1666–1708): Master of the White Hawk*. Oxford University Press, 2019.

Grewal, J.S. *The Sikhs of Punjab*. Cambridge University Press, 1990.

Grewal, J.S. "The Khalsa of Guru Gobind Singh," in *Essays in Sikh History: From Guru Nanak to Maharaja Ranjit Singh*. Gyan Books, 1982.

Grewal J.S. and Bal, S.S. *Guru Gobind Singh: A Biographical Study*. Punjab University, 1967.

Gupta, H. R. "Origin of the Sikh Territorial Chieftainships, 1748–1759," in *Proceedings of the Indian History Congress* 3 (1939): 1172–88.

Habib, Irfan. "Jallianwala Bagh Massacre," in *Social Scientist* 47, 5/6 (2019): 3–8.

Imam, Hassan. "Dara Shikoh: A Forgotten Mughal of Interfaith Personality in Indian History," in *International Journal of Applied Social Science* 6, 9 (2019): 2185–2190.

Imam, Hassan. "Jallianwala Bagh Proscribed Literature," in *Proceedings of the Indian History Congress*: Volume 73. Indian History Congress, 2012.

Jayapalan, N. *History of India*. Atlantic Publishers, 2001.

Judge, Paramjit S. and Kaur, Manjit. "The Politics of Sikh Identity: Understanding Religious Exclusion," in *Sociological Bulletin* 59, 3 (2010): 89–110.

Kapur, Rajiv A. *Sikh Separatism: The Politics of Faith*. Allen & Unwin, 1986.

Kaur, Kanwaljit. "Communal Violence In Princely States During Partition (1947)," in *Proceedings of the Indian History Congress* 72 (2011): 931–35.

Kaur, Karmajit and Bhullar, Surbhjit Kaur. "Banda Singh Bahadur's Contribution for Establishment of a Great Sikh Kingdom," in *IJCRT* 6, 2 (2018).

Kaur, Madanjit. *Guru Gobind Singh: Historical and Ideological Perspective*. Unistar Books, 2021.

Kaur, Ramandeep. "Sikhism Under the Religious Leadership of Guru Angad Dev," in *Journal of Sikh Studies*, XL (2016): 93–102.

Khalidi, Omar. "Ethnic Group Recruitment in the Indian Army: The Contrasting Cases of Sikhs, Muslims, Gurkhas and Others," in *Pacific Affairs* (2001): 529–552.

Khola, Cheema and Tohid, Ahmad. "Maharaja Ranjit Singh, Court and Culture of Lahore Darbar," in *JRSP*, 58, 2 (2021).

Macauliffe, Max Arthur. *The Sikh Religion: Its Gurus, Sacred Writings and Authors*: in Six Volumes. Oxford at the Clarendon Press, 1909.

Malhi, Ranjit Singh. "Malayan Sikhs' Participation in The Ghadar Movement: From Loyal British Subjects to Ardent Revolutionaries," in *Sikh Formations*, 17, 4 (2021), 435–449.

Mandair, Arvind Pal-Singh. *Sikhism: A Guide for the Perplexed*. Bloomsbury, 2013.

McLeod, W. H. *Guru Nanak and the Sikh Religion*. Oxford at the Clarendon Press, 1968.

McLeod, W. H. *The A to Z of Sikhism*. The Scarecrow Press, Inc., 2009.

Naeem, Nadhra Shahbaz. "Life at the Lahore Darbār: 1799-1839," in *South Asian Studies* 25, 2 (2010): 283–301.

Neki, Jaswant Singh. *Pilgrimage to Hemkunt*. National Institute of Punjab Studies, 2007.

Nesbitt, Eleanor. *Sikhism: A Very Short Introduction*. Oxford University Press, 2005.

Oberoi, Harjot. *The Construction of Religious Boundaries: Culture, Identity, and Diversity in the Sikh Tradition*. University of Chicago Press, 1994.

Oberoi, Harjot. "Ghadar Movement and its Anarchist Genealogy," in *Economic and Political Weekly*: (2009) 40–46.

Omissi, David E. "Sikh Soldiers in Europe During the First World War, 1914–18," in *Sikhs Across Borders*, eds. Knut A. Jacobsen and Kristina Myrvold. Bloomsbury, 2012.

Puri, Harish K. "Revolutionary Organization: A Study of the Ghadar Movement," in *Social Scientist* (1980): 53–66.

Ramnath, Maia. "Two Revolutions: The Ghadar Movement and India's Radical Diaspora, 1913–1918," in *Radical History Review* 2005 92, (2005): 7–30.

Rinehart, Robin. *Debating the Dasam Granth*. OUP, 2011.

Sagoo, Harbans Kaur. *Banda Singh Bahadur and Sikh Sovereignty*. Deep & Deep Publications, 2001.

Sarna, Navtej. *Guru Gobind Singh: Zafarnama*. Penguin Books, 2012.

Sarna, Navtej. *The Exile: A Novel Based on the Life of Maharaja Duleep Singh*. Penguin Books, 2010.

Siali, M.S. and Rajguru, Suparna. *Gurdwara in The Himalayas: Sri Hemkunt Sahib*. Hemkunt Press, 2001.

Singh, Bhayee Sikandar and Singh, Roopinder. *Sikh Heritage: Ethos & Relics*. Rupa Publications, 2012.

Singh, Gurnam. *Sikh Music*. Oxford University Press, 2014.

Singh, Harbans, ed. *The Encyclopedia of Sikhism*: in Six Volumes. Punjab University, 1992.

Singh, Joginder. *The Namdhari Sikhs: Their Changing Social and Cultural Landscape*. Manohar, 2013.

Singh, Kharak. *Sikhism: Its Philosophy and History*. Institute of Sikh Studies, 1997.

Singh, Khushwant, tr. *Hymns of Guru Nanak*. Orient Longman, 1991.

Singh, Khushwant. *A History of the Sikhs*: in Two Volumes. Oxford University Press, 1999.

Singh, Khushwant. *The Fall of the Kingdom of Punjab*. Penguin Books, 2014.

Singh, Kirpal. *Janamsakhi Tradition: An Analytical Study*. Singh Brothers, 2004.

Singh, Milkha and Sanwalka, Sonia. *The Race of My Life: An Autobiography*. Rupa Publications, 2013.

Singh, Nadia. "Sikhism and Covid-19: Ethics of Community Service and Activism," in *Sikh Formations* (2022): 1–13.

Singh, Nikky-Guninder Kaur. "The Myth of the Founder: The Janamsākhīs and Sikh Tradition," in *History of Religions* 31, 4 (1992): 329–343.

Singh, Pashaura. *The Guru Granth Sahib: Canon, Meaning and Authority*. Oxford University Press, 2003.

Singh, Pashaura and Fenech, Louis E. *The Oxford Handbook of Sikh Studies*. Oxford University Press, 2014.

Singh, Patwant and Rai, Jyoti M. *Empire of the Sikhs: The Life and Times of Maharaja Ranjit Singh*. Peter Owen Publishers, 2008.

Singh, Pritam. *Sikh-Concept of the Divine*. Guru Nanak Dev University, 1985.

Singh, Roopinder. *Guru Nanak: His Life & Teachings*. Rupa Publications, 2004.

Singh, Sarbpreet. *The Camel Merchant of Philadelphia: Stories from the Court of Maharaja Ranjit Singh*. Westland Publications Pvt Ltd, 2019.

Soboslai, John. "Sikh Self-Sacrifice and Religious Representation During World War I," in Religions 9, 2 (2018): 55.

Sohi, Khushbeen Kaur, Singh, Purnima and Bopanna, Krutika. "Ritual Participation, Sense of Community, and Social Well-Being: A Study of Seva in the Sikh Community," in *Journal of Religion and Health* 57, 6 (2018): 2066–2078.

Syan, Hardip Singh. *Sikh Militancy in the Seventeenth Century: Religious Violence in the Mughal and Early Modern India*. Bloomsbury, 2020.

Talib, Gurbachan Singh. *An Introduction to Sri Guru Granth Sahib*. Punjabi University, 1999.

Talib, Gurbachan Singh and Singh, Attar, eds. *Bhai Vir Singh: Life, Times & Works*. Punjab University, 1973.

Tatla, Darsham Singh. *The Sikh Diaspora: The Search for Statehood*. Routledge, 2005.

Taylor, Paul Michael and Dhami, Sonia, eds. *Sikh Art from the Kapany Collection*. The Sikh Foundation International, 2017.

Van Der Linden, Bob. "Sikh Music And Empire: The Moral Representation Of Self In Music," in *Sikh Formations: Religion, Culture, Theory* 4, 1 (2008): 1–15.

Van Der Linden, Bob. "Sikh music and empire: The Moral Representation of Self in Music," in *Sikh Formations* 4, 1 (2008): 1–15.

Van der Linden, Bob. "Sikh Sacred Music, Empire and World Music: Aesthetics and Historical Change," in *Sikh Formations* 7, 3 (2011): 383–397.

Acknowledgments

The publisher would like to thank the following for their assistance in the preparation of this book:

Roopinder Singh, reputed author and Indian journalist, for sharing his insights on Sikh history and philosophy, and taking the time to read through these pages and share his invaluable feedback and critique throughout the development of the book.

Davinder S. Toor, author and leading figure among Indian and Islamic art collectors, for opening up his beautiful collection of Sikh art to us and graciously providing images from the Toor Collection, and sharing invaluable feedback and critique throughout the development of the book.

Arpana Caur, contemporary artist, for allowing us access to her beautiful, poignant works of art, and for taking the time to read the book and share her words of encouragement.

Montek Singh Ahluwalia, former Deputy Chairman of the Planning Commission, Government of India and currently Distinguished Fellow in the Centre for Social and Economic Progress for taking the time to go through the book and share his valuable feedback.

Punita Singh for her invaluable guidance and unwavering support from the early stages of the development of the book.

Vikram Singh Sodhi, Managing Trustee of the Anandpur Sahib Heritage Foundation, for taking the time to read the book and offer his invaluable thoughts.

The Sikh Foundation International for giving us permission to use images from its expansive Sikh art collection.

Panjab Digital Library, which houses a rich collection of art, photographs, manuscripts, newspapers, articles, and books relating to the Punjab region, for allowing us access to its wealth of knowledge.

Vatsal Verma and **Avanika** for content planning; **Saanika Patnaik** and **Nehal Agarwalla** for researching and writing the book; **Anant Partap Singh** and **Vatsal Verma** for writing the following pages: **Anant Partap Singh**: 26–27, 28–29, 40–41, 42–43, 48–49; **Vatsal Verma**: 298–299; **Madhavi Singh** and **Kritika Gupta** for editorial support; **Priyal Mote** for illustration support; and **Seetha Natesh** for proofreading.

Disclaimer:
Every effort has been made to acknowledge those individuals, organizations, and corporations that have helped with this book and to trace copyright holders. DK apologizes in advance if any omission has occurred. If an omission does come to light, DK will be pleased to insert the appropriate acknowledgment in the subsequent editions of the book.

The publisher would like to thank the following for their kind permission to reproduce their photographs:

(Key: a-above; b-below/bottom; c-center; f-far; l-left; r-right; t-top)

1 Alamy Stock Photo: PBL Collection (c). **2 Toor Collection:** . **2-3 Alamy Stock Photo:** Olaf Krger. **4 Getty Images:** Richard I'Anson. **5 Alamy Stock Photo:** Dinodia Photos / Alamy Stock Photo (tr). **7 Toor Collection:** (crb). **8-9 Alamy Stock Photo:** Dinodia Photos RM (c). **10-11 Khanuja Family Collection:** . **12 Alamy Stock Photo:** Heritage Art / Heritage Images (ca). **12-13 Wellcome Collection:** Wellcome Collection. Public Domain Mark (bc). **14-15 Toor Collection**. **16 The Cleveland Museum Of Art:** Bequest of Mrs. A. Dean Perry (cl). **16-17 Dreamstime.com:** Designprintck. **17 © The Metropolitan Museum of Art:** Louis E. and Theresa S. Seley Purchase Fund for Islamic Art, 2009 (cra); The J. H. W. Thompson Foundation Gift and Gifts of friends of Jim Thompson, in his memory, 2002 (ca). **18-19 Dreamstime.com:** Blaz Kure; Benjawan Sittidech (ca). **Dreamstime.com:** Designprintck (b). **20-21 Los Angeles County Museum of Art:** Purchased with funds provided by Dorothy and Richard Sherwood ((c). **Dreamstime.com:** Designprintck (b). **22 Alamy Stock Photo:** The History Collection (tr). **22-23 Dreamstime.com:** Anjali Kumari (cb). **24-25 Wellcome Collection:** Wellcome Collection. Public Domain Mark. **26-27 ©Asian Art Museum Of San Francisco:** (cl). **Dreamstime.com:** Weedezign. **29 Getty Images:** Richard I'Anson. **30-31 Alamy Stock Photo:** ArkReligion.com (c). **Dreamstime.com:** Designprintck (b). **32-33 Kapany Collection - Sikh Foundation:** Kapany Collection - Sikh Foundation (cla). **33 Gurjit Singh Rehill:** (bc). **34-35 Seema Kohli:** . **36-37 Seema Kohli:** (c). **38-39 © The Metropolitan Museum of Art:** The Crosby Brown Collection of Musical Instruments, 1889 (c). **40 Getty Images:** Tuul & Bruno Morandi (c). **41 © The Metropolitan Museum of Art:** Purchase, Friends of Islamic Art Gifts, 2009 (tr). **42 Wellcome Collection:** Wellcome Collection. Public Domain Mark (tc). **43 123RF.com:** singhramana (bc). **44-45 Alamy Stock Photo:** Dinodia Photos / Alamy Stock Photo. **47 Toor Collection:** . **48 Alamy Stock**

Photo: Asar Studios (cra). **Courtesy: Panjab Digital Library:** (clb). **49 Alamy Stock Photo:** Nick Bobroff (cr). **50 Khanuja Family Collection:** (c). **50-51 Dreamstime.com:** Designprintck (bc). **51 Getty Images:** Hindustan Times / Contributor (clb). **52 Alamy Stock Photo:** Album / British Library / Alamy Stock Photo. **52-53 Dreamstime.com:** Designprintck (b). **55 Khanuja Family Collection:** . **56 Alamy Stock Photo:** ArkReligion.com (cla). **057 Alamy Stock Photo:** Album / British Library / Alamy Stock Photo. **58-59 Getty Images:** Nitish Waila (bc). **59 Dreamstime.com:** Brphoto (cra). **60 Alamy Stock Photo:** World Religions Photo Library. **61 123RF.com:** naturewild (cb). **62 Toor Collection:** Image courtesy of Prahlad Bubbar. **63 Dreamstime.com:** Bjrn Wylezich (crb). **64-65 Alfaaz photography:** . **66 Alamy Stock Photo:** Helene Rogers / ArkReligion.com. **67 Dreamstime.com:** Natwar Lal Bhargawa (crb). **68-69 Alamy Stock Photo:** Dinodia Photos RM. **70-71 Dreamstime.com:** Hiteshsinghstock. **72-73 Alamy Stock Photo:** history_docu_photo. **74-75 Alamy Stock Photo:** Historic Collection (c). **76 Toor Collection:** . **77 Alamy Stock Photo:** The History Collection (cra). **79 © The Metropolitan Museum of Art:** Purchase, Rogers Fund and The Kevorkian Foundation Gift, 1955. **80-81 Dreamstime.com:** Dmitry Rukhlenko. **82-83 Alamy Stock Photo:** Dipper Historic. **84 The Cleveland Museum Of Art:** Gift of J. H. Wade 1920.1969 (clb). **85 Gurdwara Baba Atal Rai:** (cla). **86 Alamy Stock Photo:** ArkReligion.com. **87 Kapany Collection - Sikh Foundation:** Kapany Collection - Sikh Foundation (crb). **88 Alamy Stock Photo:** The History Collection (cl). **89 © The Metropolitan Museum of Art:** Louis V. Bell Fund, 2003 (cr). **90-91 Alamy Stock Photo:** The Picture Art Collection. **92-93 Collection:** Academy of Fine Arts and Literature Miniature **Paintings Museum: Collection:** Academy of Fine Arts and Literature Miniature Paintings Museum. **94-95 Getty Images:** IndiaPictures / Contributor. **96-97 © The Metropolitan Museum of Art:** Bequest of George C. Stone, 1935. **98-99 Arpana Caur:** . **100 Toor Collection:** . **101 Getty Images:** Hindustan Times / Contributor (cra). **102-103 Getty Images:** Richard I'Anson. **104 Raghav Kohli:** (crb). **105 Toor Collection:** (cra). **106-107 Alamy Stock Photo:** Asar Studios / Alamy Stock Photo. **108-109 Khanuja Family Collection:** . **110 Alamy Stock Photo:** ArkReligion.com (ca, crb); David South (clb); Atthapon Kulpakdeesingworn (c). **Shutterstock.com:** uV15o6 (cra). **112-113 Getty Images:** redtea. **114 Wellcome Collection:** (clb). **114-115 Toor Collection:** . **116 Courtesy: Panjab Digital Library:** (clb). **117 Alamy Stock Photo:** The Picture Art Collection (cr). **118-119 Alamy Stock Photo:** The Picture Art Collection. **120-121 Alamy Stock Photo:** Dipper Historic. **122 Toor Collection:** . **123 Raghav Kohli:** (crb). **124 Roopinder Singh:** (ca). **124-125 Roopinder Singh:** (tc). **125**

Roopinder Singh: (c). **126-127 Getty Images:** STRDEL / Stringer. **126 Alamy Stock Photo:** Dinodia Photos (clb). **128 Alamy Stock Photo:** Ambuj Khanna (cra). **Dreamstime.com:** EPhotocorp (c). **Getty Images:** Dinodia Photo (clb); NurPhoto / Contributor (crb). **129 Dreamstime.com:** Shalender Kumar (cla, cra); Takepicsforfun (clb). **Unsplash:** Ritul Bhattacharjee (crb). **130-131 The University of Melbourne Archives:** . **132 Khanuja Family Collection:** (clb). **133 Alamy Stock Photo:** Piero Cruciatti / Alamy Live News. **134-135 Wellcome Collection:** Wellcome Collection. Public Domain Mark. **136 Wellcome Collection:** Wood engraving by A.H., 1874. Wellcome Collection. Public Domain Mark (clb). **136-137 Getty Images:** B P S Walia / IndiaPictures / Universal Images Group via Getty Images (b). **138-139 akg-images:** Yvan Travert. **141 Getty Images:** B P S Walia / IndiaPictures / Universal Images Group via Getty Images (crb). **142 Bhagat Singh:** Bhagat Singh (cra). **143 Collection of Gursharan S. and Elvira Sidhu:** . **144 Getty Images:** Hindustan Times / Contributor (cla). **145 American Numismatic Society:** (cra). **146 Khanuja Family Collection:** . **147 Khanuja Family Collection:** (cra). **148 Courtesy: Panjab Digital Library:** . **149 Kapany Collection - Sikh Foundation:** Kapany Collection - The Sikh foundation (cb). **150 Alamy Stock Photo:** V&A Images (cra). **151 Alamy Stock Photo:** Historic Collection. **152-153 Kapany Collection - Sikh Foundation:** Kapany Collection - The Sikh Foundation (b). **152 Alamy Stock Photo:** Pictures From History. **154-155 Alamy Stock Photo:** Art Collection 2 / Alamy Stock Photo. **156-157 Toor Collection:** . **158-159 Anuj Arora:** . **160 Courtesy: Panjab Digital Library:** . **162-163 Kapany Collection - Sikh Foundation:** Kapany Collection - Sikh Foundation (tc). **Dreamstime.com:** Designprintck (b). **166 Alamy Stock Photo:** The Granger Collection. **168-169 Courtesy: Panjab Digital Library:** . **169 Toor Collection:** (cra). **170-171 Alamy Stock Photo:** Art Collection 3. **172 Alamy Stock Photo:** © Fine Art Images / Heritage Images. **173 Alamy Stock Photo:** World History Archive. **172-173 Dreamstime.com:** Designprintck (b). **174 Alamy Stock Photo:** Art Collection 3. **174-175 Alamy Stock Photo:** Art Collection 2. **175 Toor Collection:** (cra). **176 Alamy Stock Photo:** Dinodia Photos RM. **178-179 Alamy Stock Photo:** Barbara Cook. **180-181 Toor Collection:** (ca). **180 Courtesy: Panjab Digital Library:** (lb). **181 Alamy Stock Photo:** Asar Studios. **182 Alamy Stock Photo:** The History Collection. **183 Digital image courtesy of the Getty's Open Content Program.:** Attributed to Samuel Bourne (cra). **184-185 Toor Collection:. Dreamstime.com:** Designprintck (b). **186 Toor Collection:** (cla, bl, tr, cr). **187 Toor Collection:** (tl, cra). **187 ©Asian Art Museum Of San Francisco:** (clb). **188 Alamy Stock Photo:** Tom Hanley (br). **189 Gurjit Singh Rehill:** Gurjit Rehill. **188-189**

Acknowledgments

Dreamstime.com: Designprintck (b). **190-191 Getty Images:** Rohaan Ali Photographics. **190 Getty Images:** ilbusca (lb). **192 Dreamstime.com:** Ndwarraich (cr); Otmar Winterleitner (lb). **Getty Images:** Aliraza Khatri's Photography (tr); Farrukh Saeed (cl). **193 Dreamstime.com:** Mortenhuebbe (cr); Jahanzaib Naiyyer (cla); Aleksandar Pavlovic (cl, clb). **Getty Images:** Tibor Bogna (cra); Nadeem Khawar (c); Jeremy Woodhouse (cb). **Getty Images:** Tibor Bognar (crb). **194 Alamy Stock Photo:** Jon Bower- art and museums (clb). **Dreamstime.com:** Alexmax (bc). **Wellcome Collection:** Wellcome Collection (ca). **195 Alamy Stock Photo:** Pump Park Vintage Photography. **196-197 Dreamstime.com:** Designprintck (b). **197 Getty Images:** Pictures from History / Contributor (clb). **198 Alamy Stock Photo:** The History Collection / Alamy Stock Photo (cla). **199 Gurjit Singh Rehill:** (crb). **200-201 Digital image courtesy of the Getty's Open Content Program.:** Samuel Bourne (English, 1834 - 1912). **202 Khanuja Family Collection:** (bl, cl). **202-203 Toor Collection:** (ca, cb). **Victoria Memorial Hall, Kolkata, India:** (bc). **203 Toor Collection:** (cb, cra). **204-205 Alamy Stock Photo:** The Print Collector / Heritage Images. **206-207 Alamy Stock Photo:** Chronicle. **208-209 Alamy Stock Photo:** GRANGER - Historical Picture Archive. **210-211 Alamy Stock Photo:** Archive Collection / Alamy Stock Photo. **212 Alamy Stock Photo:** 19th era / Alamy Stock Photo (c). **212-213 Alamy Stock Photo:** The Print Collector (cra). **213 Alamy Stock Photo:** INTERFOTO / History (c). **214 Toor Collection:** (cl). **215 Toor Collection:** (ca, lb, cr). **216 Alamy Stock Photo:** Chronicle (tl). **217 Gurjit Singh Rehill:** (crb). **Toor Collection:** (tl). **218-219 Gurjit Singh Rehill:** (c). **Dreamstime.com:** Designprintck (b). **220-221 Getty Images:** Felice Beato (b). **Dreamstime.com:** Designprintck (b). **222-223 Khanuja Family Collection:** . **224 Alamy Stock Photo:** Uber Bilder (lb). **Dreamstime.com:** Chris Dorney (r). **225 Getty Images:** Hulton Archive (tr). **226-227 Alamy Stock Photo:** Anil Dave (c). **228-229 Dreamstime.com:** Designprintck. **229 Getty Images:** INDIAPICTURE. **230 Alamy Stock Photo:** Olaf Krger. **232 Courtesy: Panjab Digital Library:** (br). **Dreamstime.com:** Wayne Mckown | (c); Anton Petukhov (bc). **233 Alamy Stock Photo:** History and Art Collection (tr). **234 Courtesy: Panjab Digital Library:** (c). **235 Courtesy: Panjab Digital Library:** (crb). **236-237 Getty Images:** NARINDER NANU. **238 Alamy Stock Photo:** Ira Berger (clb). **238-239 Courtesy: Panjab Digital Library:** (c). **239 Courtesy: Panjab Digital Library:** (lb). **Dreamstime.com:** Vnlit (cr). **240-241 Gurjit Singh Rehill:** . **242-43 Library of Congress, Washington, D.C.:** Girdwood, Hilton Dewitt, World Digital Library. **244-245 Alamy Stock Photo:** Pictures From History. **246-247 Alamy Stock Photo:** History and Art Collection / Alamy Stock Photo (c). **249 Khanuja Family Collection:** . **250 Alamy Stock Photo:** GL Archive / Alamy Stock Photo (clb). **250-251 Getty Images:** NARINDER NANU. **252 Dreamstime.com:** Aniketkadam8181 (clb); Sisirbanga (tr); Jagannathan Narayanan (cra); Singhramana (c). **Getty Images:** Hindustan Times (cb). **252-253 Alamy Stock Photo:** Graham Prentice (c). **253**

Dreamstime.com: Christopher Bellette (tr); Singhramana (cb). **Getty Images:** Hindustan Times (cra, cr). **Tamanna:** . **254 Alamy Stock Photo:** The History Collection (c). **255 Alamy Stock Photo:** The History Collection (crb). **256 Photo Division, PIB, Ministry of Information and Broadcasting:** PIB (c). **257 Getty Images:** The The India Today Group (cb). **258-259 Alamy Stock Photo:** John Frost Newspapers. **260 Dreamstime.com:** Rudolf Tepfenhart (cla). **260-261 Dreamstime.com:** Weedezign. **261 Toor Collection:** (cra). **262 Shutterstock.com:** William Vandivert / The LIFE Picture Collection / Shutterstock (clb). **263 Courtesy: Panjab Digital Library:** (cra). **Getty Images:** James Jarche / Popperfoto (crb). **264-265 Getty Images:** Hulton Archive (b). **266-267 Library of Congress, Washington, D.C.:** United States Office Of War Information, Collector (br). **268-269 Alamy Stock Photo:** Olaf Krger. **270-271 Dreamstime.com:** Jaroslaw Baczewski. **272-273 Getty Images:** NARINDER NANU. **275 Mary Evans Picture Library:** © Illustrated London News Ltd / Mary Evans (c). **276-277 Getty Images:** Keystone (t). **278-279 Alamy Stock Photo:** Anil Dave. **280 Getty Images:** Hulton Archive (clb). **Dreamstime.com:** Designprintck (b). **282 Alamy Stock Photo:** ArkReligion.com (ca); Dinodia Photos (clb). **Dreamstime.com:** Denisvostrikov (bl); Singhramana (tr). **Getty Images:** Kirti Dayanani (crb). **283 Alamy Stock Photo:** Lucas Vallecillos (tr). **Dreamstime.com:** Asafta (bl); Elena Odareeva (tl, cl, crb); Wing Travelling (bc); Mkopka (br). **Getty Images:** Christopher Pillitz / Contributor (cb). **285 British Library Board:** Europeana Collections 1914-1918 (clb). **Getty Images:** Fairfax Media (crb). **286-287 Shutterstock.com:** AP / Shutterstock (cb). **286 Khanuja Family Collection:** (cra). **288 Alamy Stock Photo:** Roth TJ (clb). **Bridgeman Images:** Christie's Images / Bridgeman Images (cla). **288-289 Getty Images:** Marco Secchi / Contributor (c). **Dreamstime.com:** Designprintck (b). **289 Bridgeman Images:** Christie's Images / Bridgeman Images (crb). **Getty Images:** Fine Art / Contributor (cra). **290 Getty Images:** Mint / Contributor (c). **291 Getty Images:** Ken Kelly / Popperfoto (cra). **292 Alamy Stock Photo:** s&g (cl). **293 Alamy Stock Photo:** s&g (clb). **Getty Images:** AFP / Stringer (tr). **294-295 Dreamstime.com:** Leszek Glasner. **294 Getty Images:** Sondeep Shankar / Contributor (c). **296-297 Getty Images:** Jacques Langevin. **298 Alamy Stock Photo:** Matteo Omied (clb). **Getty Images:** The India Today Group (crb). **298-299 Dreamstime.com:** Okawarung. **299 Getty Images:** Ulf Andersen / Contributor (clb). **300-301 Dreamstime.com:** Designprintck (b). **Getty Images:** Hindustan Times / Contributor. **302-303 Alamy Stock Photo:** Marcin Rogozinski (t). **Dreamstime.com:** Okawarung. **304-305 Alamy Stock Photo:** picture that. **306-307 Dreamstime.com:** Zoom-zoom (c). **Shutterstock.com:** Harjot Bajwa. **307 Khanuja Family Collection:** (tr). **308-309 Getty Images:** Hindustan Times / Contributor (tc). **310-311 Alamy Stock Photo:** michael smith. **315 Toor Collection:** (crb). **319 Alamy Stock Photo:** Jon Bower- art and museums (crb)

All other images © Dorling Kindersley